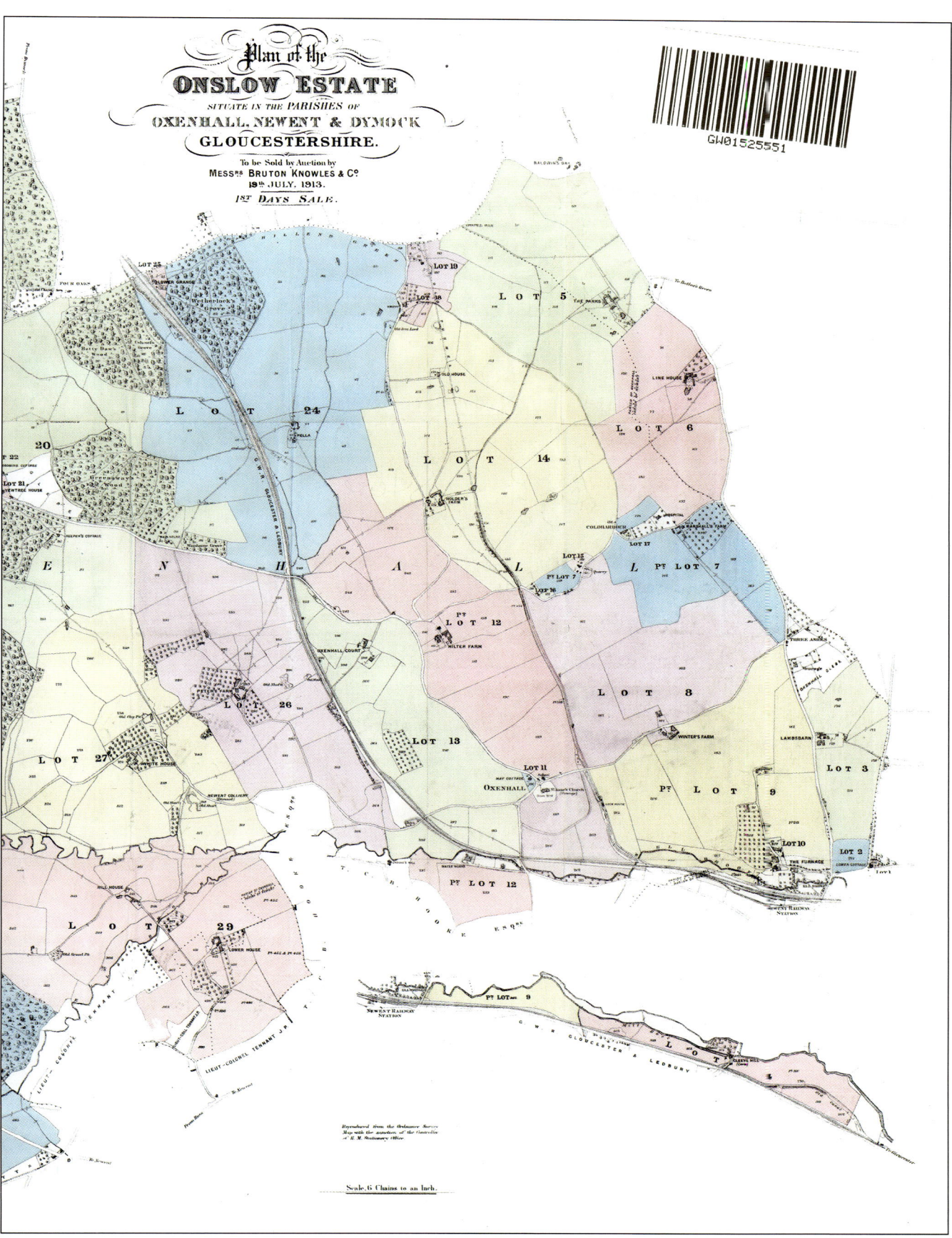

Happy 70th Birthday

Mike

love from

Chris, Leigh, Steve,
Sharon, Amber, Jade.

Oxenhall
1913-2013

Oxenhall
1913-2013

written by
Lyn Martin, Kathleen Rees and Evangeline Goulding

Pictures edited by Dave Farrants of Foxvideo Productions

Logaston Press

LOGASTON PRESS
Little Logaston Woonton Almeley
Herefordshire HR3 6QH
logastonpress.co.uk

First published by Logaston Press 2015
Copyright © Oxenhall Parish History Group 2015

All rights reserved. No part of this publication
may be reproduced, stored in a retrieval system,
or transmitted, in any form or by any means,
electronic, mechanical, photocopying, recording
or otherwise, without the prior permission,
in writing, of the publisher

ISBN 978 1 906663 95 7

Typeset by Logaston Press
and printed and bound in Poland by
www.lfbookservices.co.uk

Cover photograph by Dave Farrants

Note on names

In the sale details of 1913 the names of most of the farms that end in an 's' appear with an apostrophe (e.g. Winter's), except for Peters which never had an apostrophe. Over the intervening years the apostrophe was dropped by the owners except for Lamb's Barn. Thus, an apostrophe has been included when writing about these farms up to the First World War, but not when mentioning them in relation to subsequent years.

Similarly, in 1913 Whitehouse Farm was one word but by 2013 it was White House, and in 1913 Line House farm and cottage each had an 'i' but in 2013 Lyne House farm had gained a 'y'. We have adopted a similar dating rule regarding these spellings.

The use of the names Elmbridge and Ellbridge can also cause some confusion. Here the difference is that the iron works in Oxenhall in the 17th century was called Elmbridge while the area around the old site and the Ell brook is known as Ellbridge.

In all cases, names have been left as they appear on printed maps.

Contents

	Acknowledgements	*viii*
1	Oxenhall, the Exhibition and this Book	1
2	Oxenhall before 1913	11
3	The Background to the Onslow Sale	29
4	Farms in 1913	37
5	Cottages in 1913	89
6	Oxenhall in 1913	105
7	Timelines 1914-2013	115
8	Farms and Houses in 2013	147
9	Cottages and Houses in 2013	175
10	Oxenhall in 2013	195
	Bibliography	205
	Index of Places	207
	Index of Names	210

Acknowledgements

This book would not have come together without the help of many people. We would like to thank the residents of Oxenhall, past and present, who lent us photos and documents, filled in questionnaires, answered questions, told us their stories and gave consent for this information to be used in the book. You loved the Exhibition – now enjoy the book!

Thanks are also due to the members of the Oxenhall Parish History Group for their research, delivering and collecting questionnaires, and for their support and encouragement. Members of the Group involved in this project in addition to the three authors were Mary Bowers, Tricia Brooks, Libby Drew, Sue Teire, Anne Thompson, Gwen Tutt and Chris Wright; Gwen and Chris also read and reviewed early drafts. Other members of the community whose research we used were John Anderson, Richard Martin and Roger Tutt, and some photographs were taken by John Teire.

In compiling this book we trawled through many sources listed in the bibliography which included visits to Gloucestershire Archives and Hereford Record Office where the staff were always extremely helpful. Time was also spent in Newent Library looking through their excellent selection of books on local history.

Several individuals gave specific help, for which we are indebted: Mary Bowers, for drawing the maps showing the areas and cottages; Dave Farrants of Foxvideo Productions who took some of the photographs and ensured pictures and illustrations were of the highest quality; Lee Hines for her help, advice and encouragement throughout this process; Richard Martin for collating and organising the pictures and providing technical expertise when required.

We would also like to thank the following for permission to use material and photographs: Bruton Knowles for permission to use the Onslow Estate sale details, plans and photos; The National Portrait Gallery for the images of Thomas Foley and Paul Foley in Chapter 2; The Governors of Ottery St Mary Parish Church for the photograph of Bishop John Grandisson in Chapter 2; C.T. and G.H. Smith, Estate Agents for the photograph of Oxen Hall in Chapter 5; Gloucester Speleological Society for the photographs of the entrance to Oxenhall tunnel in Chapter 2 and the interior of the canal tunnel in Chapter 6; Derek Pearce for the photographs of Newent Station and the Pumping Station engine in Chapter 2 and of Newent Pumping Station in Chapter 6; Shirley Bailey (LBIPP) for the wedding photograph in Chapter 10; Robin Madge for 'Last Passenger Train at Newent Station' with an altered caption 'Last Passenger Train on the Daffodil Line'; and Darren Powell, Research Manager, Skyviews Aerial Archives, Springwell Cottage, 3a Rakehill Road, Berwick in Elmet, Leeds LS15 4JJ, (tel: 0113 2811043, (mobile: 07707 303943, mail@skyviewsarchives.co.uk, www.skyviewsarchives.co.uk) for the use of aerial photographs.

Thanks to the Heritage Lottery Fund who financed the 'Then and Now' project and who were always supportive with prompt and useful advice.

Finally our thanks go to Andy Johnson of Logaston Press who was helpful, thorough and unflappable.

1 Oxenhall, the Exhibition and this Book

Oxenhall is a small, rural parish in north-west Gloucestershire situated between Newent and Dymock. Roughly rectangular in shape, it is two miles east to west, where it borders Herefordshire, and one mile north to south. It is 11 miles from the city of Gloucester. Visitors are sometimes baffled that there is no village, just St Anne's Church and the Parish Hall on a steep hill, built on an outcrop of the local red sandstone. Farmhouses and barns dot the gently rolling land surrounded by orchards and fields; cottages and houses with large gardens edge the 11 miles of lanes. There are footpaths through fields and tracks in the woods for walkers to follow.

Most of the Oxenhall History Group outside The George Hotel, Newent, scene of the second day's sale of the Onslow Estate in 1913

For over a thousand years the economy has been based mainly on agriculture and forestry and it seems the landscape has not changed much. The woods of the west, the streams fed by underground water, the red ploughed soil of the undulating fields turning green in spring and gold at harvest time, the orchards in blossom and sheep grazing in the fields, all these remain today to delight those who live and visit here.

The community may be scattered but Oxenhall is fiercely protective of its heritage. The Oxenhall Parish History Group has been active since 1994, researching the area and its residents, recording and exhibiting their findings. Most of the farms and cottages in Oxenhall were once part of the Onslow Estate of over 2,000 acres. In 2010 the group realised that in 2013 it would be 100 years since the estate was sold in 1913. From this realisation came a germ of an idea which grew into a plan to mount an exhibition at the Parish Hall in July 2013, 100 years since Bruton Knowles auctioned off the farms and cottages of the estate. An application for a grant from the Heritage Lottery Fund was successful and in August 2012 research began in earnest.

A meeting with landowners in Oxenhall to explain our aims generated a lot of interest and the group started by interviewing owners of all the major farms and publicising our plans to everyone in the parish. The original aim was to produce two contrasting snapshots of Oxenhall life – in 1913 and 2013 – titled 'Then and Now'. As the responses snowballed, it became clear that the intervening years could not be ignored and so the project grew!

Alongside preparation of the exhibition, it was decided to produce a DVD showing the Oxenhall year 2012-2013. Dave Farrants of Fox Video Productions provided equipment and invaluable technical expertise, and worked with Van Goulding and Gwen Tutt as producers. The DVD was finished and on sale in November 2013, four months after the exhibition, and was received with glowing reviews from all who watched it, near and far.

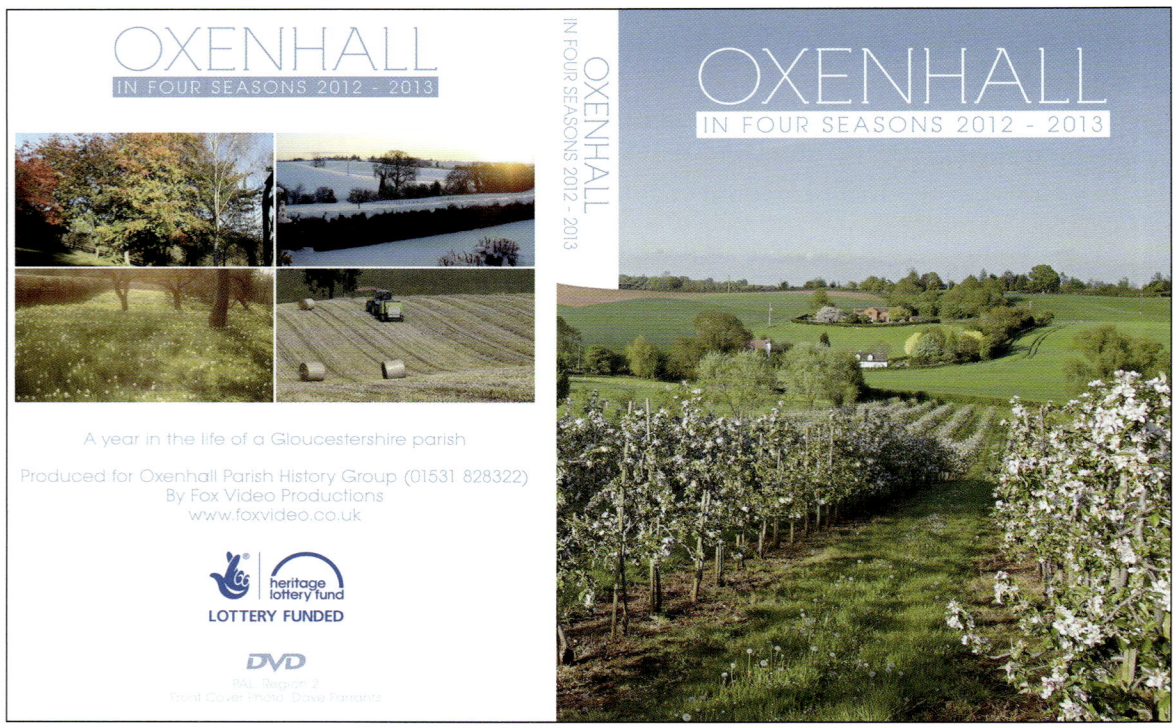

All too soon the big week of the exhibition arrived. The opening ceremony featured Bruce Fowler, from the present-day property firm Bruton Knowles, arriving in a vintage car from the 1913 era, driven by John Bowers.

Bruce delivered the original speech from the 1913 auction to an audience which included Cherry Anne Knott from the Heritage Lottery Fund.

It probably added to the sense of occasion that it heralded the start of a heatwave which lasted through the five days of the exhibition and beyond!

SALE OF THE CENTURY
THE PURCHASERS
TENANTS BECOME OWNERS
"Before 1914 few people owned their own houses." DanSnow

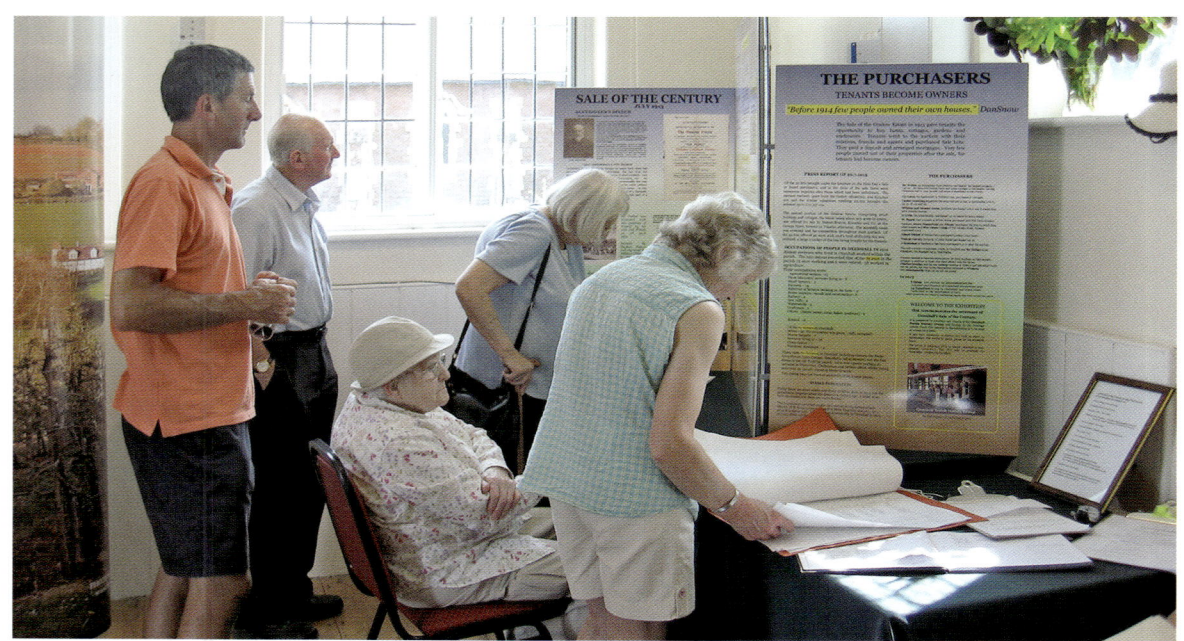

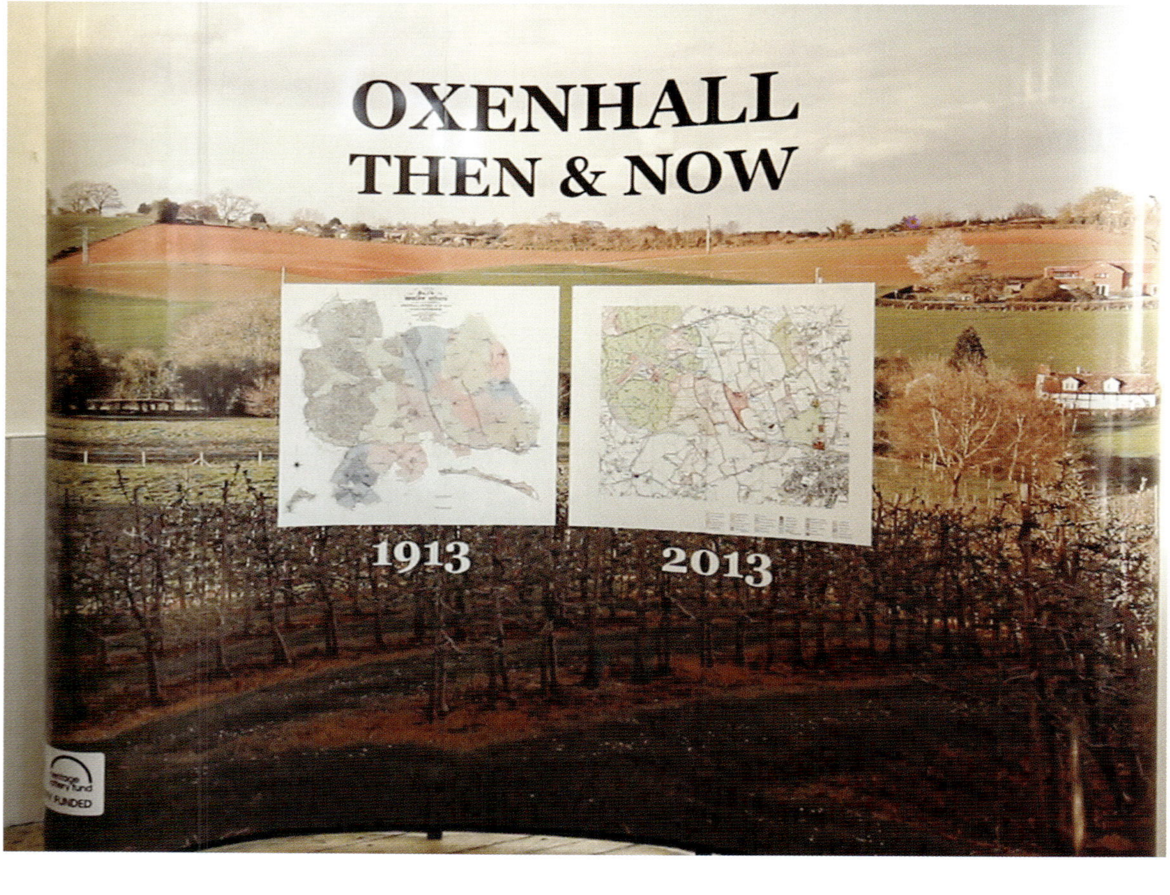
OXENHALL
THEN & NOW
1913
2013

The Parish Hall housed the part of the exhibition detailing the farms and cottages of the estate. Introductory boards explained the background to the Onslow sale.

A parabolic display showed two maps: one of Oxenhall in 1913 with the sale lots marked, and one with the present-day property names and landholdings marked.

To link events in Oxenhall with what was happening nationally and internationally from 1913-2013, a time line with photos and dates was produced by Richard Martin and mounted on a stand along the side of the hall. Richard's vision for presentation, and Phil Peachey of Gloster Photographic's expertise in printing, underpinned the look of the whole exhibition.

There was a display board for each farm with pictures and text showing changes from 1913 to 2013 and a folder with more detailed information underneath the board for visitors to sit and read.

The cottages were grouped in areas on boards in the smaller room and there were more detailed folders of the five communities: Shaw Common, Four Oaks, Three Ashes, Ellbridge and the centre of the parish.

There was also a display on Oxenhall School (the Parish Hall was the school from 1842 until 1935), including children's toys and clothes typical of 1913.

In a marquee outside were displayed farming implements, household equipment and other everyday objects that people used from 1913 onwards. These appealed especially to older folk, who remembered them, and to children, who were fascinated to see how things worked, some of them before electricity!

Visitors in the marquee reminiscing about the home and agricultural artefacts borrowed from local people

A demonstration of seed sowing by Bob Taylor of Parks Farm Nurseries using a 'fiddle'. The children are a group from Gorsley Goff's School

In St Anne's Church were displays produced by Roger Tutt about water and the canal, and information about the railway and transport. The 400-year-old Oxenhall Bible, usually kept in Gloucester Archives, was also on display.

John Anderson, an Oxenhall resident who worked for the Forestry Commission, produced a display at the back of the church showing the Oxenhall woods and how the management of them had changed from 1913 to the present day.

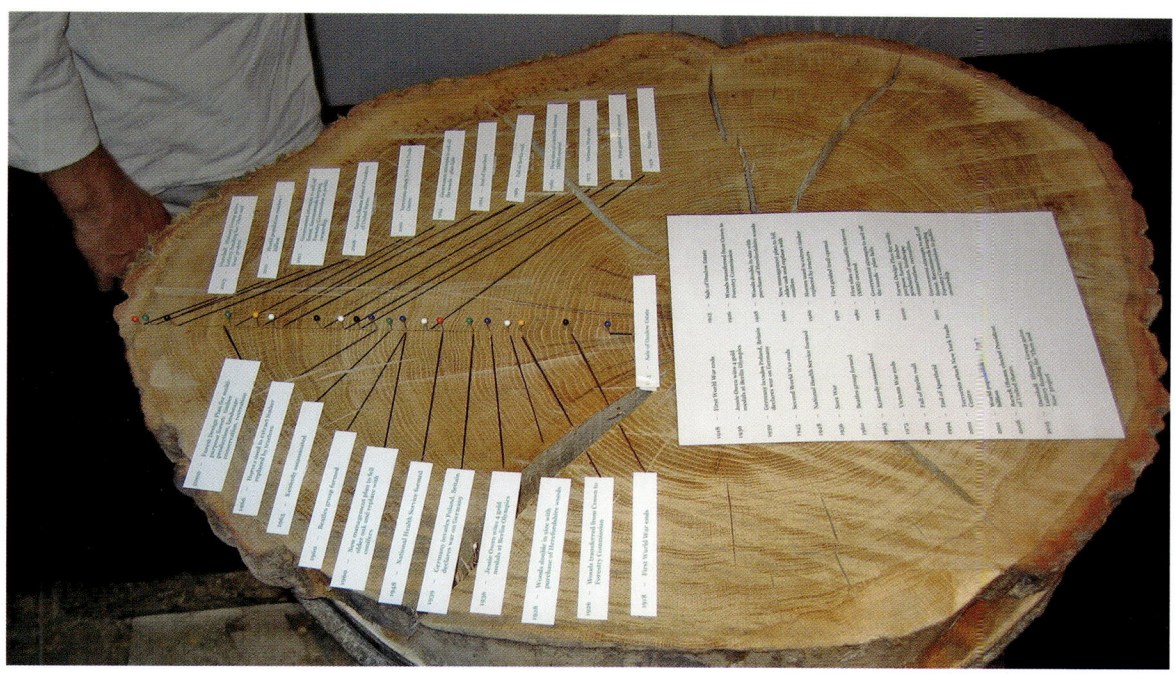

On the font was a huge cross-section of an oak trunk showing the annular rings and a time line of important national events as well as those in woodland management.

Outside, on the path leading up to the church porch, was a display of all the products produced from the local woods and the tools used to produce them.

John gave our school visitors demonstrations of how the tools were used.

The exhibition was a great achievement for such a small community with many residents lending photos, artefacts and expertise and volunteering to help with refreshments and at the exhibition itself. Over 900 visitors came, some from far afield, and some returned several times. Many commented on how much detailed work had gone into the displays. The History Group also became aware of how much we had discovered and not had time to absorb. It was decided to put up the information in the main hall again in January 2014 for a couple of days, so the group had time to study everything.

The History Group had always hoped to produce a book based on our research and this experience crystallized our ideas. The aim of this book is to provide information on Oxenhall's earlier history and a picture of how Oxenhall has changed. We hope to show that though the description of an unchanged, rural landscape at the beginning of this chapter still holds, the lives of people living in Oxenhall have changed immensely over those 100 years.

This book is limited to the properties sold on the first day of the Onslow sale, with the emphasis on life in 1913 and 2013, with changes in the intervening years summed up more briefly. The hope is that this format will provide an interesting book to read or browse through; it does not include detail which is covered much better in more specialist books.

2   OXENHALL BEFORE 1913

For almost a thousand years, five nationally powerful and influential families had charge of Oxenhall. These families have been highlighted because their ownership illustrates historical trends over the millennium. The first of them was the de Lacy family.

The De Lacy Family – Powerful Norman Lords
The Domesday Book of 1086 tells us that before 1066 the Saxon, Thorkell, held the Manor of Oxenhall from King Harold but after the Norman Conquest William the Conqueror granted Oxenhall and Kempley to the De Lacy family:

> Roger de Laci holds Horsenehal in Botelau hundred. ... It is worth and was worth 40s.

Roger de Lacy had inherited 21 estates in Gloucestershire, 75 in Herefordshire plus many in Shropshire from his father, Walter. Oxenhall Manor contributed to the de Lacys' great wealth. Income from their estates supported military campaigns and promoted the Church. The de Lacy family were powerful lords and had great skill in overseeing construction: they built fortresses, churches and monastic houses such as St Peter's Priory, Hereford and Llanthony Prima. They gave money to St Peter's, Gloucester where Roger's brother, Walter, was a monk and later the Abbot (1130-1139) and they also gave land to support religious institutions. Kempley Church was probably built by Hugh de Lacy (Roger's brother) and the 12th-century lead font in the church at Oxenhall may have been provided by the de Lacy family. Of the nine surviving lead fonts in Gloucestershire, six came from the same mould. Three were in parish churches associated with the de Lacy family: Tidenham, Frampton and Oxenhall. The de Lacy family held the Manor of Oxenhall for six generations over 175 years.

The power of the de Lacys decreased after the death of Hugh, Roger's great-nephew, in 1185 when his son Walter was a minor and became a royal ward. Henry II retained some of the de Lacy possessions in the Marches, subsequently dividing these among three other families. This pattern of the manor being passed on to other large landowners in the favour of the king continued for another hundred years.

The font in St Anne's Church, Oxenhall

Not part of the manor, St Anne's Church, the rectory farm (now Oxenhall Court Farm), the glebelands and all the tithes of the parish belonged in 1291 to the Knights Hospitaller of the preceptory of Dinmore in Herefordshire. Although originally founded to care for sick and injured pilgrims, the Knights Hospitaller were among the most famous of the western Christian military orders undertaking crusades in the Holy Land during the Middle Ages.

The De Grandisson Family – Knights in the King's Service
From 1280 William de Grandisson, a knight in the service of the king, held the Manor of Oxenhall as a part of his vast estates. He guarded the southern part of the Welsh/English border, built and maintained castles, attended parliament as a baron, travelled with the king, to whom he supplied horses and men, and led armies in Gascony, Scotland and Ireland. He and his wife, Sibyl, a wealthy heiress, had six children. Peter and Otto became knights and joined the Templars in Crusades to the Holy Land.

Another son, John, became one of the most famous and wealthy bishops of Exeter and recorded that he stayed with his family in Oxenhall on his way to take up his appointment as bishop in 1327, suggesting that after his retirement from the king's service William may have been one of the few lords of the manor to reside in Oxenhall. His main home had been at Ashperton. The three Grandisson daughters married into influential families and descendants of their families inherited Dymock. Family members from three generations succumbed to the Black Death in 1348.

Bishop John Grandisson – a carving in Ottery St Mary Church, Devon

During the 14th century five members of the de Grandisson family were lords of Oxenhall Manor in succession – William, his sons Peter and John, his grandson Thomas, and Margaret, the widow of Thomas, who died in 1394. On the death of the lord of the manor there was a court hearing or *Inquisition post mortem* to ascertain the size and value of the estate and who was the heir. At the *Inquisition* on the death of Peter in 1358, 12 local men declared to the escheator (the court official) that the free tenants paid rent and that the customary tenants, who worked on the lord's demesne (that part of the manor farmed directly by its lord, which was in the sandy part of the manor) paid a small rent. There was a manor house, a dovecote and a deer park. As the three field system of farming was followed, two of the three large open fields were planted with crops whilst one field lay fallow (rested) for a year in order for the soil to regain nutrients. The manor's tenants had the right to graze their animals on the arable land after the corn harvest, on six acres of meadow after haymaking until 2 February, and throughout the year on the large wood with its pasture. There was no regular income from the main woods though there was underwood in the park of some value.

The Piggott and Finch Families – First Local Owners

Thus far in Oxenhall's history the power of the king and the Church had determined who owned it. After the Reformation there was a big change; land began to be sold rather than granted as a reward for services to the king. This meant that many more people had the opportunity to become landowners. In 1544 the Crown mortgaged Oxenhall to a group of London merchant tailors who sold it to Lord Grey of Wilton in 1547. In 1551 he sold Kempley and Oxenhall Manors to William and Margery Piggott, who lived in Kempley.

Their granddaughter Ann and her second husband, Henry Finch from Buckinghamshire, became lords of the Manors of Oxenhall and Kempley in 1608. They built themselves a new manor house at Stonehouse in Kempley. When Henry Finch was High Sheriff of Gloucester in 1615 he commissioned a survey to be made of his woods in the western part of Oxenhall. The resulting map on parchment shows boundaries to the woods and fields that have hardly changed since then and gives the names of the woods, the tenants of the fields and small dwellings around the woods.

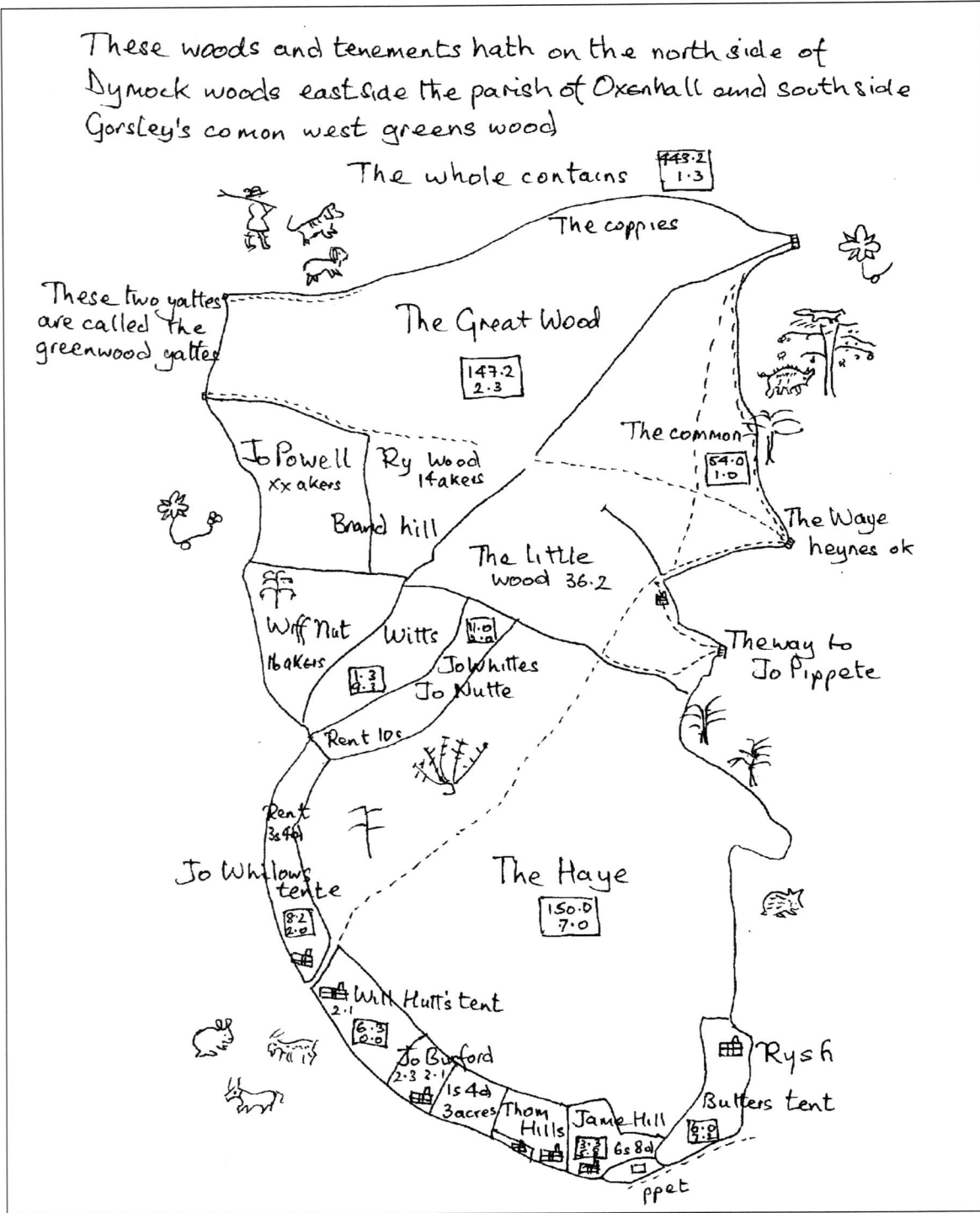

A drawing based on Henry Finch's map

The map does not include Upper Wayhouse wood, part of Greenaway wood, which Henry had rented as early as 1574. Fifteen years later he leased the wood and nearby Way House with its buildings, arable land and meadow (recently known as St Anne's Vineyard). Henry's interest in woodland suggests he was making money from the woods. Perhaps he was already coppicing the trees and making charcoal for the iron industry, for neighbouring lords of the manor, such as John Kyrle (Marcle) and John Wintour (Forest of Dean) were involved in the iron industry.

By 1639 Henry's son, Francis, had set up a charcoal blast furnace at Elmbridge in Oxenhall. He dammed the stream to the east of Oxenhall Church and created a channel to carry water to drive the bellows of the furnace and forge. The timber from the woods, already used for farm repairs, buildings, transport, furniture, tools, storage barrels, fuel and bark for tanning, was now definitely also coppiced for charcoal used in iron-making. Francis Finch made a big impact on Oxenhall during his 30 years as lord of the manor. He raised the finance to prepare the site and build the furnace, and utilised natural resources – iron ore from the northern part of Oxenhall, charcoal and water – as well as using cinders left over from previous iron workings. He recruited skilled workers and trained local labourers to work in the foundry and found markets for the pig iron produced. Ultimately Francis failed because he ran into debt buying up woodland locally to make more charcoal, a financial position not helped by the Civil War. He mortgaged the ironworks to Thomas Foley, an ironmaster, but could not repay his debts. So in 1658 Francis Finch sold the manor to Foley.

The Foley Family – from ironmasters and industrial entrepreneurs to landed gentry

Thomas Foley was born in 1616, the son of Richard Foley, the Mayor of Dudley and a wealthy industrialist. Between 1624 and 1633, Richard acquired leases on five furnaces, nine forges and other ironworks on his own and in partnerships with others. From an early age his three sons took over parts of the business. The Foleys soon controlled mines, woodlands, furnaces, forges, slitting mills to cut metal, wireworks, warehouses and trows (Severn sailing barges) in Worcestershire, Staffordshire, Shropshire and the Forest of Dean. The family developed accounting methods and trained salaried clerks to supervise the day to day running of the various works. They created policies and enforced routines which held together the whole enterprise. They demanded accountability from all those involved.

Thomas Foley (1616-77)

In 1655, Thomas purchased the manors of Great Witley and Little Witley which he made his base, and in 1656 he served as High Sheriff of Worcestershire. Thomas acquired 97 leases and partnerships, expanding into the Forest of Dean where the furnaces produced exceptionally high grade iron from local ores. In 1658 he purchased the manor of Oxenhall with its blast furnace and two years later he purchased the manor of Newent with its woods, minerals, watercourses and market.

For 90 years the Elmbridge furnace was the centre of activity in Oxenhall. The iron founder, the agent who ran the estate and the iron business, and the woodward who managed the woods, were all employed full-time. Many of the manor's tenants and family members gained extra employment as day labourers. Some worked day and night at the foundry. Carters with horses and carts hauled ore, cinders, limestone and sandstone to Elmbridge and they also hauled pig iron from the furnace to Ashleworth, from where it was transported to Stourbridge on Severn trows. Several men were engaged in the woods, cutting and cording coppice and making charcoal, whilst others dug the iron ore and earlier cinders which were reprocessed. Tenants gained extra income from the lord of the manor if hauliers crossed their land. Foley was anxious to conserve all the water available, so tenants and others were paid to clear channels and keep the banks of lakes and dams in good order.

The furnace was 'in blow' continuously for up to nine months of the year – as long as the iron founder was in good health and there was sufficient water to drive the water wheel that powered the two 18ft leather bellows used to help combustion. Records show that from 350 to 550 tons of high grade pig iron was produced annually, over 1% of the national production. Firebacks, cannon balls and other items were made from molten iron poured into moulds of sand. In 1669 Thomas handed over control of the Forest of Dean furnaces and forges, including Elmbridge, to his son Paul, who bought the estate of Stoke Edith in Herefordshire, rebuilt the manor house and made it his home. Paul was respected as a good financier and lawyer and was elected Speaker of the House of Commons in 1695. This provided access to government contracts for the business. He died in 1699 leaving an estate reputed to be worth £4,000 a year (probably over £400,000 at today's value).

Paul Foley (1644-1699)

For six generations the Foleys were leaders of a dynamic sector of industrialisation, but from 1710 they gradually disposed of their ironworks. Elmbridge continued until 1751 when it closed abruptly, two years after the blast furnace had been rebuilt. There were several reasons: changing technology meant that 21 coke furnaces were built in England in 1750, coke providing a hotter, more efficient heat, helping make coke pig iron cheaper to produce than charcoal pig iron. In addition local resources were exhausted, increasing haulage costs. The final blow was the lifting of duty on imported iron from America in 1750, which caused the market price of pig iron to drop. The Foleys could no longer compete.

Agriculture continued to be important in Oxenhall throughout the industrial period, but during the 18th century the lords of the manor sought to increase the revenue from farming and forestry. They encouraged the use of manure, marl and clay to improve the soil and the planting of fruit trees, especially cider and perry varieties. They employed a cooper to make barrels for alcohol and dried goods. When the blast furnace ceased, brick-making gained importance and men who formerly dug iron ore and cinders were engaged to dig clay, and those who had hauled raw materials and pig iron used their horses and carts to haul clay or faggots of gorse to the brick kilns at Shaw Common, White House Lane and the Furnace. One man could mould 1,000 bricks a day. The bricks were left to dry for six weeks and then they were put into clamps holding up to 100,000 bricks, tiles and crests. The brickmaker controlled the firing and any mistakes meant the bricks would be spoilt.

Whereas sandstone, Gorsley stone and timber with wattle and daub had been the building materials of the past, from 1750 red bricks were used to renovate and enlarge farm buildings and houses. Many Oxenhall buildings have a sandstone foundation, followed by low walls of Gorsley stone and then red brick. Tiles replaced thatch and windows began to be glazed. The design of farmsteads changed from the linear hall, mill house and cowshed, to farm buildings forming a square around a yard or fold where stock sheltered in the winter. Bricks were also used to line wells, culverts and the canal tunnel and to build bridges.

The increasing population in the 18th century created a need for additional housing for young married couples from Newent, Gorsley and Oxenhall. The Foleys allowed people to encroach and enclose land on the estate, especially around the woods and on the edge of the parish. The settlers, most of whom were labourers and craftsmen, built their own houses but they were charged ground rents. In line with national trends, the Foleys changed the way land was tenanted. Their estate agents made agreements for short leases and rents were collected twice a year. Previously land was passed on by copyhold (under which the tenant had a copy of the agreement written in the lord of the manor's court rolls), or by long leases for 99 years or 'for three lives'. Tenants were no longer so attached to one property and they began to move around. They also had fewer rights, and the lord of the manor could refuse them a new lease.

Andrew Foley, the third son of Thomas Foley, inherited Oxenhall in 1777 just two years after a detailed survey and map had been made of the estate. He lived the life of a country gentleman at Newport House, Almeley, Herefordshire with its walled garden, stables and kennels. He was a Member of Parliament for 44 years and was involved in legislation for canal building. He benefited from the annual rents of houses he purchased near Cavendish Square in London, which must have provided him with a good income. Needing an agent to manage the Oxenhall estate, he appointed William Deykes, who came to live in Oxenhall at Furnace House for 50 years, serving Andrew Foley and his two sons, Thomas and William. The latter each died unmarried before they reached the age of 40. When William died in 1828 his sister Elizabeth inherited Oxenhall and Newent manors. She continued to live on the Newport Estate and enlisted the help of her nephew Richard Foley Onslow to manage affairs.

During the time that Elizabeth Foley was lady of the manor the payment of tithes gave rise to national controversy concerning the inequitable treatment of food producers and the reluctance of non-conformists and Catholics to pay towards the established church. Before 1836 all occupiers of land had to give a tenth (a tithe) of their income annually for the support of the church and its clergy. Tithes were payable on three sources of income: 'All things rising out of the ground', which covered grain, wood and vegetables; 'All things nourished by the ground', which included cattle, sheep, poultry and their produce – wool, eggs and milk; and 'Produce of man's labour' such as profits from mills and fishing.

The Tithe Act of 1836 replaced payment in kind with money payments known as tithe rent charges. These varied annually according to the price of corn over the whole country. Land cultivated as market gardens, hop yards or orchards was subject to an additional rent charge as the value of the produce was greater. As a result of the Act a Tithe Survey was carried out in parishes and by 1841 the Tithe Apportionment listed the name of the owner and occupier, the name of each piece of land, its area in acres, roods and perches and the cultivation code. The accompanying Tithe Map showed watercourses, cottages and gardens, houses and buildings and all of the fields. These were given numbers that related to the apportionment.

The survey accounted for 1,886 acres in Oxenhall, made up of 490 acres of woodland, 398 acres of meadow, 956 acres of arable and 42 acres of common or 'waste' land, some of which was used for roads and the canal. On the clay the crop rotation was fallow, then wheat followed by beans or oats, whilst on the light sandy lands the rotation was turnips, barley, grass seeds and wheat. Oak flourished on the clay and elm grew on the sandstone. The stock in Oxenhall included 35 cows, 52 bullocks, 65 horses, and 800 sheep. The rateable value of arable land was 34 shillings whilst pasture was 30 shillings.

The surveyor met the owners and tenants to hear about any changes that needed to be made in the records and an agreement was then signed. The average annual tithe paid over a period of seven years for Oxenhall was £447 15 shillings. In 1841 the tithes were payable to the lay impropriator, Mary Ann Symonds, who owned Oxenhall Rectory. The Symonds/Beale family retained their right to the tithes until the 1930s, by which time many owners had redeemed the tithes on their property. Payment of tithes on land only ended in 1996.

Coal and Canals

Mines to extract coal and iron were opened up in the late 1700s on land between White House, Hill House and Lower House farms, but the quantity and quality proved disappointing.

In 1791 an Act of Parliament was passed for the construction of the Herefordshire and Gloucestershire Canal in order to link the rich agricultural areas of the region with the Bristol Channel. The original route, from Ledbury to Gloucester, was along the Leadon valley with a branch to Newent. However, this plan was revised when many investors were led to believe that, although the coalfields had not been worked for the last 24 years, they could be reopened if there was a market for the coal. They thought this coal would provide half the anticipated revenue, an idea reinforced by the announcement that 'additional veins of coal have been discovered so as to leave no apprehension of a scarcity'. In order to get closer to these coalfields the route was changed to go through Newent.

Choosing this route ultimately led to the decline of the canal. Substantial extra costs were incurred because a tunnel had to be constructed through the northern ridge of Oxenhall. Horse-operated machinery was first used to remove water and spoil from the 17 shafts. This proved extremely strenuous for both men and horses and eventually steam engines brought in from Cornwall had to be used. The tunnel, which was 2,192 yards long, was officially opened in 1798 when four vessels passed through it in 52 minutes. Many Oxenhall residents stood at both ends of the tunnels and on the bridges along the canal. It must have been a wonderful sight!

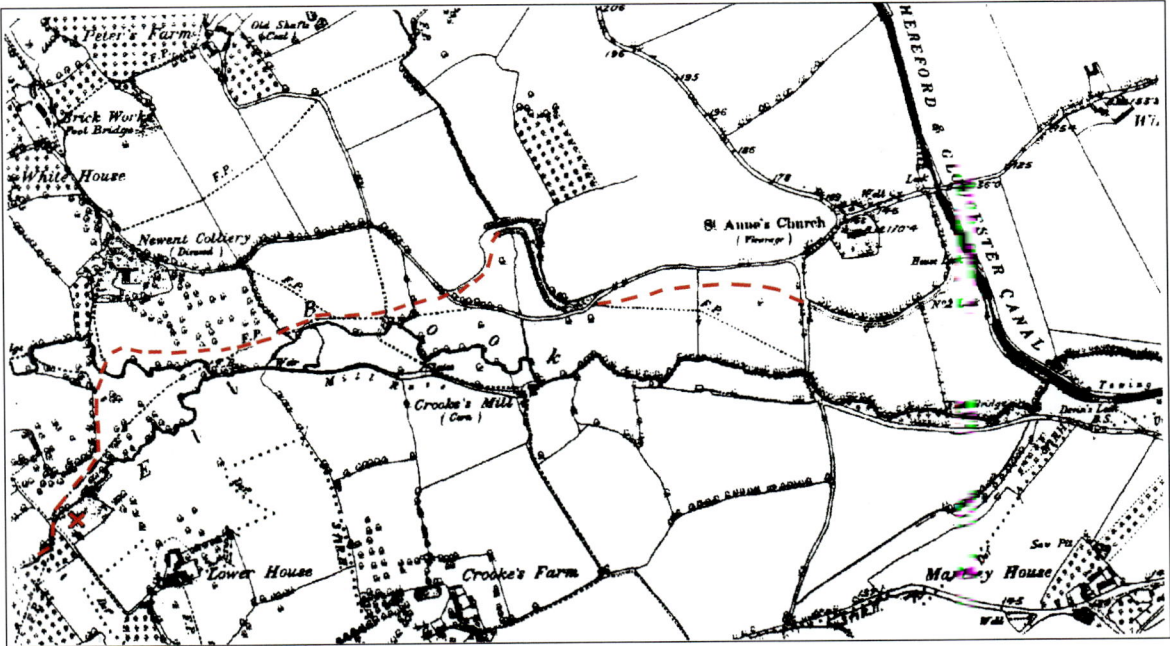

Part of the Newent coalfield in the 1880s, showing Hill House Colliery (marked x), Newent Colliery and workings at Peters. The Oxenhall branch of the canal is shown as a broken red line.

Costs were increasing all the time, whilst the coal mined at Newent proved to be of poor quality, resulting in the branch of the canal quickly falling into disuse. Railways were becoming a much more reliable mode of transport and it was hoped that losses could be cut by selling a section of the canal to the railway company, which planned to build a railway to Hereford. As this rail link to Hereford did not materialise, the sale of the canal fell through, leaving the canal company with no alternative but to try to boost trade. Things did improve, resulting in the creation, in 1849, of a timetable for barges using the Oxenhall Tunnel. Unfortunately this did not always work. For example, in 1851 two boats met in the middle and as neither would give way there was deadlock for 58 hours!

Bad weather also caused problems for traffic on the canal. The *Hereford Times* reported in July 1853:

> There was an incredible cloudburst at Dymock which sent so much water into the channel that a boat in Oxenhall Tunnel was driven back, and then drawn forth at a great rate when the banks burst on the Dymock side. Laden with lath, slate and timber, it eventually grounded in the darkness of the tunnel, and water rose up to the third stair of the Lock-keepers cottage in Oxenhall.

In 1862 the canal was leased to the Great Western and Midland Railway but trade was not helped by severe winters. Frost frequently interrupted canal traffic. Early in 1871, when the canal froze for several weeks, six horses had to haul an icebreaking boat right along the canal from Hereford to the Severn. More expense!

Eventually, on 30 June 1881, the canal was closed and the section through Oxenhall became part of the rail track between Gloucester and Ledbury. It wasn't until 1948, when the railways were nationalised, that the Canal Company was formally wound up.

The entrance to the Oxenhall Tunnel in the present day

The coming of the Railway

Just imagine the reaction of local people when they first heard that there were plans to build a railway line through Oxenhall! There would have been speculation about the route and the disruption to their peaceful lives. Local farmers and landowners especially would have been worried about the noise frightening their animals and the smoke and steam destroying their crops. But there must have been excitement too. After all, most people would have heard about the train service through Gloucester and would look upon this as a chance to travel further and faster and to transport animals and goods to market.

Plans to use the bed of the Oxenhall canal, including the tunnel, as the route of the Newent to Ledbury line were published in 1872 and authorised in 1873. The Newent Railway Company would construct a single track railway from the line of the Great Western Railway at Over, near Gloucester, passing through Newent to Dymock, where it would join the double track line of the Ross to Ledbury Railway.

However, in 1874 the plans were changed to include a new section of rail avoiding the tunnel. At this time the canal company was struggling for funds so it must have been a relief to sell their land to the railway companies. Much of the stone used for the railway bridges came from the old canal locks. Lack of capital delayed the start until an agreement was made between the two local companies and the Great Western Railway by which the latter would provide the capital to build the line.

In the summer of 1881 construction work commenced south from Ledbury, using the canal to convey materials from the River Severn. In 1883 construction work began from Dymock towards Newent. Obviously the canal had to be drained, and apparently the men who drained the canals placed nets across the mouths of the outlets and caught great quantities of fish which they sold at market!

Newent Station in 1905

By the middle of the 19th century it was estimated that 2,500 navvies were employed nationally for the physical work involved in railway construction, mostly using picks and shovels. These navvies, who lived in huts by the line, paid a certain amount to sleep in a bed and less to sleep on the floor. Their work was dangerous and many lives were lost in collapsed tunnels or through the use of explosives. Stations were built at Dymock, Newent and Barber's Bridge and on Monday 27 July 1885, the day of the Gloucester Agricultural Society Summer Show, a train service began.

Lancaster Saw Mills
Oxenhall's timber was transported to Gloucester by canal from a timber yard near the bridge in Coldharbour Lane until the canal closed. The railway attracted timber merchant Herbert Lancaster to move to Newent from Sussex sometime before 1901 and he developed a timber-yard next to Newent Station to which the GWR built a private railway siding. The road entrance was at the junction of Horsefair Lane and Ross Road. Trees from woods and hedgerows, mainly oak and elm, were felled and hauled by gangs to the sawmills. In 1913 Herbert Lancaster was demonstrating that steam traction engines were more efficient than teams of horses for hauling timber. The company, the biggest employer in the area, continued for over 60 years. The siren that sounded to mark the start and end of working time resounded through Newent and Oxenhall. The site is now used by Ladder and Fencing Industries (Newent) Ltd.

The Onslow Family – last owners of the Oxenhall Estate
Throughout the 18th century the Oxenhall Manor Estate was passed down through the Foley family. In 1857 Oxenhall Court and the rectory lands were sold to Richard Foley Onslow, a nephew of Elizabeth Foley. Onslow had been brought up at Court House, Newent, and had moved with his wife Catherine to Furnace House on the death of William Deykes in 1827.

The Onslows had several family members who were either clergymen or wives of Church of England clergy, and Richard and his son gave land, building materials and money generously to support local churches. Unlike many landowners who refused to allow non-conformists to be their tenants, the Onslows welcomed them on their farms and as employees on their estate, for they had a good reputation as workers. Richard Baldwin, a trusted woodward and lay preacher who died in 1866, was one of them. A school and non-conformist chapel built in Gorsley in 1821 was one of 32 enterprises set up by Edward Goff's Trust offering free education for poor children in rural areas. Goff, born in Hengoed, near Kington in north-west Herefordshire, left his home and work as an agricultural labourer and made his wealth as a coal merchant based at Scotland Yard, Westminster. The Trust appointed John Hall, formerly a sawyer, as teacher/minister in 1831 and he continued as schoolmaster for 34 years and remained an influential Baptist minister for 50 years. As part of his pastoral work he wrote letters for the illiterate, assisted families with legal matters and health problems and set up a Friendly Society to provide men with money when they fell sick. The school and chapel had a lasting impact on families within a five mile radius and several became tenants on the Onslow Estate.

Elizabeth Foley often stayed at Newent Court with her sister Harriet, wife of Archdeacon Richard Francis Onslow, vicar of Newent. She was interested in her tenants and the day to day running of her estate; for example, she was pleased when the Cothers, who had been tenants for 60 years, became farm owners. She took pride in the appearance of the farms and was annoyed by the damage at Holder's and Waterdines caused by the mounds of spoil that had been dumped at the top of the canal tunnel shafts.

Elizabeth was the last of the Foleys, and on her death in 1861 Richard Foley Onslow inherited the estates in Oxenhall and Newent when he was 59 years old. This was the first time all the lands in Oxenhall had been owned by the same family. His hopes of prospering from the reopening of Newent Colliery in the 1870s, on the site of the earlier White House Colliery, were dashed when the enterprise failed. However, the family still gave generous help to the community. Richard Onslow already had over 30 years' experience in estate management and as acting squire, for he had always been Elizabeth's deputy. As his assistant he promoted Richard Warne, who had served on the estate as the Foleys' gamekeeper. Warne married a trusted domestic servant of the Onslow family, Anne Pritchard, and they moved to Little Furnace, which was converted into a house from two workmen's cottages. They farmed at Furnace Farm and at Richard's former home at Way House, a total of 80 acres, and Anne helped the Onslows with their family of ten children.

Richard Onslow lived the life expected of Victorian landed gentry, building a mansion, entertaining influential guests, running social events, owning stables (he loved riding) and kennels and taking a leading role in local events and sports.

Richard Foley Onslow, 1802-1879

He served as a magistrate in Newent and Gloucester and was appointed Deputy Lieutenant of Gloucestershire in 1856. He engaged John Middleton, a Yorkshire architect who moved to Cheltenham, for several building projects. The first and most expensive was the conversion of a farmhouse called Stardens into a neo-gothic style mansion for his family, begun in 1864. Sadly Catherine never moved to the house for she had a heart attack as she walked to church in August 1865 and died later that day, aged 65. So Richard Onslow moved to the mansion with some of his sons.

Middleton also rebuilt Oxenhall Church and The Parks, built as a property to let. In 1869 the house was rented out at £46pa to Mrs Thurston, who farmed Holder's and The Parks farm. After 1871 the tenants were from outside the area and were of independent means.

Building other schools and churches and the restoration of the 16th-century Market House in Newent, as well as giving the land for a livestock market held in Newent fortnightly, provided work for local people but continued to deplete Richard Onslow's capital. It was difficult to meet such expenses from the estate's regular income.

Stardens – from the 1910 Sale brochure

Oxenhall School

In 1842 a day school had been opened in a building on land given by Elizabeth Foley, opposite the church. In 1847 the school, known as the Vicar's School, had an income from subscriptions and school pence (each child had to pay three pence per week) and taught 21 boys. It had closed by 1868, probably from lack of funds, and some Oxenhall children

The board in the present day Parish Hall which records the donations given to set up the school

then went to Newent's National School while others, perhaps girls and infants, were taught by Richard Onslow's daughters, and about six boys attended a night school taught by T.P. Little, the vicar. There was also a dame school in the parish attended by about 15 children. So at this time education for the children of Oxenhall's tenant farmers and labourers was patchy, had to be paid for, and was often provided by the Church and the lord of the manor. Without a benefactor the children of the poor would have received no education. Elizabeth Foley and Richard Onslow had also given land for the building of Picklenash School in 1848.

By 1883 a National School, established under the 1870 Education Act, had opened in Oxenhall under the management of the vicar and a temporary committee of parishioners. It then had an average attendance of 38 boys and girls in a single all-age class. This was an improvement in that both boys and girls were taught and that the parishioners of Oxenhall had some say in the running of the school.

Management of the school was taken over by the County Education Authority in 1903 and in 1905 the building was enlarged to provide a separate infants' classroom. Like all schools, it had to keep a log book and registers, and notify the authority of any infectious diseases, and it was inspected regularly. Called Oxenhall Church of England School from 1907, it had an average attendance of 44 in 1910. The link with the Church was kept with both the name of the school and the vicar's close involvement, but ultimately power now rested with the local authority.

St Anne's Church, Oxenhall

Throughout the ages Oxenhall Parish Church, dedicated to St Anne, mother of the Virgin Mary, had been the main focal point for this scattered community. The earliest reference to a church building in Oxenhall was in 1186 but only the exceptional early medieval lead font remains from this church, dating from about 1130. The tower, built soon after 1300, is the only external part of the church not rebuilt in the 19th century.

In 1604 scholars began the arduous task of translating the Bible into English as decreed by James I. By 1611 this work was completed and in 1613 St Anne's Church purchased its copy of the King James Bible.

In 1663 Robert Kerfoot, appointed vicar by the crown, appealed to the Court of Chancery for the establishment of an income for the benefice, as the appointment of the vicar had lapsed. The subsequent enquiry discovered that there had not been a vicar in Oxenhall for 60 years! After the matter had been referred to the bishop of Gloucester, a house for the vicar was built on glebe land, close to the church. Unfortunately this building was destroyed by fire in 1664. The Revd Kerfoot lost most of his possessions and the parish registers in the fire, leaving a regrettable gap in the parish's historical record.

Following this fire, for many years curates lived outside the parish, probably supplementing their meagre stipend with other work. Only when the church was restored in 1865 was a new vicarage provided; it was built at Three Ashes, now a private residence, called Oxen Hall.

In 1688 'A Survey of Railes and Walls of the Churchyard' recorded the names of 38 people, the names of the property they occupied and the length of the churchyard wall that they were responsible for repairing. This survey was signed by churchwardens John Hill, Josias Barnwood and Thomas Phillips.

By 1865 the walls of the church were leaning badly and it was decided to rebuild the nave and chancel, retaining most of the internal furniture, including the pulpit of 1632. The work was carried out by the architect John Middleton at a total cost of £925, a principal benefactor being Richard Onslow. The east window is a memorial to his wife, Catherine Onslow. Major repairs were carried out to the chancel in 1898.

Change of Parish Boundary

Until 1883 Brockmore Brook and the Ell Brook formed the southern boundary of the parish. Then the detached part of Pauntley was added to Oxenhall by an Act of Parliament, enlarging the civil parish by 341 acres and five or six additional farms. Altering the civil parish boundary led to some confusion because the ecclesiastical parish boundary was not changed until 1922, 40 years later. When Ruth Notley, who lived in part of what had been the civil parish of Oxenhall since 1883, but part of Pauntley ecclesiastical parish until 1922, was interviewed in the 1990s she said: 'We lived at Hill House from 1915-1922. We did not live in Oxenhall – we lived in Pauntley.'

Isolation Hospital

In 1897 Newent isolation hospital was moved to the eastern part of a field in Coldharbour Lane opposite Marshall's Farm, purchased by Newent Rural District Council from the owner Edward Little. This tiny wooden and corrugated iron building consisted of two small rooms, one for the nurses and the other to accommodate one or two patients. In 1923 it was sold and removed to Greenway. Mr and Mrs Fumpson lived in a caravan on the site with their goats in the 1950s.

Water and The Onslow Agreement

The Ell Brook watercourse has always been an important resource for farmers in Oxenhall. In the past several water mills operated along its length – the remains of one near Crooke's Farm can still be seen today. The brook's many tributaries formed lakes and ponds and fed the canal, while a reservoir of water powered the bellows for the ironworks' furnace.

Below ground in Oxenhall are many aquifers formed by the presence of permeable rock which can hold and transmit water. This can be both a blessing and a curse. Too much underground water was a factor in the failure of the coalmining venture at Newent Colliery in the 1870s. Farmers dug out and lined ponds for their animals and many farmhouses still have very deep wells in their yards, which must have been a blessing before mains water.

After the drought of 1891, the city of Gloucester searched for an additional supply of water as their supplies were inadequate. Oxenhall was chosen and a borehole sunk in 1893. The water was pronounced 'very pure but hard' by the Medical Officer of Health. In 1894 the Mayor of Gloucester removed the first sod of earth for the well, which was completed in 1896. It is said that the pressure of water was so great that the workmen completing it had to drop their tools to escape the fast rising water! A fine Victorian building housed the steam engine that pumped water to a reservoir at Madam's Wood in Upleadon.

The pumping station engine

The land for this venture was, at that time, being administered by the trustees of the R.F. Onslow Estate. An agreement between the trustees and Gloucester Corporation included a free water supply for 18 properties and farms on the estate. A further 11 properties received a supply of water at the rate of one shilling per 1,000 gallons and the Furnace, the Onslow residence, 500,000 gallons of water every month free of charge. This agreement lasted until 1986 when the water supply was privatised.

Oxenhall's Setting – Local Links

Newent has always provided the parish with markets, shops and small businesses. In the midst of this rural area most of the tradesmen dealt in goods and services essential to agriculture. Local farming and horticulture provided raw materials for cottage industries in the past, including weaving (wool and flax), dyeing, hosiery, tanning, glove making, brewing, cider and perry making, boot and shoe making and even wig making.

In 1801, the earliest reliable record of population, 2,351 people lived in Newent. The opening of the canal in 1798 brought tradesmen with different skills to the town and, by 1851, census records tell us that many of the residents of Newent were professionals ready to give advice and assistance to local people. In 2103 the population of Newent is around 5,000, serving 13 small hinterland parishes bringing its total population to just over 13,000.

In the past the roads in Oxenhall, still in use today, were ancient, narrow, sunken lanes very difficult for vehicles and even horses. These lanes, giving access to the scattered dwellings, joined major roads in and around the parish. In 1726 the local Turnpike Trust was ordered to increase the width, and generally improve the road between Gloucester and Hereford, including the road through Newent. In 1810 the present B4221 was opened as a new road to Hereford.

These roads, together with the canal and the railway, allowed the residents of Oxenhall to travel more easily, not only to the city of Gloucester with its port, cathedral, industry and larger businesses, but also to Ledbury, Ross-on-Wye, Hereford and Malvern.

Oxenhall's farmers and cottagers were not isolated from the growing town of Newent or the city of Gloucester, 12 miles away. Yet in 1912 Oxenhall was still a rural village, reliant on agriculture and forestry.

This history of Oxenhall through the ages shows that until 1861 the manor/estate always belonged to someone other than the inhabitants. Under Saxon landlords, the Church, Norman barons, large landowners and industrial entrepreneurs, Oxenhall folk worked their land (or underneath it) and lived their lives, paying their rents and tithes and looking after their families. The woods, used for hunting with bows and arrows, by hawks, horses, dogs, guns and snares, had provided food for the king's table as well as for that of the lord of the manor. They are reduced in number now and no longer the haunt of wily poachers supplementing their diet or income. From the Middle Ages onwards farms have been amalgamated into larger units, with some holdings lost, but new cottages have been built and farmhouses and buildings improved, particularly during the time of the Foley Estate. The population has remained at around 200 inhabitants from 1775 to 2014, apart from an additional 150 people in 1811, perhaps drawn by the benefits brought by the canal. The scars of this time have to be searched for now, but they are still there, as are the canal and the railway bridges. It could be argued that Oxenhall is a microcosm of what happened to rural areas, but how many such villages have an industrial past, coal mineshafts, a canal, a railway and a pumping station? Yet the landscape remains much as it was in former times, though with improved roads and lanes, the subject of much complaint from earlier travellers into Oxenhall, such as by S. Rudder in *A New History of Gloucestershire* in 1779: 'The roads cannot be commended at any times, but in the winter they are almost impassible.'

An Oxenhall resident of 1912 would stand by the church and Parish Hall today and notice some changes, but in 1912 the changes to their lives which would take place in the next few years would have been unimaginable. The old order of things was about to change forever.

3   The Background to the Onslow Sale

Richard Onslow had spent a great deal on maintaining his position as one of the county's landed gentry, gradually reducing his capital as he did so. This in turn reduced his income, creating a cycle of sales. In 1866 he mortgaged Lamb's Barn for £1,151, a sign that he was running into financial difficulties. Nevertheless, he continued to spend money on his property and he improved the drainage on his land at Cleeve Mill and at Pound Farm, where his son the Revd William Arthur Onslow, was tenant.

In 1875 he leased the rights for the mineral deposits of fireclay, ironstone and the coal seam under 836 acres of the estate. Mr Aston agreed to pay £1,200 a year for these rights and set up a coalmining business. Richard Onslow bequeathed eight equal shares of the income from this lease to his surviving children, but they gained nothing. Initially successful, by 1880 the venture was employing 60 men to extract coal but a year later it had closed. By the time of his death in 1879 Richard Onslow had not only lost his fortune, he was in deep debt from which his descendants never recovered.

In his will, Richard Onslow left the estate in the hands of his two sons-in-law, Major William Hill of Worcestershire and the Revd Robert Burroughes of Norfolk, with his eldest son Captain Andrew George Onslow as tenant for life, to be followed by his grandson Andrew Richard Onslow. By this means he hoped to protect the estate and avoid death duties. The value of Richard Onslow's personal estate was less than £14,000 but in his will he left £6,000 to each of six younger children – William Arthur, George, Mary Charlotte, and Emma Francis Onslow, and Anna Theodosia Hill and Caroline Burroughes.

Andrew George Onslow was 49 years old when he took over the running of the estate. He had studied at Oxford University and had a career in the army. He rose to the position of Captain of the 97th Regiment and of the 13th Light Infantry, so he had a reasonable pension. The family are recorded as living at Stardens on the census of 1871, after which they lived at various places in Herefordshire before returning to Stardens by 1879. Following his father's death, Captain Onslow spent the rest of his life working with the trustees attempting to clear his father's debts. In addition to their financial difficulties the Onslows were victims of economic, climatic, social and technological changes.

Lot No	Holding	Tenant 1880	Acres 1880	Rent 1880	Tenant 1891	Acres 1891	Rent 1891	Tenant 1902	Acres 1902	Rent 1902	Tenant 1913	Acres 1913	Rent 1913
3	Lamb's Barn										W. Fowler Beckett	29	£50
4	Cleeve Mill	C.J. Faulks	3	£40	J. Cummins	¼	£55	Exec. Humphrey Jones	7	£66	Exec. H. Jones Mrs F. Jones	7 13	£66 £25
5	Parks House	Mrs Gregorie		£60	Revd H.E. Hodson		£40	A.W.M. Campbell	1	£64	A.W.M. Campbell		£55
5	Parks Farm	In hand	92	£135	J. Lodge	83	£110	W.W. Pope	93	£60	George & John Goulding	94	£135
6	Line House										D. & G. Goulding	60	£78
7	Marshall's						£39	L.B. & J. Robinson	39	£65	Robert & George Savidge	43	£72
8	Winter's	George Tranter	113	£150	William C. Jones	106	£175	W.C. Jones	104	£120	W.C. Jones	104	£122
9	Furnace Farm	Capt. Byron			J. Lodge	96	£140	James Lodge	97	£144	Late J. Lodge	104	£150
	The Furnace House	Capt. Byron	105	£250	In hand		£40	A.R. Onslow	5	£40			
12	Hilter's	William Faulks	101	£175	Robert Savidge	10	£150	Robert Savidge	114	£150	Robert Savidge	117	£151
13	Oxenhall Court Farm	Thomas Hale	51	£106	John Niblett	69	£83	John Niblett	72	£82	Amos Scott	77	£91
14	Holder's	S.A. Cadle	175	£107	In hand	175	£194	Daniel & George Goulding	138	£94	Daniel & George Goulding	139	£94
20	Pound Farm	William A. Onslow	151	£148	In hand	110	£87	George Chapman James Davies	98 13	£61	George Chapman	103	£70
	Little Pound				Thomas Boulter	51	£45	Elijah Gurney	53	£30	George Gurney	53	£32
20	Murrell's	Allen	15	£20	John Jones	14	£16	James Jones	15	£16	C. Lane	15	£18
24	Pella	In hand	120	£120	In hand	113	£87	Daniel Goulding Henry Jones	159	£113	Henry Jones Daniel Howley	187	£126
26	Peters	Mr Gardner	109	£138	George Brook	108	£65	T.D.J. Dowdeswell	118	£70	Late John Niblett	112	£95
27	Whitehouse	Late Price	138	£160	Edwin Jones	140	£154	Samuel Jones	141	£125	Samuel Jones	129	£117

Lot No	Holding 1880	Tenant 1880	Acres 1880	Rent 1880	Tenant 1891	Acres 1891	Rent 1891	Tenant 1902	Acres 1902	Rent 1902	Tenant 1913	Acres 1913	Rent 1913
28	Brassfield's	Joseph Cummins	79	£100	R. Dobbins	92	£45	Edmund Higgins	91	£76	R.J.C. Honeyfield	157	£82
29	Lower House & Hill House	Late Capt. George Onslow	148	£225	Thomas Dowdeswell	145	£180	Reps Thomas Dowdeswell	156	£150	Daniel Dowdeswell	139	£143
Day 2	Brockmore Head							Charles Matthews	72	£54	Late C. Matthews	49	£41
Day 2	Gorsley Court	Daniel Goulding	31	£34	Thomas Overton	34	£37	Alfred Drinkwater	38	£37	Alfred Drinkwater	33	£37
	Gorsley	John Jones	49	£76									
Part 12	Hydes	Samuel Wood	18	£36	Mrs Wood		£34				Now part of Hilter's		
Day 2	Poplars							John Hartley	19	£26	John Hartley	18	£24
Day 2	Bull Hill	Nathan Freeman	40	£40	John Jones	43	£40	W. Beard/ C. Jones	43	£25	W. Beard	39	£26
	Newtown	John Cummins	350	£500	John Cummins	330	£566	W.W. Pope	294	£375	SOLD		
	Stardens Mansion	In hand	3	£350	Major How		£200		36	£200	SOLD		
	Nelfields	Josiah White	175	£260	SOLD								
	Dales	Joshua Smith	37	£116	SOLD								
	Black House	William Crook	137	£180	W. Crook	132	£167	Mrs C.M. Hall	138	£119	SOLD		

A selection from the Onslow Rentals 1880-1913

The annual income expected from rents of the 3,648 acre estate was £3,670, with an additional £1,400 from timber sales, a total of £5,070. In 1880 the trustees re-mortgaged 156 properties on the estate for £46,300 at 5% interest so that the interest payable was £2,315. They also had to pay interest on £16,000 to the family members for money left in the Estate at 4%, a further £640, leaving £2,000 for personal expenses and the running of the estate.

Agriculture suffered severe setbacks from bad weather and the effects of cheap imported food, so that tenant farmers were struggling to pay their rent. Between 1874 and 1896 there were only six good harvests. After the volcanic eruption of Krakatoa in August 1883, sunlight was diminished and temperatures were lower than normal for five years. Periods of continuous rain caused animals to suffer from liver fluke and cattle plague. Corn harvests were poor. The government allowed merchants to import even more cereals from America to feed the increasing population. Another blow was the introduction of refrigerated shipping that transported cheaper meat from Australia, New Zealand and Argentina, lowering the price of British lamb and beef. The first refrigerated ship arrived from New Zealand in 1882 and five years later 172 shipments arrived carrying frozen Canterbury lamb. It was hard for farmers to be motivated to continue and landowners had to reduce rents in order to keep tenants on the farms, and this reduced the overall income of the estate.

The banks called in the money they had loaned 25 years earlier when government encouraged landowners to improve land and invest in building projects. Many landowners could not repay their loans and were forced to sell their land. So much land was on the market that its value fell dramatically. Nationally in the 1870s land was worth about £54 per acre but its value had fallen to £19 per acre by the 1890s. In 1873, 36 acres at Marshall's Farm were sold to James Heane for £2,300, almost £64 per acre, but the value had dropped to £25 per acre by 1890.

Captain Onslow made bold decisions regarding his finances that affected his social status. Firstly, he reduced the farm rents in order to keep his tenants on the farms. Secondly, in 1890 he agreed with the trustees and mortgagees to sell two of the largest farms, Nelfields and part of Newtown Farm and properties in High Street, Newent, to Andrew Knowles, who became joint Squire with him. Thirdly, he decided to lease Stardens and the sporting rights of the estate to Major How. He and his family moved back to Furnace House so his costs were reduced and he could benefit from the additional rent obtained from Stardens. The new railway station was very near the house so he could travel by train to local towns, allowing him to reduce the number of horses he kept.

In 1894 Andrew Richard Onslow, who was 23 years old, inherited the estate on the death of his father. Two years later he married 18-year-old Margaret Finch Dawson, the daughter of a barrister, but the marriage soon broke down and the couple were divorced in 1908. Andrew had no children but was restricted by the terms of Richard Onslow's will to pass the estate to a male heir.

Early in 1910, 76-year-old Major William Hill resigned as a trustee and 76-year-old Mary Charlotte Onslow, who was a mortgagee, died. The remaining two trustees, Charles

Burroughes and Hugh Thursby, had no alternative but to sell the estate. By September 1910 the Stardens part of the estate, bounded by the Tewkesbury Road, Redmarley Road and Strawberry Hill Lane, was on the market together with Newent woods, Cleeve Mill and three farms in Newent.

The remainder of the Onslow Estate was on the market in July 1913. All the residents of Oxenhall and people in neighbouring communities were poised for a change in their circumstances. There was the chance that the estate might be sold as a whole to one new owner, but it was more likely to be sold in separate lots. Tenants had to consider their future. Did they want to remain in their farms and cottages or move out of the parish? If they wished to stay, they needed to make a successful bid at the sale and find money to purchase the property. The alternative was for farmers to take up new tenancies elsewhere, for agricultural labourers to find new employers, and for non-agricultural workers and craftsmen to find new homes. Many local people might have the opportunity to become land and home owners for the first time in their lives.

The estate sale included property in Oxenhall, Newent, Dymock, Linton and Aston Ingham. It was planned for 1912, but the two-day sale was postponed until July 1913. Buyers had to pay a 10% deposit on the day of the sale. Most smallholders and farmworkers did not have bank accounts so they asked friends and acquaintances to loan them cash. Those who were not familiar with the procedures of an auction chose someone to represent them, especially at the second day's sale when 45 smaller lots were on offer. Farmers sought loans from family and mortgages from banks. As they faced major changes, several tenants engaged a photographer in 1912 to record their families outside their homes.

Almost all the land and buildings in Oxenhall, except for a few small freehold properties at Three Ashes and two farms formerly in Pauntley, were part of the estate. Kews Farm was owned by Lt-Colonel Tennant, a relative of the tithe owners, and Crookes Farm had been awarded to the Hooke family by King Henry V. The vicarage, the school and the glebe lands were owned by the Church. Land used for the Great Western Railway, the isolation hospital and the waterworks had previously been purchased from the Onslows.

Auctioneers Messrs Bruton, Knowles and Co. were engaged to run the auction. Sale books were prepared with details of each property, its acreage, the name of the occupier, the land tax, the rent tithe charges payable to the various parishes and the value of the timber. These charges had to be paid in addition to the purchase price. The woodward, Richard Baldwin, estimated the value of every tree that was in the hedgerows of the farms (see table on page 36).

The first day's sale was held at the Bell Hotel in Gloucester on Saturday 19 July and the second day's sale of smallholdings and cottages at the George Hotel in Newent on Tuesday 22 July. Henry W. Bruton, aged 69, came out of retirement to run the auction. His grandfather, the butcher William Bruton, had lived at Lower House cottage and rented a field called Butchers Field adjacent to Blue Lane and Kews Lane in 1841. Henry's father was the auctioneer who founded the Bruton and Knowles partnership in 1862. He had lived in Church Street, Newent and had been encouraged in his career by Richard Onslow. His partner William Knowles was from Cirencester and not apparently related to the late Andrew Knowles of New Court, Newent.

Because the value of agricultural land had fallen so low, many tenants found themselves able to purchase their farms and cottages, some paying as little as £10 per acre. Furnace Farm and Lower House were sold for about £17 per acre, whilst Line House fetched the highest price at £20 per acre. Many of those who had borrowed money from friends and family or from the Newent branches of Lloyds Bank and Gloucester Banking ended up paying considerably less in interest on their loan than the amount they had been paying in annual rent. At Winter's Farm the rent was £122 per year but interest on a full loan, if at 5%, would have been only £92. Likewise at Furnace Farm the rent was £150 whilst interest on the loan would have been £108.

Henry W. Bruton, the auctioneer

Mr Weller, an accountant from Malvern purchased the largest property – Lot 20. He then sold Pound Farm and some cottages to the tenant, George Chapman and in 1914 he sold 638 acres of woodland to the Crown.
A.E. Jones, the blacksmith in Holders Lane, purchased six cottages.
Daniel Goulding supported his sons and son-in-law in purchasing Lots 6, 14, 15, 16, 24 and 29.
William and Samuel Jones, brothers, purchased Lots 6 and 8, where they were already tenants. Their nephew James Jones, who had lived at Murrells, did not purchase the property sold as part of Lot 20.
H. Little, the wheelwright, purchased Lot 10, where he was a tenant.
W. Beard, once a tenant at Whitehouse, purchased Bull Hill Farm, Gorsley at the second day's sale.
Farmers Messrs **Honeyfield** and **Niblett** purchased the lots on which they were tenants and **Mrs James Lodge** of the George Hotel, Newent purchased Lot 9, which the family had farmed for over 20 years.
Albert Niblett of Peters Farm purchased Gorsley Court Farm on Day 2.
George Gurney, formerly of Little Pound, purchased Lot 13.
J. Robinson of Baldwin's Oak Farm purchased Lot 12 after the auction.
The only outsider to purchase a farm in Oxenhall was **Mr Hulme** from Cheshire and he purchased Lot 5, 'The Parks', which included Parks House and Parks Farm.
Farmers needed to have accommodation for their workers, so they bought cottages in addition to those that were offered with the farms.
Robert Savidge and his son **George,** farming at Hilter's and Marshall's, both left the parish, but later descendants returned to Winters as Charles Junior married W.C. Jones' daughter.
The **Dowdeswells** from Lot 29 and the **Scotts** from Lot 13 left the parish.

Purchasers at the Onslow sale

THE ONSLOW ESTATE SALE ON 19TH JULY

In opening the sale Mr. H.W. Bruton said it was his privilege to conduct one of the most important sales ever held by his firm, and he wished to take the earliest opportunity of thanking the trustees for having entrusted the sale to his firm. He might claim to have known the Onslow Estate intimately for nearly half a century and he had no hesitation whatever in saying, after going over the whole of the property, that he had never seen the homesteads and the buildings generally in such a good state of repair, that he had never known a better class of tenants, and he had never seen the prospects of the farms more encouraging.

On all sides one saw unmistakable evidence of excellent treatment of the land; the arable land, with very few exceptions, being in a clean condition and the crops most promising. The rents of the farms were very considerably reduced some years ago when the agricultural outlook was by no means encouraging and they have remained undisturbed. Anyone with a practical knowledge of farming must admit that the present rents were moderate.

1912 – ABNORMALLY WET SEASON

Continuing, Mr. Bruton said he thought he might fairly claim that agricultural prospects were encouraging, the hay crop was abundant and the prices of all description of stock excellent. Last season had been undoubtedly a most discouraging one – an abnormally wet season following an abnormally dry one – but probably there was no estate in that district which suffered less from the prolonged wet than the Oxenhall estate. As they knew, the greater portion was a sandy loam, and of a character, therefore, which suffered less from a wet season than land of a heavier nature.

SQUIRE R.F. ONSLOW

He had the privilege, like his father before him, of enjoying the friendship and full confidence of Mr. Richard Foley Onslow, so well known as the old Squire. It might be truthfully said of him that no man more worthily sustained the best traditions of a country gentleman than he did. He exemplified a politeness which marked the old school of gentlemen. He was a sportsman of the truest type, a practical farmer, a scholar of a cultivated mind and taste. He was one who realised the responsibilities attached to the ownership of a landed estate.

Mr. Bruton said that the Trustees had done all in their power to ensure a profitable occupation of their farms by their tenants. Mr. Bruton then proceeded with the sale.

Excerpts from a national newspaper report dated 26 July 1913

Of the 30 lots brought under the hammer on the First Day's Sale 21 found purchasers, and at the close of the sale there were numerous inquiries after those which had been withdrawn. The amount realised, apart from the timber valuations, was £23,642 10s and the timber valuations totalling £3,615 brought the amount up to £27,257 10s.

The second portion of the Onslow Estate, comprising small holdings and cottages, the whole being about 222 acres in extent, was offered for sale by Messrs. Bruton, Knowles and Co. at the George Hotel, Newent on Tuesday afternoon. The assembly room was crowded and the competition throughout most spirited. Of the 45 lots offered 42 were sold, and a total of £6,082 10s was realised, a large number of the lots being bought by the tenants.

Another press report gives an overview of the two-day sale

The craftsmen of the parish, the blacksmith and the wheelwright, also purchased their homes, land and buildings so they could continue their work unhindered. The tenants of the cottages were delighted to become owners of their orchards, gardens and homes. They could look forward to a stable and independent future, though hard manual work was needed for them to earn a living. They also worked in the woods and undertook seasonal farmwork such as haymaking, harvesting and picking up cider fruit. They grew flowers and vegetables for sale. A few had jobs working on the railway, at the timberyard or the waterworks.

When the Onslow Estate was sold in 1913 the break-up of the large estates in Newent and Oxenhall was complete. In *Champagne and Shambles*, her book about the break-up of the Hampton Court Estate in Herefordshire, Catherine Beale wrote that 'One quarter of the land in England changed hands between 1912 and 1920.' For the Onslow family the sale was a disaster as the income generated was not enough to pay off the debts. For the tenants it was a challenging opportunity to own their own homes, land and buildings and farm as they wished, without reference to the lord of the manor.

Farm Name	Lot No.	Elm	Oak	Black Poplar	Ash	Other	Woodward's Value	Sale book Value
Lamb's Barn	3	572	15	185				£69
Furnace	9	1536	322	470			£75..02..0	£57
Winter's	8	2070	55	200	154		£83..12..0	£75
Marshall's	7	1757		120	20			£56
Line House	6	910	23	435	30			£34
Parks	5	1569	796			Larch 337	£115..12..0	£104
Holder's	14	4642	156	20	5		£142	£128
Pella	24	702	659		96		£51	£270
Little Pound	20	103	36		7			£
Hilter's	12	2107	91		89	Beech 100	£80..04..0	£72
Oxenhall Court	13	1287	40		77		£54..12..0	£49
Gt Pound	20	277	205		34			£
Peters	26	1217	377		51		£58	£53
Whitehouse	27	1272	631		28			£63
Lower House & Hill House	29	1086	380		71		£54..19..0	£49
Brassfield's	28	143	226		16			£91
Brockmore Head	Day 2	20 trees	3 trees		5 trees			
Gorsley Court	Day 2	26 trees	6 trees		1 tree			

Value of timber on Onslow Estate farms at January 1913
The woodward, Mr Richard Baldwin, measured all timber trees on the farms in cubic feet and estimated their value ready for the estate sale.
This information is from a notebook with entries in pencil at GRO Ref D2299/7/144/3

4   Farms in 1913

> **GLOUCESTERSHIRE**
>
> PARTICULARS, PLAN AND CONDITIONS OF SALE
> OF THE REMAINING PORTION OF
>
> ## The Onslow Estate
>
> An Important Agricultural and Sporting Property
> Lying in a ring fence, and adjoining or within a short distance of Newent Station on the Great Western Railway, comprising:
>
> A MODERN RESIDENCE KNOWN AS
> ### "THE PARKS"
> CHARMINGLY PLACED IN FINELY TIMBERED GROUNDS
>
> ### Thirteen Excellent Farms
> WITH CAPITAL HOMESTEADS
>
> WATER MILL, WITH RICH MEADOWS ATTACHED THERETO
>
> **SEVERAL SMALL HOLDINGS**
>
> ENCLOSURES of ACCOMMODATION LAND & COTTAGES
> AND
> A Capital Sporting Estate of 850a. 3r. 7p. including well placed
>
> ### WOODS AND PLANTATIONS
> THE WHOLE BEING
>
> ### About 2410 Acres
> IN EXTENT
>
> **Messrs BRUTON, KNOWLES & CO.**
>
> Will offer this IMPORTANT FREEHOLD ESTATE for
> *Sale by Auction*
> **AT THE BELL HOTEL, GLOUCESTER**
> On SATURDAY, the 19th JULY, 1913
> at 2 o'clock most punctually
>
> Particulars, Plan and Conditions of Sale may be had of Messrs Radcliffes & Hood, Solicitors, 20 Craven Street, Strand, London; Messrs Blofeld & Burroughes, Estate Agents and Surveyors, 37 Lincoln's Inn Fields, London; or of the Auctioneers, Albion Chambers Gloucester.

Although the front page of the sale is titled 'The Onslow Estate', as the previous chapter explained, the main house, Stardens, together with land and farms in Newent had already been sold in 1910. There must have been some hope that a purchaser could be found for the whole Oxenhall Estate, as it is described as 'An important Agricultural and Sporting property'. On the second page the possibilities for playing golf, hunting, rearing game for shooting, and managing farms and extensive woodlands paint a picture of a lifestyle which was already disappearing.

This 'remaining portion' of properties and land in Oxenhall was still a considerable 2,410 acres. Lot 20 with 850 acres of mostly woodland together with three farms and numerous cottages, was the largest lot and its sale must have been critical to the success of the auction.

The position of the Oxenhall Estate, with the railway providing good access to local towns and London, and its good soil and timber, is also emphasised.

The details of properties that follow start with those picked out on the front sheet of the sale brochure: The Parks, then Cleeve Mill, then Lot 20 consisting of woods, plantations, a farm, smallholdings and cottages. The remaining larger farms of the Estate are detailed after that.

LOT 5   The Parks

The Parks is given top billing on the front sheet and there is a picture of the house inside with the details. Its modernity, situation and wooded grounds are highlighted and the marketing may have suggested it as a replacement for the main estate house. The imposing dwelling, surrounded by a tennis court and pleasant gardens, was in an excellent position well away from the main road and approached by a carriage drive. It included a butler's pantry, a housekeeper's room, coach house and associated 'man's room'. It is also the only house on the estate where an indoor WC is mentioned! (Some houses are listed as containing 'dressing rooms', but the WC was outside.) Certainly the wording makes the house appealing to those with their own means, the kind of people who could afford servants to run the house.

TENANT	A.W. Montgomery Campbell
	Sub Tenant Mrs Glegg
ACREAGE	94 acres 2 Roods 12 Perches
LAND	Pasture, Arable, Tennis Court, Well-Timbered Grounds, Pleasure Garden and Kitchen Garden
LIVESTOCK	Horses, Cattle, Pigs and Poultry
RENT	Lease at £55 for 14 years
SOLD	In 1913 to Charles Hulme
PRICE	£1,850

LOT 5

"THE PARKS"

AN ATTRACTIVE RESIDENTIAL ESTATE

comprising a gabled residence and about **94a. 2r. 12p.** of pasture and arable land, of which the following is a particular:—

No. on Ordnance Map	Description	Quantity A. R. P.	Total A. R. P.
	PARISH OF NEWENT		
	ARTHUR WM. MONTGOMERY CAMPBELL, Esq., Tenant		
Pt. 72	"The Parks" Stabling	0 0 8	
74	"The Parks," Gardens, Lawns, Cottage, &c.	1 0 0	1 0 8
	Messrs GEORGE and JOHN GOULDING, Tenants		
68	Pasture	8 0 16	
69	Arable	12 3 4	
70	Pasture	19 1 21	
71	Arable	3 2 35	
Pt. 72	Yards and Buildings	0 2 2	
73	Pasture	1 3 20	
	PARISH OF OXENHALL		
115	Arable	7 2 26	
116	Do.	17 0 6	
117	Pasture	0 3 35	
118	Arable	3 2 39	
119	Pasture	2 0 30	
121	Do.	15 2 10	93 2 4
		A.	94 2 12

"The Parks" is approached by a carriage drive, occupies an exceptionally pleasant position well set back from the main road, and contains:—

On the ground floor: Dining-room, 16 ft. 7 in. × 14 ft.; Drawing-room, 18 ft. 6 in. × 14 ft. inclusive of bay; Breakfast-room, 16 ft. 3 in. × 16 ft. 3 in.; Butler's Pantry, Kitchen fitted with range, Scullery with hard and soft water supply, Larder, Housekeeper's room, and on the first floor: 6 Bedrooms, Dressing-room, and w.c. Cellar in the basement. In yard in the rear are coal-house, knife house, and w.c.

"The Parks" is surrounded by a tennis lawn and well timbered pleasure grounds.

In the kitchen garden is a potting shed (the greenhouse belongs to the tenant).

Near thereto is a range of excellent brick and tile stabling, comprising coach-house, 4 stalls, 2 loose boxes, with loft over, washing-box and harness-room with man's room over.

With "The Parks" is let an excellent cottage containing sitting-room, kitchen, back-kitchen, dairy, 3 bedrooms, and underground cellar.

"The Parks" with gardens, cottage and stabling, is let on lease at £55 for 14 years from the 25th March, 1902, with option for lessee to determine the tenancy by twelve months' notice, to A. W. Montgomery Campbell, Esq., whose sub-tenant is Mrs Glegg.

The land and farm buildings are in the occupation of Messrs George and John Goulding, on a Michaelmas tenancy, at the yearly rent of £80. The buildings (which are brick-built and tiled) in their occupation are around a yard, and comprise open sheds, loose-box, cow-house, barn, a range of poultry-houses, 3 piggeries, with boiling-house, wagon-shed, cart stable for 4, and harness-room with loft over.

This Lot is subject to the right of the purchasers of Lots 18 and 19 to take water from No. 70 on the plan.

It is subject to Tithe rent charges, that of Oxenhall amounting to £11 14s 2d, that of Newent to £9 8s 10d, the total value thereof on the 1st January last being £15 7s 6½d.

It is also subject to a Land Tax of £5 1s 10d.

The Timber on this Lot has been valued at the sum of £104.

"The Parks" may be viewed by card to be had of the Auctioneers, and by appointment with Mrs Glegg.

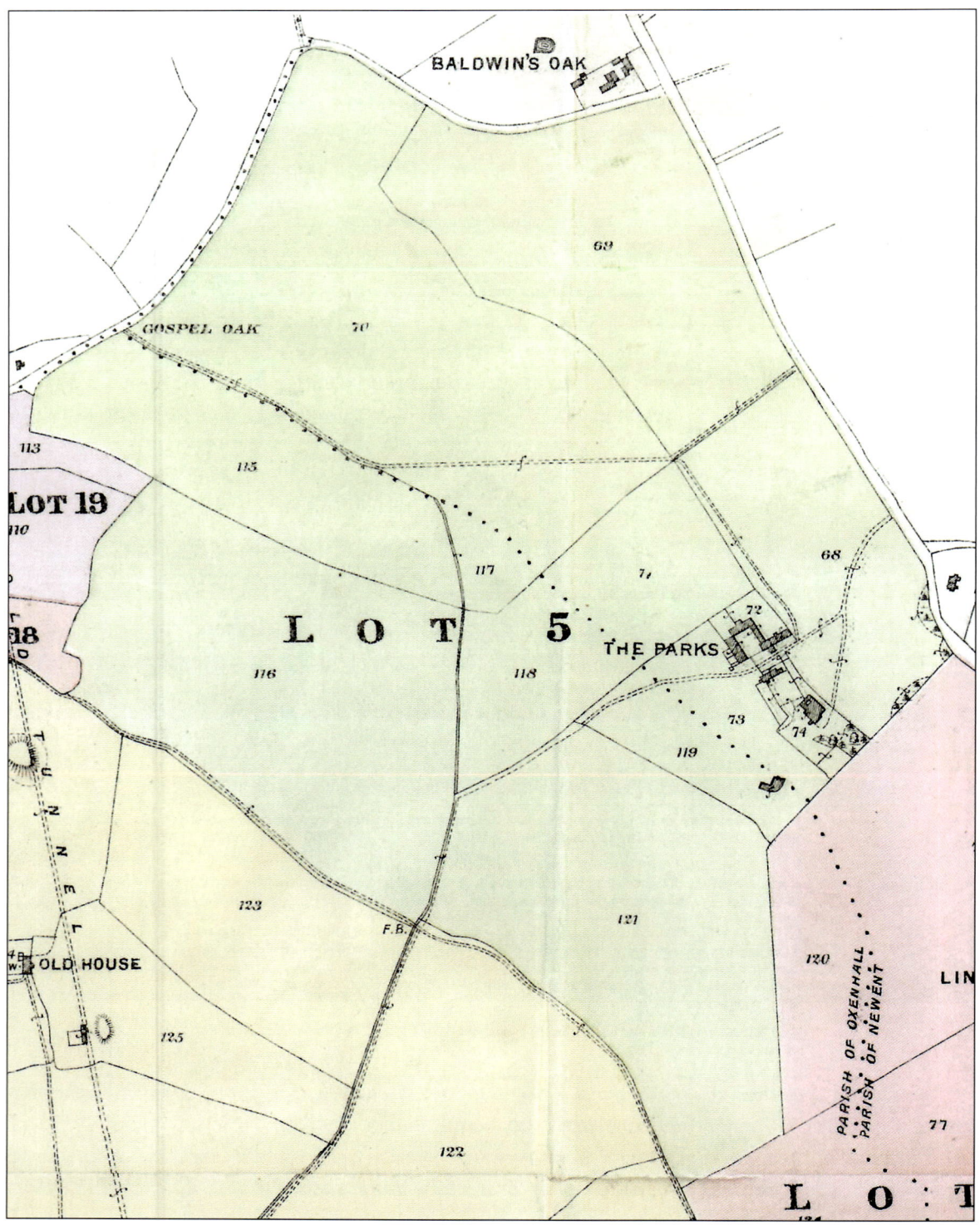

The tenant, A.W. Montgomery Campbell, had moved to the area from Hertfordshire. As a keen huntsman he was well aware of the problems caused to horses and riders by wire on the ground so he decided to do something about it, as an article in *Hunting with the Ledbury* written in 1996 recalls:

> Mr Montgomery Campbell, of The Parks, Newent, came to 'the Ledbury' from Hertfordshire and is remembered for his efforts to clear the country of wire. In 1908 the committee was determined to deal with the problem and so with the support of landowners and farmers, he obtained permission to remove over 15,000 yards of wire, thus clearing most of the country.

In 1913 The Parks was bought, along with Parks Farm, by Mr Charles Hulme of Cheshire. Increasing deafness had made it impossible for him to continue as an auctioneer and purchasing The Parks gave him the opportunity to take up farming. Charles and his wife, Hannah Mary, had two sons, Charles and William, who attended Sir Thomas Rich's Grammar school in Gloucester. Son Charles and his wife, Evelyn Elizabeth, were to make their home in Malswick with their three sons and one daughter. William remained on the farm and eventually took it over.

> After the sale The Parks was sold by private contract to Mr C. Hulme of Field House, Biddulph near Congleton, Cheshire. It is a residential estate comprising a gabled residence etc and about 94a 2r 12p of pasture and arable land in the parishes of Newent and Oxenhall, approached by a carriage drive and let at £135. The lot is subject to tithe rent charges amounting to £21 3s value, on first of January £15 7s 6½d and to a land tax of £5 1s 10d. Timber valued at £104.

The sale of The Parks as reported in a newspaper

Parks Farm
   TENANTS   George and John Goulding
   RENT   £80 per annum
   SOLD   Charles Hulme
   PRICE   Included in Lot 5

This is where Charles Hulme and his family lived after they bought Lot 5 at the sale, farming the land.

Charles and Hannah Hulme

LOT 4   Cleeve Mill

Cleeve Mill was not in Oxenhall but was a part of the Onslow Estate that had been put up for sale in 1910, but not sold. The mill had been worked by Humphrey Jones and his wife Florence. Her father farmed at Brockhampton, south of Hereford. They had one daughter, Margaret. In 1900 Humphrey died, leaving Florence a widow after only six years of marriage. In 1901 the census shows Florence at the mill with her daughter, her nephew, a fellow widow and a servant. She employed Joseph Kidney as manager.

In the following census of 1911 she is described as a 'grist miller'. Her daughter was by then at school and her mother was living with them. She still had Mr Kidney as manager. Her sister married Charles H. Jones, the elder son of Charles Jones, the blacksmith of Hill End cottage in Oxenhall.

At the auction Mr Kidney bought the mill for £950. He probably bought it on Mrs Jones' behalf, for when he died in 1917, aged 52, Mrs Jones continued working the mill. She is still the miller in Kelly's Directories for 1923 and 1927. Kelly's lists J.H. Lawrence as the miller in 1939 and he is still there in 1953 but not in 1955. It seems likely that competition from Pridays' mill in Gloucester had made working Cleeve Mill unprofitable.

LOT 4
CLEEVE MILL

comprising a brick and tiled dwelling house, water mill, buildings, and enclosures of rich meadow land, the whole being about **20a. 3r. 15p.** in extent, of which the following is a particular:—

PARISH OF NEWENT

No. on Ordnance Map	Description	Quantity A.	R.	P.
276	Old Canal	0	3	26
Pt. 310	Pasture	8	3	29
311	Do.	2	3	38
313} 403}	Do.	6	0	20
314	Cleeve Mill, House, Garden and Buildings	0	1	31
315	Pasture Orchard	0	2	28
405	Mill Race	0	2	1
1102	Old Canal	0	1	2
		A 20	3	15

The dwelling house contains two sitting-rooms, kitchen, back-kitchen, pantry, five bed-rooms, and two attics.

The Water Mill has three floors, and an overshot wheel driving two pairs of stones. Close to the Mill is a cart-house, in part 310 is a stone and tiled stable, with four stalls and loft over, and there is a newly-erected large piggery.

A large sum was spent last year on structural work. With the Mill is sold the shafting and main gearing.

The Executors of Mr Humphry Jones are tenants of the mill, orchard, etc., **7a. 3r. 2p.** in extent, at £66 0s. 0d. a year, their tenancy terminating at Candlemas, 1914. Mrs Florence M. Jones is the occupier of the remainder of the land, **13a. 0r. 13p.** in extent, at £25 a year on a Michaelmas tenancy.

The Lot is subject to a tithe (Newent Parish) of £4 3s 3d, the value thereof on the 1st January last being £3 0s 6¼d, and to a Land Tax of about £1 6s 9d.

It has a long frontage to the road leading to Upleadon, and is bounded on other sides by the Mill Race, the Great Western Railway, and Lot 9.

The Timber on this Lot has been valued at the sum of £49.

The Woodlands and Pound, Little Pound and Murrell's

On the front sheet the size of the type used to detail the woods is much larger than that for the sporting estate, suggesting that the value of timber was more appealing to a potential buyer than hunting, game rearing and shooting. The ability of the landed gentry to support these activities was certainly declining. Pound Farm (103 acres) was an equivalent size to the other farmhouses on the estate, with four bedrooms in the farmhouse and the usual outbuildings, though it did have the only hop kiln on the estate. Little Pound and Murrell's were more like smallholdings, and there were about 10 cottages as part of the lot. It is interesting that three of the cottages were still thatched so not all the estate cottages had been tiled in the improvements carried out after 1750. The head keeper's cottage was empty, which may suggest that the pheasants' house in the details was not a thriving enterprise any more, despite the insistence that the lot offered 'unusual facilities for the rearing and preservation of a large head of game'.

The 'prime quality of the oak timber' and the increasing demand for coppice wood was probably more successful in attracting interest from purchasers.

LOT 20   Pound Farm

TENANTS	George and Alice Chapman
CHILDREN	8 Children (one died)
ACREAGE	103 Acres 1 Rood 30 Perches
LAND	Approximately 87 acres Pasture, 6 acres Arable
	8 acres Orchard/ Pasture, and possible Hop Growing
LIVESTOCK	Pigs, Poultry, Horses and Cattle
RENT	£70 per annum
SOLD	Archibald Weller (re-sold to George Chapman)
PRICE	Unknown

George Chapman and his wife, Alice had eight children, though one had died by the time of the auction. In 1891 they were living in Tewkesbury and he was a butcher. By 1901 they were at Pound Farm with six children. The 1911 census shows them at Pound Farm with sons Frederick (18) and Howard (15), both described as workers, probably on the farm. A daughter, May (4), was also at the farm, not yet attending Oxenhall School. The other three children, aged 13, 22 and 23 were living at and managing Gamages, a farm in Much Marcle.

> **THE POUND FARM**
>
> The Dwelling House on the Pound Farm contains 2 sitting-rooms, kitchen, dairy, larder back-kitchen with furnace and baking oven, 4 bedrooms, and underground cellar.
>
> There is a lean-to in the rear of the house in which is a galvanised soft-water tank.
>
> In the orchard in the rear of the house is a large stone-built enclosed shed with corrugated iron roof.
>
> The Agricultural Buildings comprise a range of timber and tiled sheds and nag stables for 2, in enclosed yard, tie-up shed for 7, mill-house with mill and press and with granary over, hop kiln adjoining, range of 4 piggeries, with meal-house and poultry-house adjoining ; in a second yard, two open tie-up sheds for 16, with mangers and feeding passages, cart stable for 4, and chaff-house, both having lofts over, large barn with two bays and stone driving way, loose-box, and 5 bay wagon shed.
>
> Nearly all the above buildings are brick-built and tiled.
>
> The Whitehall Cottage on No. 7 on this Farm is stone or brick-built and tiled, and contains four rooms, together with piggery, lean-to shed with furnace and open and enclosed sheds.
>
> The Farm is let to Mr George Chapman, on a Candlemas tenancy, at £70 a year, and possession may be had at Candlemas 1914.

LOT 20

AN EXCEPTIONALLY ATTRACTIVE

Sporting and Agricultural Estate

COMPRISING:

THREE CAPITAL FARMS

KNOWN AS

POUND, LITTLE POUND & MURRELL'S

Enclosures of Accommodation Land

HEAD KEEPER'S COTTAGE.   COTTAGES & GARDENS

AND THE FOLLOWING WOODS

DYMOCK WOOD	GREAT & LITTLE HAY
OXENHALL WOOD	WOODS
PARK WOOD	GREENAWAY'S WOOD
BRANDHILL WOOD	BETTY DAW'S WOOD

AND

COLONEL'S GROVE AND WAINHOUSE GROVE WOODS

THE WHOLE BEING

ABOUT **850a. 3r. 7p.** IN EXTENT

AND OF WHICH THE FOLLOWING IS A PARTICULAR:—

No. on Ordnance Map	Description	Quantity A. R. P.	Total A. R. P.
	PARISH OF OXENHALL		
	POUND FARM, Mr GEO. CHAPMAN, Tenant		
6	Pasture	2 2 2	
7	Cottage Garden and Pasture Orchard	0 1 34	
8	Pasture Orchard	0 1 35	
9	Arable	0 3 34	
12	Pasture (laid down by tenant)	0 3 15	
10	Do.	0 1 30	
11	Do. (laid down by tenant)	0 2 29	
16	Pasture	12 3 25	
17	Do.	28 3 39	
19	Do.	8 0 23	
56	Pasture Orchard	0 3 8	
60	Do.	0 2 35	
66	Do.	0 2 34	
87	Pound Farmhouse, Garden, Yards and Buildings and Orchard	2 0 9	
88	Pasture Orchard	3 0 39	
91	{ Pasture	15 3 21	
	{ Arable	6 0 0	
		21 3 21	
261	Pasture	6 1 32	
262	Do.	5 1 24	
263	Pasture Orchard (laid down by tenant)	5 3 2	103 1 30
		Carried forward	103 1 30

15

No. on Ordnance Map	Description	Quantity A. R. P.	Total A. R. P.
	Brought forward		103 1 30
	LITTLE POUND FARM, Mr GEO. GURNEY, Tenant		
65	Arable	2 3 3	
68	Pasture	1 1 25	
69	Do.	1 3 3	
70	Pasture, with a few trees	0 3 36	
71	Pasture	6 0 23	
72	Pasture, with a few trees	1 0 0	
73	Lane	0 2 30	
74	Pasture Orchard	1 0 6	
75	Pasture	5 0 4	
78	Do.	4 1 4	
80	Do.	5 3 30	
82	Pasture Orchard	2 0 31	
83	Pasture	0 3 22	
84	Pasture Orchard	0 2 37	
85	House, Yards and Buildings	0 0 26	
86	Pasture Orchard	0 2 17	
93	Pasture Orchard	1 2 31	
95	Pasture	1 1 24	
97	Do.	5 1 0	
264	Old Cottage, Pasture Orchard, &c.	0 1 19	
265	Pasture, with a few trees	0 2 24	
266	Pasture Orchard	1 1 13	
375	Pasture	6 2 17	
376	Roughet	0 1 7	
			53 0 32
	PARISH OF DYMOCK		
	MURRELL'S FARM, Mr C. LANE, Tenant		
46	Pasture	4 0 6	
47	Do.	2 0 19	
48	Do.	2 3 19	
48a	Pasture Orchard	1 0 2	
49	House, Yards and Buildings	0 0 35	
50	Arable	1 3 6	
70	Pasture	3 1 17	
			15 1 24
	PARISH OF OXENHALL		
	Representatives of Late Mr CHAS. MATTHEWS, Tenants		
332	Pasture	1 1 0	
333	Do.	5 0 8	
334	Do.	5 0 22	
371	Do.	5 2 13	
373	Do.	3 0 36	20 0 39
	Mr SAMUEL JONES, Tenant		
269	Arable	3 2 3	
326	Do.	6 3 31	
330	Brake	0 3 31	
			11 1 25
	Mr JOHN GRIFFIN, Tenant		
51	Cottage and Garden	0 1 25	
52	Pasture Orchard	0 1 32	
53	Do.	0 1 10	
			1 0 27
	Mr W. S. BEAN, Tenant		
Pt. 22	Pasture	0 0 32	
24	Pasture Orchard	1 2 27	
			1 3 19
	Mr RICHD. HOWLEY, Tenant		
21	Cottage and Garden	0 1 31	
Pt. 22	Pasture	0 0 35	
			0 2 26
	Mr HENRY LOAD, Tenant		
94	Cottage and Garden	0 1 25	
	Carried forward		207 3 7

16

No. on Ordnance Map	Description	Quantity A. R. P.	Total A. R. P.
	Brought forward		207 3 7
	Mr E. SYSUM, Tenant		
372	Garden, pt. Pasture	0 2 8	
374	Arable Orchard	0 3 19	
377	Pasture Orchard	1 0 22	
378	Pasture	0 1 17	
379	House and Garden	0 0 34	
381	Garden	0 0 36	
	PARISH OF NEWENT		
476a	Pasture	0 1 3	
477	Do.	0 1 7	
			3 3 26
	PARISH OF OXENHALL		
	Mrs KEYSE, Tenant		
18	Cottage and Garden		0 0 23
	IN HAND		
90	Head Keeper's Cottage, &c.		0 2 35

WOODS, PLANTATIONS, &c.

PARISH OF DYMOCK

No.	Description	Quantity A. R. P.	Total A. R. P.
41	Dymock Wood	86 1 11	
43	Do.	85 1 15	
45a	Do.	0 1 10	
	PARISH OF OXENHALL		
3	Oxenhall Wood	48 2 10	
4	Do.	1 3 9	
5	Woodground Plantation	14 1 38	
13	Ellis's Cross Wood	2 1 25	
14	Do.	0 0 30	
64	Park Wood	35 3 14	
2	Brand Hill Wood	73 1 15	
79	Mount Pleasant Plantation	7 0 13	
76	Wood	0 1 23	
81	Little Hay Wood	57 1 30	
268	Great Hay Wood	152 2 2	
89	Do.	21 3 2	
50	Greenaway's Wood	26 1 1	
20	Betty Daw's Wood	12 2 35	
28	Colonel's Grove	9 1 4	
96	Wainhouse Grove	2 0 29	
			638 3 31
		A.	850 3 7

The Chapman family washing at the pump

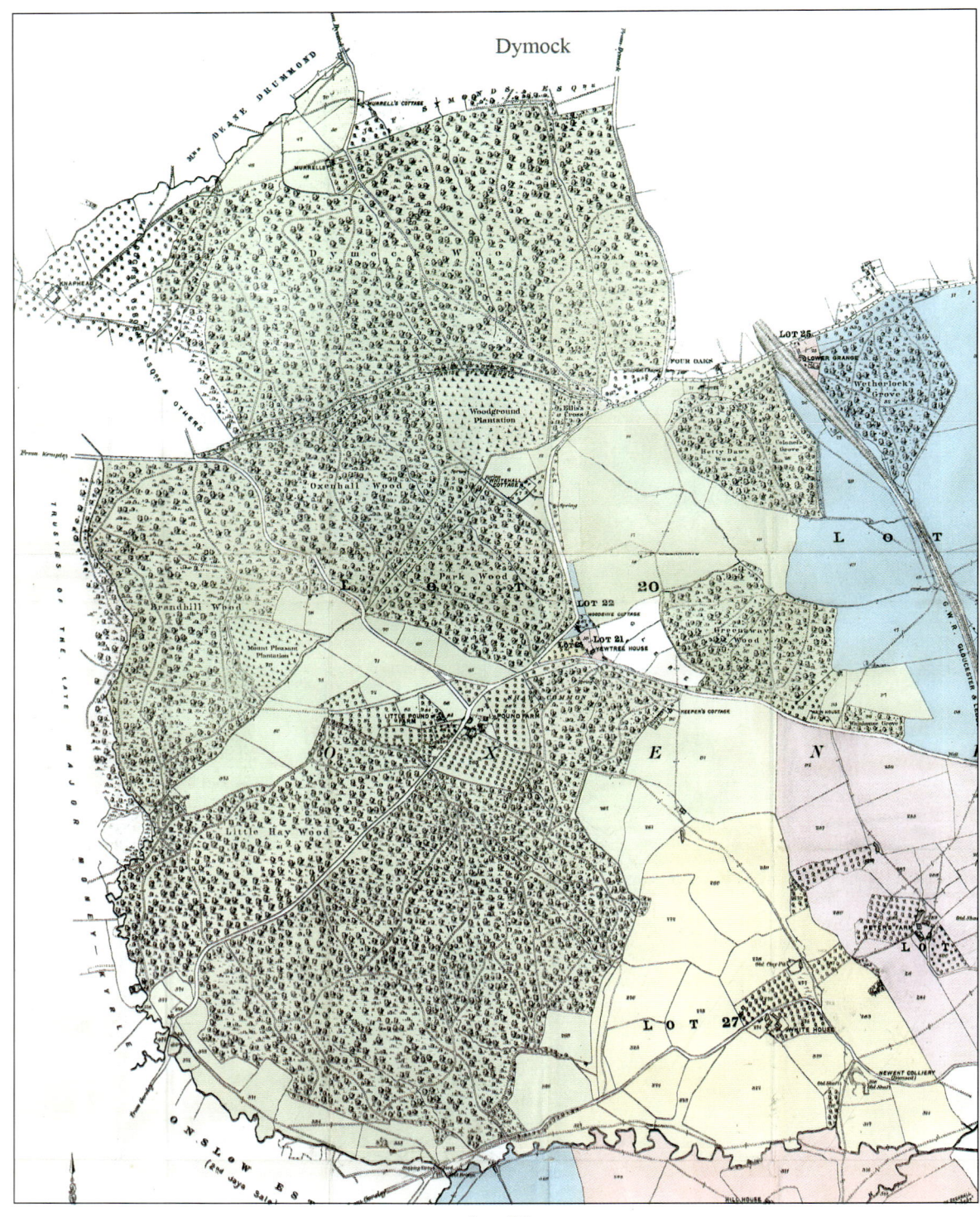

Lot 20

The house at Pound Farm in 1924

Howard Chapman watching his father George mowing grass

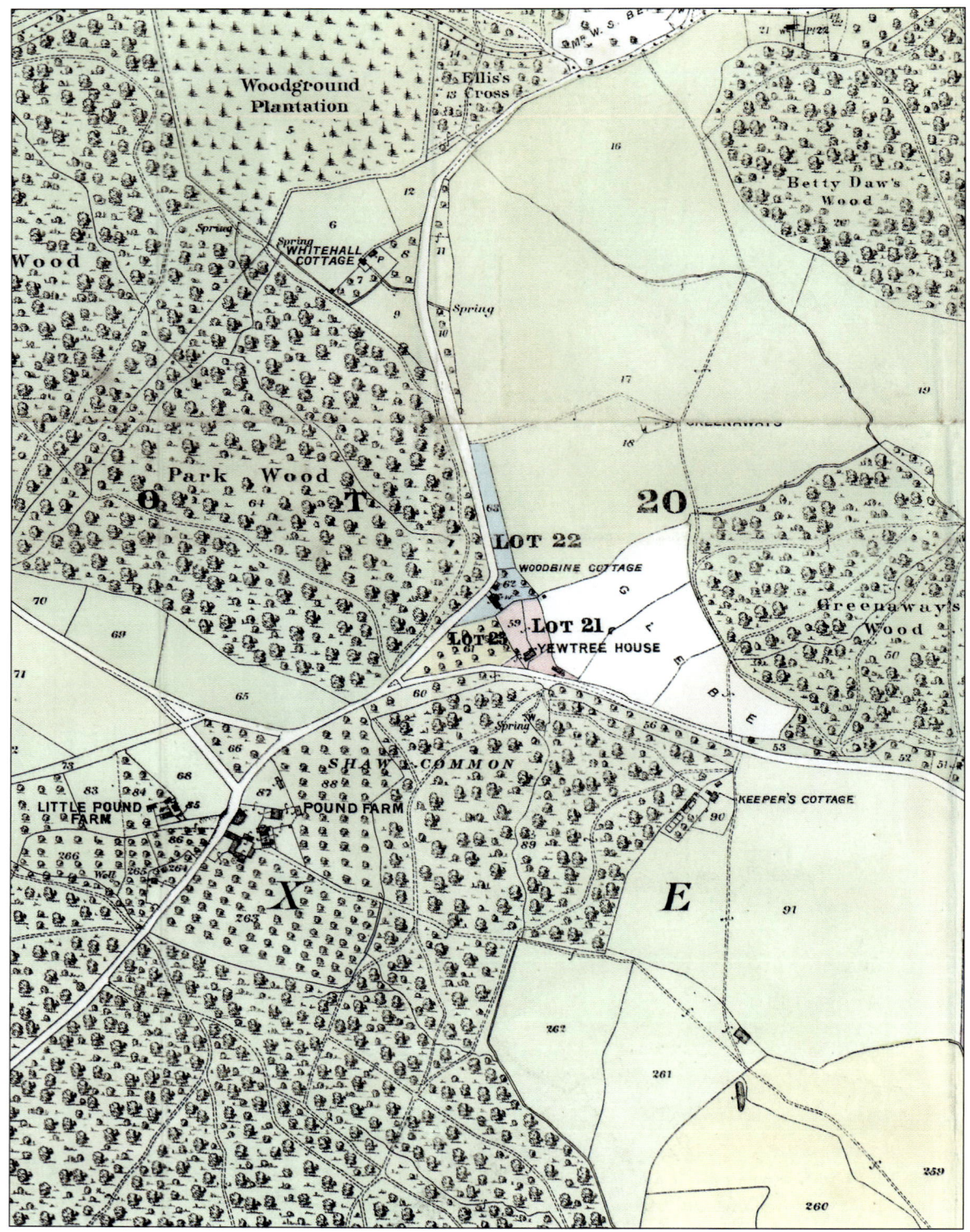

At the auction all of Lot 20 was bought by Mr Archibald Weller. He was a chartered accountant, living in Malvern with his wife and a 15-year-old son, who was a clerk working for an accountant, presumably his father. They also had a servant living with them. It is not known for how much Lot 20 was purchased, or if Mr Weller bought for himself or on behalf of someone else. In any event, George Chapman bought the farm from Mr Weller four months after the auction.

Little Pound Farm

TENANT	George Gurney
CHILDREN	Single, no Children
ACREAGE	53 Acres 0 Roods 32 Perches
LAND	Approximately 41 Pasture, 2 acres Arable and Orchards
LIVESTOCK	Horses, Cattle and Pigs
RENT	£32 per annum
SOLD	Archibald Weller (re-sold to Ambrose and Margaret Preece, 5 Children)
PRICE	Unknown

The tenant at the time of the sale, George Gurney, was 44 and single. In 1901 he was a labourer boarding at a house in Kempley. By 1911 he was farming at Little Pound Farm, but at the auction he bought the smaller Oxenhall Court Farm for which he paid £1,250.

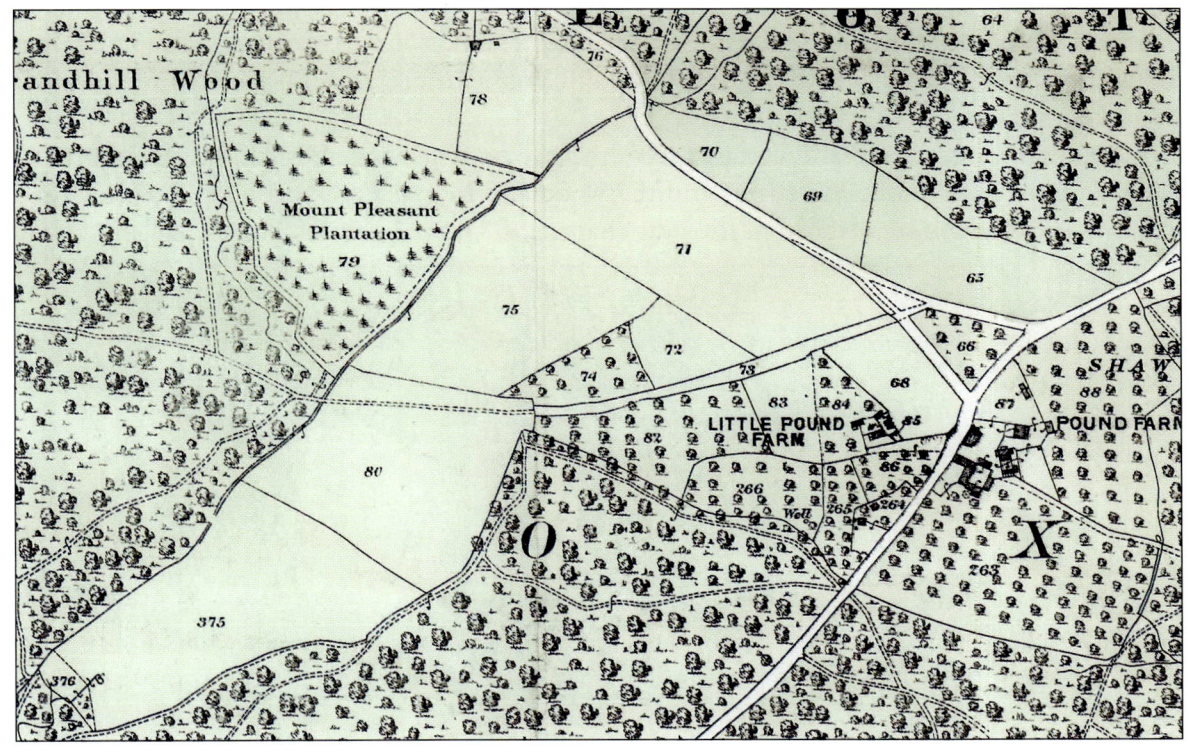

Archibald Weller bought Little Pound Farm at the auction and then sold it a few months later to the Preece family, who were farming in Cradley near Malvern.

He may have known them; perhaps, as an accountant, he even prepared the farm accounts. By the time of the 1911 census, Ambrose Preece and his wife Margaret had had five children, four of them still living: Adolphus, Mabel, Francis and David. They also had a lodger, a timber feller, living with them.

> **THE LITTLE POUND FARM**
>
> The Little Pound Farm is a compact holding with a dwelling house, brick and timber-built, with tiled roof, containing sitting-room, kitchen, back-kitchen with furnace, wash-house with furnace, dairy, and four bedrooms.
>
> The buildings comprise wagon house, yard with two open sheds, a brick and tiled barn with stone and brick floor, cart stable for 2 with loft over, cider-house, cow-house, and three piggeries.
>
> The Farm is in the occupation of Mr George Gurney, on a Candlemas tenancy, at the annual rent of £32, and possession may be had at Candlemas, 1914.

Murrell's

Though the heading of the sale details makes Murrell's sound like a farm, in fact it was a smallholding of about 15 acres. In 1891 John Jones was tenant there and his nephew James had taken over the tenancy by 1902. The Jones brothers, John's sons, had several tenancies in Oxenhall – Samuel was at Whitehouse, William at Winter's and Henry at Pella, and granddaughter Annie married George Goulding of Holder's. In 1913 at the time of the sale Charles Lane, the brother-in-law of James Jones, was the tenant. Murrell's, as part of Lot 20, was bought by Mr Weller who sold the properties on later. Murrell's is in Dymock so we have not traced later owners.

The other plots of land and cottages seem to have been put together for the sale as one lot with Pound and Little Pound Farms and the woodland to make a 'Sporting and Agricultural Estate'. The cottages are detailed in the next chapter.

> **MURRELL'S FARM**
>
> Is a compact desirable small holding with a dwelling house, brick-built and tiled, containing sitting-room, kitchen, back-kitchen with bread oven, pantry, and two bedrooms, and a good wash-house with fireplace, furnace, and pump.
>
> The Buildings include mill-house with cider mill and press, 2 enclosed sheds, wagon-house, barn with stone driving way, cart stable for 2, and 3 piggeries.
>
> The Farm is in the occupation of Mr Charles Lane, on a Candlemas tenancy, at the yearly rent of £18.
>
> The enclosures of pasture land (**20a. 1r. 0p.** in extent), in the occupation of the Representatives of the late Mr Charles Matthews, are let at an apportioned rent of £11.
>
> The **11a. 1r. 25p.** in the occupation of Mr Samuel Jones, form part of the Whitehouse Farm, Lot 27, and are, with the remainder of the Farm, let to him on a Candlemas tenancy, and possession may be had at Candlemas, 1914. The rent apportioned to the **11a. 1r. 25p.** is £8 0s 0d.
>
> The brick and timber-built Cottage, with thatched roof, in the occupation of Mr John Griffin, is situate at Shaw Common, and contains four rooms, with lean-to shed, and together with the pasture orchards, the whole **1a. 0r. 27p.** in extent, is let at the yearly rent of £6.

The Pasture Orchard in the occupation of Mr W. S. Bean, at £2 a year adjoins Four Oaks Bridge, and has a long frontage to Four Oaks Road.

The Cottage in the occupation of Mr R. Howley, is brick and timber-built, with tiled roof, contains four rooms, has a well of water and a good garden, well planted, and is, together with the pasture paddock, let at the annual rent of £5 19s 2d.

The Cottage in the occupation of Mr H. Load, is brick, stone, and timber-built, with tiled roof, contains 5 rooms and cellar, together with lean-to shed, piggery, and has a good well of water.

It is let at the yearly rent of £5.

The Cottage on Mr E. Sysum's holding is stone-built and newly thatched; it contains 4 rooms, and the buildings include a small barn, stable for two, trap-house and two piggeries. The Cottage Buildings and 3a. 3r. 26p. are let at £9 5s 4d a year.

Mrs Keyse's Cottage is stone-built with thatched roof, contains four rooms, and is let at £3 18s. od a year. There is a well of water, and in the garden is a pigs'-cot.

The Head Keeper's Cottage (late in the occupation of Arthur Williams, but now void) is a brick and timber-built dwelling house with tiled roof, containing sitting-room, kitchen with range, scullery with furnace and oven, pantry and 3 bedrooms. Adjoining is a brick and tiled shed, and near thereto are pheasants'-house, timber and tiled divided shed and piggery.

This Lot is subject to the following Tithe rent charges:—

	£	s	d
Oxenhall	107	12	2
Newent	0	1	4
Dymock	25	10	4
	133	3	10

the total value of the Tithes on the first January last being £96 16s 10d.

It is also subject to a Land Tax of £19 4s 10d.

The Woods, which form so important a feature of this Lot, consist almost entirely of oak coppice with oak standards. The practice has been to cut the coppice wood in each "fall" about every sixteen years, and sell such timber as is selected in that "fall" in the following year.

For the past sixty years or more Messrs Bruton, Knowles & Co. have held the annual sales of timber and coppice wood on the Onslow Estate. The returns from the woods included in this Lot for the past fourteen years show an average annual sale of £412.

The prime quality of the oak timber in these woods, which is particularly free from sap, has always proved attractive to timber merchants, and the demand for the coppice woods has steadily increased of recent years, as much as £22 5s. 0d. an acre having been realised for the coppice wood in Greenaway's Wood on the occasion of the last sale in that wood.

The purchaser shall pay the sum of £3462 for the timber growing on this Lot, this sum being inclusive of the Larch Plantations in Woodground and Mount Pleasant Plantations (Nos. 5 and 79 on plan); or he may have the option of taking such timber as he selects by valuation in the usual way, such option to be exercised on or before the 6th September, 1913, in which case the vendor reserves the right of selling such timber as is not selected, by auction or private contract before the end of 1913, subject to the Conditions of Sale usual on this estate (which may be seen at Messrs Bruton, Knowles & Co.'s office), which provide for clearance by December 31st, 1914; and he also reserves the right of clearing the said timber without compensation to the purchaser.

The coppice woods are included in the sale except in the case of the following, which the vendor reserves the right of selling and clearing in like manner to the timber as above mentioned, except that the conditions of sale will provide for clearing the coppice wood by the 25th March, 1915, and the cordwood by the 24th June, 1915:—

	A.	R.	P.
Ellis' Cross	2	2	0
Wetherlock's Grove	21	3	0
Hill House Grove	28	0	0
Dymock Wood—1st fall	31	1	32
" 2nd fall	29	3	20
" 3rd fall	35	0	24
	148	2	36

But the purchaser shall also have an option to take to any coppice wood included in the foregoing list by valuation in the usual way, such option to be exercised on or before the 6th September, 1913.

This Lot possesses exceptional sporting attractions. The Woods and Plantations are so well dispersed as to offer unusual facilities for the rearing and preservation of a large head of game.

Thirteen Excellent Farms

The sale details for Line House included a picture of the house, the particulars calling it 'a superior dwelling house' and picking out its veranda and garden for particular attention. Winter's Farm is noted as 'picturesque and gabled'. Apart from these details, farm particulars stick to the practical and utilitarian. The brick and tiles of the farmhouses are emphasised to show how they have been improved. To modern eyes these houses have a lot of bedrooms, between four and seven, but working farms needed rooms for servants who helped in the house and families were also much bigger in 1913. Servants were no doubt housed in the attics, and the 'back kitchen', which appears in many of the particulars, would have been their domain for food preparation, storage and washing. There was sometimes a scullery, dairy or larder as well.

If there was no mains water to the house it was pumped from a well in the yard or collected from a rainwater tank.

The 'furnaces' referred to in the farmhouse particulars were very important. Water for laundry would have been heated in a copper, and cooking done on a range with oven and hotplates. Rooms had open fires, big fireplaces in the drawing and dining rooms and small cast iron grates in the bedrooms, burning wood or coal.

Just as the house details show us how farming families lived in 1913, the descriptions of outbuildings show us what crops they grew, what livestock they kept and how they worked the land. The farms had big barns with a 'stone driving way' for bringing in the carts and wagons and providing space for threshing grain. Working horses needed stables and tack rooms, there were sheds for tying up animals and milking cattle, houses for keeping a bull, houses for calves, some poultry houses and nearly all of the farms had piggeries. Most farms also had a mill house with a cider press, sometimes with a granary above. Cider was still being made on farms and there were orchards of fruit trees. The timber on each lot was also given a value and this must have been an important resource for farmers for fencing, gates, repairs and for firewood. This paints a picture of mixed farms with ranges of outbuildings for keeping animals, making cider, and for storing crops and the implements and machines they used to work the land. The work must have been heavy and hard with only horse-drawn or steam-powered machinery to help them. Farmers relied on local labourers all year round, with extra manpower needed at harvest time.

Farmhouses had dairies, cold rooms (usually in the north-east of the house) and larders for storing food and keeping it cold before the advent of refrigerators. After threshing time the precious seed corn for next year was also kept in the house. A stone slab was used to salt the pig after slaughter and the joints were hung to dry from iron hooks supporting wooden slats in the ceiling. Farmers' wives were kept busy making butter, cream and cheese and looking after geese, ducks or chickens, taking eggs to market and preparing poultry for sale. Along the lanes between the farms dairy cows were herded for milking, and the full churns were put on wooden stands by the farm gates ready to be picked up by horse and cart. Supplies of groceries, coal and other essentials for the house also came up from Newent by horse and cart. Children walked to school in all weathers, the postman covered several miles on his daily round and those who had a bicycle or managed to get a lift on a passing cart counted themselves lucky.

Although farming families did move farms, it was often within a known area and Oxenhall must have been a close-knit community. Families tended to have a lot of children (George Goulding from Holder's had 12 children, though four died, and Robert Savidge from Hilter's had nine, though one son died). Second marriages would often occur when a first wife had died. By 1913, live-in servants were becoming less common but workers still lived in cottages 'tied' to a particular farm. Farmers' sons were expected to help on the farm until they married or got a farm of their own, whereas daughters often moved away to work unless they married locally.

Newent, with its railway station, shops, pubs and livestock market, was a social hub, but for Oxenhall folk social occasions were often centred on the church or chapel or their own homes. Neighbours or workers on a farm were invited for informal get-togethers – to share the ham and cider, to sing songs, tell tales, play cards and games. This sense of community is what older residents of Oxenhall have told us they remember, rather than the hard work of everyday life on the farms.

LOT 3   Lamb's Barn

In the late 17th century this property was named after the former owner of adjoining fields and sometime before 1841 a small farmhouse was built alongside the barn.

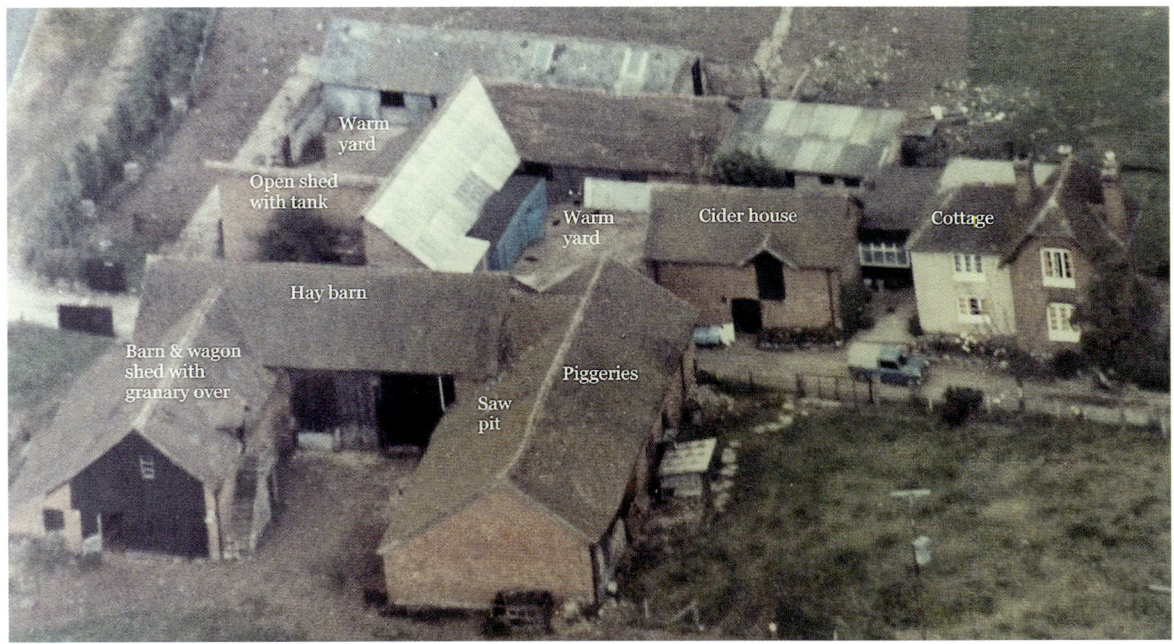

Aerial photo of Lamb's Barn in 1976 with the buildings labelled as they were in 1913

In 1911 George Evans and his wife Emily lived at Lamb's Barn with their children George aged 12, Kathleen aged 10 and baby Dora aged 3 months. George, a shepherd, was born in Stratford-on-Avon and Emily came from Cheltenham. Before coming to Oxenhall they had lived in other parts of Gloucestershire as George was born in Cobberly, Kathleen in Up Hatherley and Dora in Prestbury.

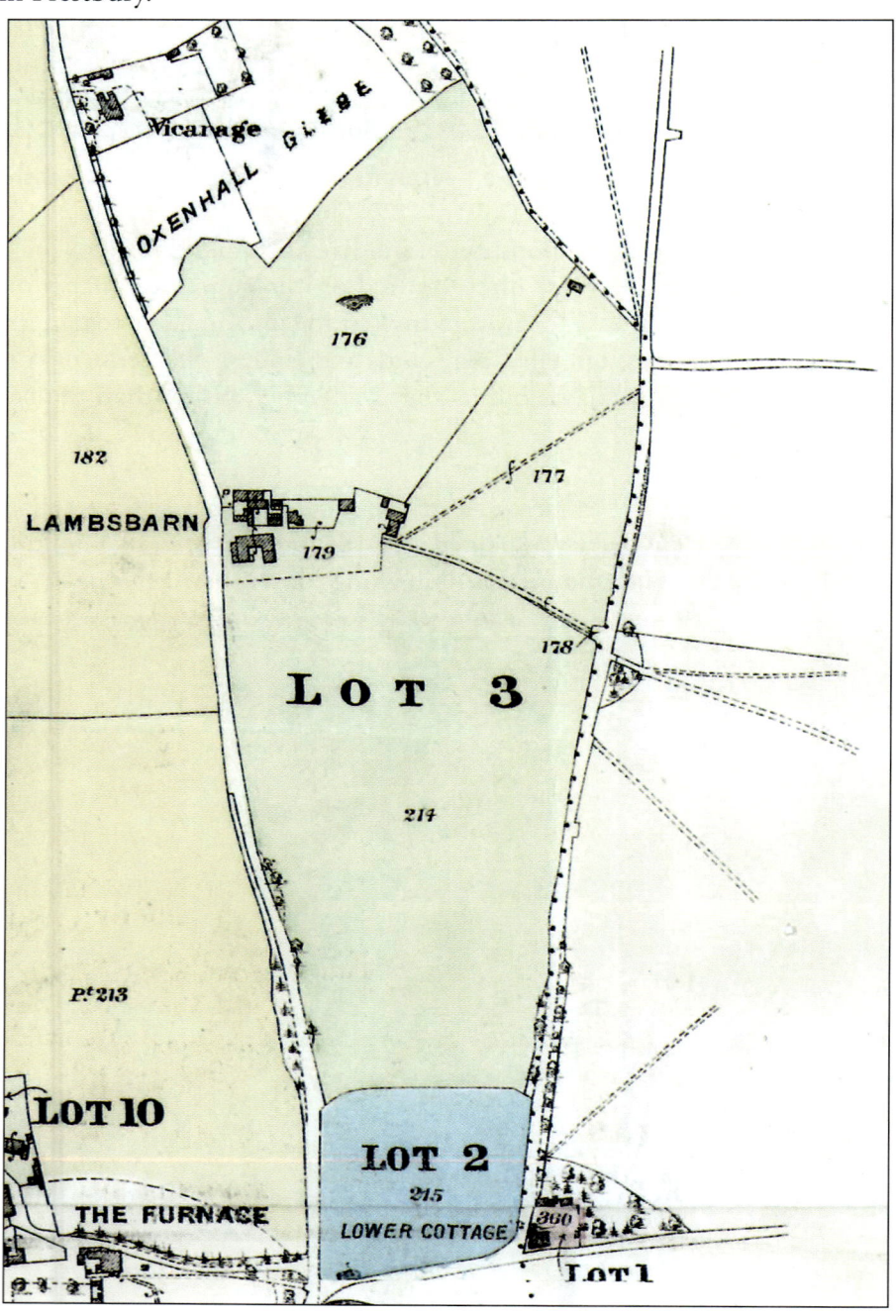

As Lamb's Barn was not sold at the sale it must have remained in the ownership of the Onslow family. Many of the buildings mentioned in the sale details can still be identified on the aerial photograph taken in 1976 (see p.53).

LOT 3

LAMB'S BARN

A VERY DESIRABLE SMALL HOLDING

comprising a cottage, superior farm buildings, and about **29a. 2r. 20p.** of pasture and arable land, of which the following is a particular:—

No. on Ordnance Map	Description	Quantity A. R. P.
	PARISH OF OXENHALL	
176	Pasture	9 1 28
177	Pasture	4 3 16
178	Roadway	0 0 2
179	Cottage, Garden, Yards, Buildings, &c...	1 0 38
214	Arable	14 0 16
		A 29 2 20

The Cottage, which is brick-built and tiled, contains sitting room, kitchen, back-kitchen, with furnace and baking oven, and three bedrooms, together with courtyard in which is a w.c., and garden.

There is a good supply of water.

The cottage, land and the following buildings are let to Mr W. Fowler Beckett on a Michaelmas tenancy, at an annual rent of £50:—Cider or root house (the loft above, in hand), two warm yards, in the first of which is an open shed with tank, and in the second: open sheds, enclosed feeding stalls for 5, loose box, two ranges of piggeries (5 in each range), barn, wagon shed (part in hand), with granary over, and implement shed.

The following buildings are in hand:—Lime shed and blacksmith's shop, carpenter's shop, saw pit, storage shed with two divisions, stable for 4, harness-room, lean-to cart-shed adjoining, barn and small enclosed shed.

Nearly all the buildings are substantially built of brick with tiled roofs.

This lot is in the centre of two roads, to each of which it has long frontages, and is bounded on the south by Lot 2, and on the north by the Sandyway Estate and Oxenhall Glebe.

This Lot is subject to a Tithe rent charge (Oxenhall Parish) of £10 0s 0d, the value thereof on the 1st January last being £7 5s 5d.

The Timber on this Lot has been valued at the sum of £69.

LOT 6   Line House Farm

TENANTS	According to the sale details Daniel and George Goulding were joint tenants. John and Charlotte Goulding lived in the house
CHILDREN	Horace, Olive, Phyllis, Marjorie and Gilbert
ACREAGE	60 Acres 0 Roods 32 Perches
LAND	Pasture, Arable, Pasture orchard and Garden
LIVESTOCK	Horses, Cattle, Pigs and Poultry
RENT	£78 10s per annum, 8s 10d for barn floor
SOLD	Sold in November 1913 to John Goulding
PRICE	£1,540

From the 1913 Onslow sale book it can be seen that the Goulding family worked their land in Oxenhall together. John and his brother George were joint tenants of the land and buildings at The Parks, while Daniel and George shared the tenancy of Line House Farm, which was occupied by John (son of Daniel) and his wife Charlotte. John started his working life as a grocer's apprentice but turned to farming when he married Charlotte Toomey in 1905.

In November 1913 John Goulding bought Line House Farm, the associated cottage and 60 acres of arable and pasture for £1,540, John and Charlotte continuing to live at Line House with their children Horace, Olive, Marjorie, Phyllis and Gilbert.

Line House was certainly a 'superior dwelling house' with its two sitting rooms and five bedrooms and large Victorian veranda. The large back-kitchen housed a pump, and the wash-house contained two furnaces and a large slate water tank.

In 1913 Percy and Minnie Williams were tenants in the cottage.

LOT 6
LINE HOUSE FARM
A VERY ATTRACTIVE PROPERTY

with a superior dwelling house, occupying an elevated and most pleasant position, with cottage, agricultural buildings, and about **60a. 0r. 32p.** of land, of which the following is a particular:—

No. on Ordnance Map	Description	Quantity A.	R.	P.
	PARISH OF NEWENT			
76	Arable	12	3	29
77	Do.	4	0	27
78	Pasture	4	2	27
79	Line House, Yards, Buildings, &c.	1	1	38
80	Pasture Orchard and Cottage and Garden	0	3	39
101	Pasture	13	2	23
	PARISH OF OXENHALL			
120	Arable	3	3	14
134	Do.	6	2	23
135	Pasture	7	1	2
137	Do.	4	2	10
		A. 60	0	32

The dwelling house contains 2 sitting-rooms, kitchen, larder, 5 bedrooms, and coal house. In the courtyard are large back-kitchen with pump, dairy, wash-house with two furnaces, and large slate water tank. Near thereto are nag stable, harness-room, and trap-house.

A verandah extends along the south side of the house, and there is an excellent garden.

The Farm Buildings comprise mill-house, with mill and press with granary over, 4 piggeries, poultry house, barn in which is a corn-shed, cart stable for 4 with harness-room, open and enclosed sheds, wagon and implement sheds.

The well-built cottage (pt 80.) contains kitchen, back-kitchen, pantry, and three bedrooms, together with good garden, shed, and piggery.

This Lot is in the occupation of Messrs Daniel and John Goulding, on a Lady-day tenancy at £78 10s 0d a year, together with interest of 8s. 10d. a year, payable in respect of a floor in Barn.

The cottage and garden (pt. 80) are let to Mr George Goulding at the nominal rent of one shilling a year.

Possession may be had at Lady-day, 1914.

It is subject to Tithe rent charges, that of Oxenhall being £7 14s 0d, that of Newent being £9 10s 0d, the total value thereof on the 1st January last being £12 10s 1¼d.

It is also subject to a Land Tax of £2 14s 1¼d.

The Timber on this Lot has been valued at the sum of £34.

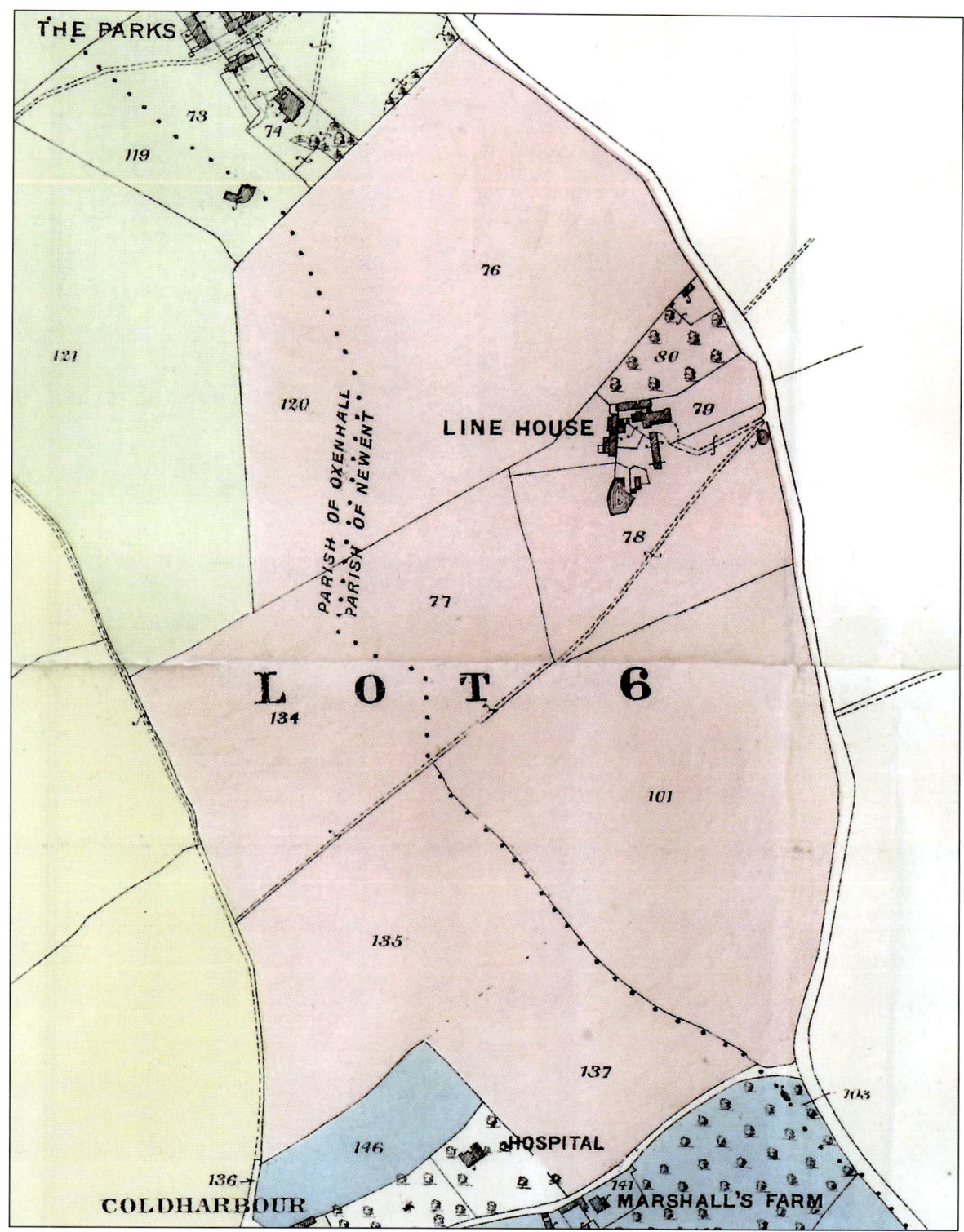

Line House in 1913

John Goulding's family in 1912.
John and Charlotte with (L-R) Marjorie, Horace, Phyllis and Olive

LOT 7   Marshall's Farm

LOT 7

MARSHALL'S FARM

A VERY DESIRABLE SMALL HOLDING

situate in the parish of Newent, and comprising an excellent dwelling house, brick-built and tiled, and about **43a. 3r. 30p.** of pasture, pasture orcharding and arable land, of which the following is a particular:—

No. on Ordnance Map	Description	Quantity A. R. P.
	PARISH OF OXENHALL	
139	Arable	7 2 38
140	Pasture, part Orchard	4 2 19
141	Marshall's Farm-house, Garden, Yards and Buildings	0 2 4
142	Arable	19 3 28
146	Do.	2 0 30
159	Do.	2 2 12
164	Roadway	0 0 39
165	Arable	1 1 27
166	Do.	4 2 0
	PARISH OF NEWENT	
103	Pasture	0 0 33
		A 43 3 30

The dwelling house, which is brick-built, and tiled, occupies a pleasant elevated position, and contains 2 sitting rooms, kitchen, larder, dairy, 4 bedrooms, and box-room, together with underground cellar, and back-kitchen, with furnace.

The buildings include a mill-house with mill and press and a granary, extending over the back-kitchen and the mill-house. In a fold-yard are 2-stall stable, open sheds, nag stable and piggeries, barn, calves'-house, and piggery in rick-yard, a detached barn, lean-to wagon shed, and enclosed cow-house.

The property has long frontage to the road leading from Newent to Ledbury.

It is in the occupation of Messrs Robert and George Savidge, on a Candlemas tenancy at the annual rent of £72 5s 0d.

Possession may be had at Candlemas, 1914.

It is subject to a Tithe rent charge (Oxenhall Parish) of £12 13s 11d, the value thereof on the 1st January last being £9 4s 7¼d, and also to a Land Tax of £3 2s 5d.

The Timber on this Lot has been valued at the sum of £56.

TENANTS	Robert and George Savidge were joint tenants but George and Ruby Savidge lived in the house
CHILDREN	One son, George
ACREAGE	43 Acres 3 Roods 30 Perches
LAND	Pasture, Arable and Pasture Orchard
LIVESTOCK	Horses, Cattle and Pigs
RENT	£72 5s per annum
SOLD	Not sold at auction
PRICE	Not Known

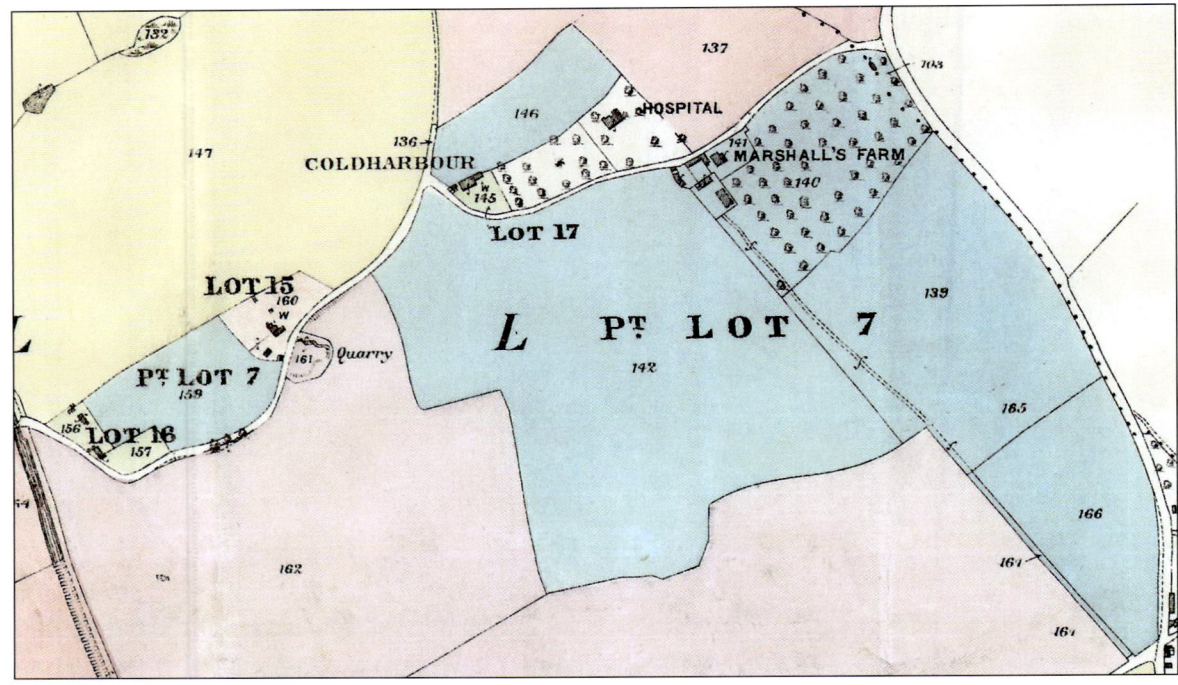

Marshall's Farm became a part of the Onslow Estate in 1890 when Richard Onslow bought it from James Heane, continuing a policy adopted by the Foley family whereby any available freehold land was bought and added to the estate.

In 1913 George and Ruby Savidge lived at Marshall's. George was born in Flaxley and married Ruby Parlour, a Newent lass, in 1909. Their son, also George, was born in 1910. John Guppy, a 32-year-old farm labourer originally from Highbridge, Somerset also lived on the farm. George and his father Robert were joint tenants but at the time of the sale Robert, born in Wolverhampton, lived at Hilter's with his family.

The farm buildings included a mill-house with press and a large granary. Marshall's was not sold at the 1913 sale and continued to be let until sold in 1922 for £1,900.

Marshall's farmhouse in 1913.
The people are probably
George and Ruby Savidge.

LOT 8   Winter's Farm

WINTER'S FARM
A VERY DESIRABLE HOLDING

situate in the parish of Oxenhall, comprising a picturesque gabled house of brick, timber, and tile, a good set of agricultural buildings, and about **104a. 2r. 35p.** of pasture and arable land, of which the following is a particular:—

No. on Ordnance Map	Description	Quantity A.	R.	P.
	PARISH OF OXENHALL			
161	Quarry and Sand Pit	0	1	3
162	Pasture	22	1	2
163	Arable	41	1	16
184	Yard and Buildings	0	1	18
185	Farmhouse, Garden, Yards and Buildings	0	3	25
187	Pasture (laid down by tenant)	16	2	7
199	Arable	7	2	14
200	Pasture	4	3	23
202	Do.	3	2	31
203	Do.	5	1	12
225	Do.	1	2	4
		A. 104	2	35

The Dwelling House contains dining and drawing-rooms, kitchen, back-kitchen, pantry, 3 bedrooms, 2 attics and underground cellar.

Near to the dwelling house are nag stable and coach-house (the partition in the latter being the property of the tenant).

A good supply of water is afforded by a pump in the courtyard, and in the back-kitchen is a soft-water tank.

The buildings in the first yard comprise open and enclosed shed, and 2 piggeries, and in the second yard, an open shed calves'-house, cart stable, calves'-shed with granary and loft over, and poultry-house.

In the rickyard is a barn having a stone driving way, one bay concreted, and with chaff-cutting floor, corn-room, with concrete floor and granary, a feeding shed in the rear of barn for tying up 7, and a second feeding stall for 7.

The Farm is in the occupation of Mr William C. Jones, on a Candlemas tenancy, at a rent of £120 a year, together with interest of £2 5s 8d in respect of the granary.

Possession may be had at Candlemas, 1914.

With this Lot is sold the right of the water from the old Canal to field No. 187 on the map, as now enjoyed by the present tenant. See note attached to Lot 12.

The Lot is subject to a Tithe rent charge (Oxenhall Parish) of £30 7s 2d, the value thereof on the 1st January last being £22 1s 5½d., and to a Land Tax of £5 15s 0d.

The Timber on this Lot has been valued at the sum of £75.

TENANTS	William and Julia Jones
CHILDREN	Kate Dorothy and Elsie Lilian
ACREAGE	104 Acres 2 Roods 35 Perches
LAND	Pasture and Arable
	Quarry and Sand Pit
LIVESTOCK	Horses, Cattle, Pigs and Poultry
RENT	£120 per annum plus £2 5s 8d interest for granary
SOLD	William C. Jones
PRICE	£1,850

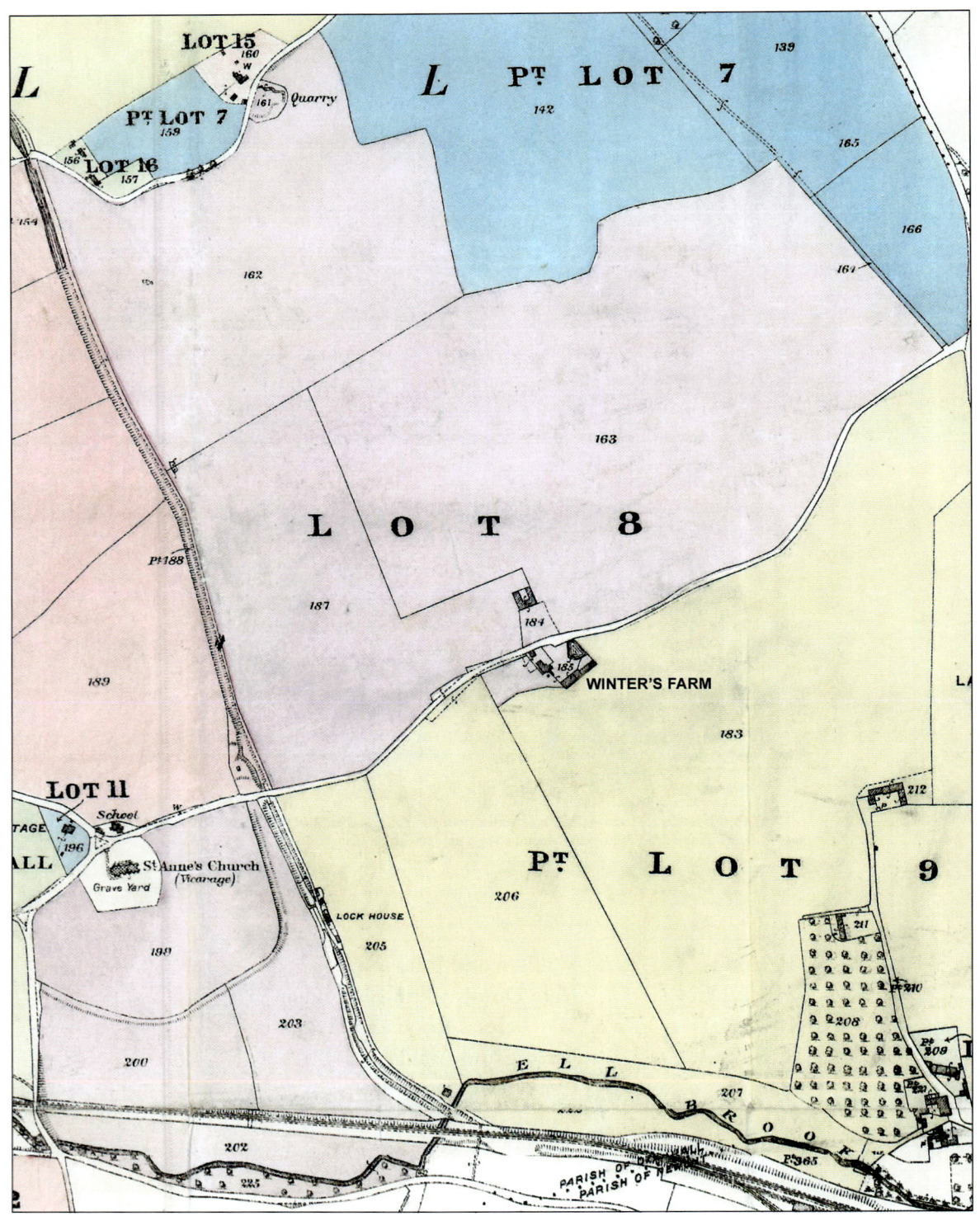

Winter's Farm in 1913

*Cattle in the fold yard. William Jones and his daughter Elsie Lilian.
The young man may be William's nephew, Carey Parry.*

In 1913 the occupants of Winter's Farm were William Charles Jones, his wife, Julia Mary [née Kingscott], and their two daughters, Kate Dorothy and Elsie Lilian, together with a nephew, Carey Parry. Carey, aged 25, worked on the farm.

A pump in the courtyard provided a good supply of water and there was a soft-water tank in the back kitchen. Interestingly, this sale lot included the right to use water from the old canal specifically for one field.

In 1915 daughter Kate married Charles Frank Savidge of Poyke's farm, Newent. They had four children: Kenneth, Elsie, Mary and Norman. Elsie continued to live at home.

William Charles farmed Winter's until his death in 1929. A year later Kate's husband Charles Frank Savidge bought the farm and the family continued to live there until 1985.

Kate Jones (born 1891) in the porch at Winter's

LOT 9   The Furnace Farm

TENANT	James Lodge (deceased)
SUB-LET	Thomas Taylor and Walter Blewitt
ACREAGE	104 acres 2 roods 30 perches
LAND	Mixed farm
RENT	£150 per annum
SOLD	Frank Treasure (solicitor) for Mrs Lodge
PRICE	£2,150

At the 1911 census Furnace Farm's farmhouse was divided into two cottages let out to men working on the farm. Thomas Taylor, born in Twyning and then aged 67, was a cowman who had worked locally for over 40 years. He had married Ann Hyett when he was aged 20 and they had had six children. Thomas had lived in different places around Oxenhall since 1871. At the time of the census he was living with a daughter, then a widow, aged 40, his wife Ann having died in 1907. He died in Gloucestershire in 1918 aged 75.

In the other cottage was Walter Blewitt, who had been born in Newent. In 1891 Walter was 21 and living in Malswick with his parents, when his father's occupation is not given in the census. Walter and his brother William, aged 15, were both general labourers, and they had a sister, Alice, aged 9. By 1901 Walter was married to Sarah and had three children: Florence aged 6, Frank aged 4 and Hubert aged 2. They were living in Bury Bar, Newent and Walter was a carter on a farm. By 1911 Walter, now listed as a waggoner, and Sarah had another child,

William aged 8, while Florence, now aged 16, had left home and was working as a housemaid in Dursley. Walter died in Gloucestershire in 1954 aged 84.

James Lodge, listed as the tenant of Furnace Farm in the 1913 sales particulars, was recorded in the 1871 census as married and listed as both a farmer and an innkeeper at the Crown Inn at Lea. In 1881 he was running The George Hotel in Newent. In 1891, as well as the tenancy of Furnace Farm, he was the tenant at Parks Farm, but he had given that up by 1902. He had died in 1909, but his wife bought the farm at the auction. James and Mary had 14 children, according to census records, although in the 1911 census, when for the first time mothers had to record child deaths, she recorded 15 children born alive and 13 still living.

In 1911 she still had four children living with her at the George, one of her sons managing the farm. She died in 1922.

THE FURNACE FARM

situate in the parishes of Oxenhall and Newent, comprising two cottages, farm buildings, and about **104a. 2r. 30p.** of pasture, pasture orcharding, and arable land, of which the following is a particular:—

No. on Ordnance Map	Description	Quantity A. R. P.
	PARISH OF OXENHALL	
182	Arable	8 2 14
183	Do.	38 3 21
205	Pasture	5 2 35
206	Arable	14 2 39
207	Pasture	3 3 6
208	Pasture Orchard	4 3 1
Pt. 210	Road	0 2 5
211	Two Cottages and Gardens	0 1 12
212	Yards and Buildings	0 1 33
Pt. 213	Arable	14 0 33
Pt. 221	Buildings and Rickyard	0 2 18
222	Pasture	2 3 17
	PARISH OF NEWENT	
362	Pasture	8 2 0
Pt. 365	Do.	0 2 36
		A. 104 2 30

Each of the two cottages which are brick-built and tiled, contains 4 rooms, one having also a lean-to shed.

The buildings on No. 212 comprise barn with concrete driving way, tie-up shed and implement shed adjoining, machine-house adjoining barn, wagon-shed together with open shed and bull-house in fold-yard, in which there is a pump.

The buildings in No. 221 comprise a stone-built barn with tiled roof (formerly the Tithe Barn), stable for 5, two stalls and loose-box, open shed and bull-house in yard, and in a second yard, open and enclosed sheds and root house. Both yards are supplied with Gloucester Corporation water, for which the tenant pays £2 0s 0d a year.

This is a most productive tract of land, close to the Newent Railway Station, is in a high state of cultivation, and is well-known to have yielded some of the finest crops of corn and roots in the district. It is now, together with a yard and buildings not included in the Sale, in the occupation of the representatives of the late Mr James Lodge, on a Candlemas tenancy, at £156 0s 0d a year, the landlord paying the rates on No. 182. The rent apportioned to this Lot is £150 0s 0d.

Possession may be had at Candlemas, 1914.

It is subject to Tithe rent charges, Oxenhall Parish being £30 11s 1d, Newent £2 8s 9d, Pauntley 9s 9d, the total value thereof on the 1st January last being £24 6s 10d., and to a Land Tax of £7 9s 4½d.

The Timber on this Lot has been valued at the sum of £57.

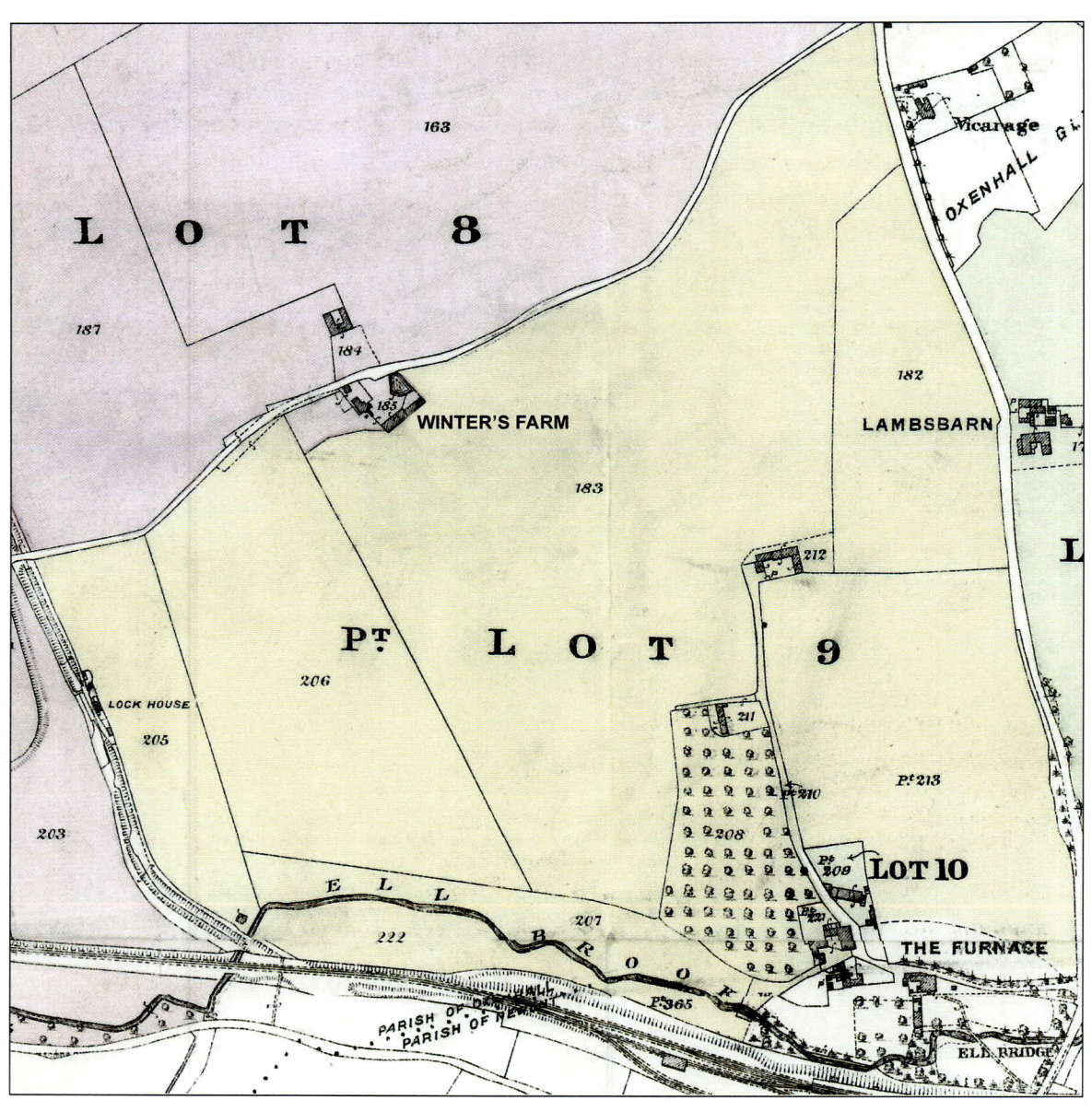

LOT 12   Hilter's Farm

In 1913 the Savidge family from Flaxley had been tenants at Hilter's Farm for over 20 years.

TENANTS	Robert and Charlotte Savidge
CHILDREN	George, Lilian, Charles, John (died aged 4), Albert, Alice, Robert Henry, and May
ACREAGE	117 Acres 0 Roods 36 Perches
LAND	Pasture: 43 Acres 1 Rood 19 Perches
	Arable : 69 Acres 3 Roods 38 Perches
LIVESTOCK	Horses, Cows, Pigs, and Poultry
RENT	£150 per annum
SOLD	Not sold at auction; but bought later by John Robinson
PRICE	Unknown

The Savidge Family at Hilter's, 1887-1913

Frank Robert Savidge and his wife Charlotte Ann both came from farming families and were living at Hilter's Farm at the time of the 1891 census. They married in 1881 in Ross and ten years later had five children and three servants – Charles Davis aged 38 of Flaxley, Joseph King

The Savidge Family at Hilter's c.1905
Standing: George, Lilian (Cis), Charlie and Robert Henry (Harry) on horseback
Seated: Alice, Robert (Frank), Charlotte and May

LOT 12

HILTER'S FARM

situate in the Parish of Oxenhall, comprising an excellent dwelling house, ample set of farm buildings, cottage and about **117a. 0r. 36p.** of pasture and arable land, of which the following is a particular:—

No. on Ordnance Map	Description	Quantity A. R. P.
	PARISH OF OXENHALL	
101	Pasture	4 3 19
102	Do.	11 3 32
151	House, Garden, Yards and Buildings	1 1 21
152	Arable	14 2 26
153	Pasture	8 2 28
189	Arable	14 1 9
190	Do.	14 0 23
233	Do.	12 2 20
237	Pasture	2 3 30
241	Do.	1 1 19
242	Arable	6 0 20
243	Pasture	13 2 11
248	Arable	8 0 20
247	Cottage and Garden	0 0 31
	IN HAND	
Pt. 154	Old Canal	0 1 2
Pt. 188	Do.	2 0 5
	A.	117 0 36

The dwelling house, brick-built, with tiled roof, contains dining and drawing-rooms, kitchen, dairy, back-kitchen with three furnaces, 5 bedrooms (approached by two staircases), and 2 attics, and underground cellar.

The Farm Buildings comprise mill-house with mill and press and with loft over, poultry, house, implement shed, calves'-house, with granary above; and in No. 1 fold-yard, a partly-enclosed shed, cart stable for 5, with loft over, feeding stalls for 6, nag stable for 2, and harness-room. In second yard, open shed with loose-box at end, 2 piggeries, and tie-up shed for 4; and also barn with two stone driving ways, one bay being pitched with brick, wagon-house, to which is attached a lean-to implement shed, and poultry-house.

Nearly the whole of the buildings are brick-built with tiled roofs.

The Dwelling House occupies a most pleasant elevated position near to the Church, and a pillar letter box is close at hand.

The Gloucester Corporation water is supplied to both house and buildings, for which the tenant pays 1s 0d per 1000 gals.

The cottage on No. 247 contains 4 rooms, together with shed, garden and piggery.

The Farm, together with a strip of garden ground, No. 251 on plan, in Lot 13, is in the occupation of Mr Robert Savidge, on a Candlemas tenancy, at a rent of £150 4s 4d. a year. Possession of the Farm may be had at Candlemas, 1914. The estimated rent of the Old Canal (2a. 1r. 7p.) is £1 10s. 0d.

The Farm has long frontages to the road leading from Oxenhall Church to Shaw Common.

This Lot is sold subject to the right of the tenant of Winter's Farm (Lot 8) to take water from the old Canal, as now enjoyed by him, and also to a right of road being reserved for the tenant of Pella Farm (Lot 24), over Nos. 243 and 101 on the plan.

It is subject to a Tithe Rent charge of £31 4s 1d, the value thereof on the 1st January last being £22 13s 9d, and to a Land Tax of £6 18s 11½d.

The Timber on this Lot has been valued at the sum of £72

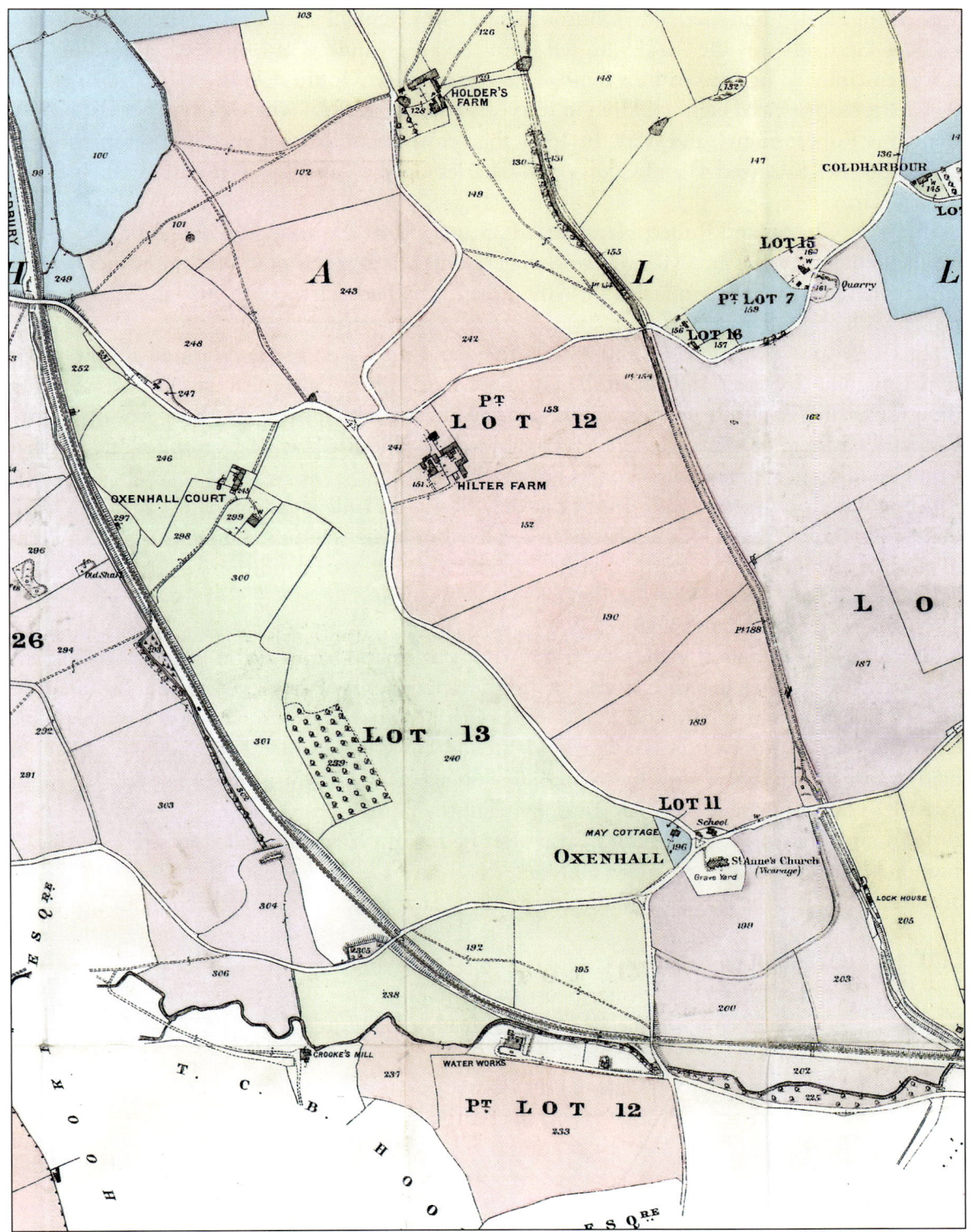

aged 19 of Flaxley, and Gertrude Johnson aged 17 of Oxenhall – living with them at the farm. Perhaps Gertrude was the maid who fell from the attic window and survived, according to a story remembered by the Griffiths family (tenants at Hilter's in the 1930s).

Charlotte produced eight children in ten years and was aged 44 when she had her last babies, the twins Robert Henry and May. In 1901 the census recorded that they had seven children (John died in 1892 aged 4) and George and Charles (aged 17 and 15) were helping their father run the farm.

By 1911 Charles and Robert Henry (aged 25 and 18) were working on the farm, Alice was a supplementary teacher and May was working at home. George was now a tenant farmer himself at Marshall's Farm, having married in 1909. Lilian, who had married in 1907, and Albert, were no longer living at home.

In 1913 Robert was aged 62 and Charlotte 64 and they had lived and farmed at Hilter's for something like 26 years. The sale of the Onslow Estate in July 1913 must have been a worrying time for them. They did not buy Hilter's at the auction but moved to a property in Yatton. Robert died there in 1915. George Savidge moved to The Rock at Lea, on the same day that Sam Goulding left there and moved to Lower House.

The cottage on the farm (247 on the sale details) was on land at the side of the road in a small quarry opposite Oxenhall Court Farm. It was lived in by agricultural workers at Hilter's Farm until about 1968, when it was demolished as it was in very poor condition.

The Robinson Family, 1913-1947

John Robinson was a local man, his family farming at Knapp Farm, Aston Ingham. He lost his first wife, Edith, after less than a year of their marriage, when they lived at Marshall's Farm. The 1901 census shows him still living there with his sister and two workers. He must have remarried shortly afterwards, for the 1911 census shows him and his second wife, Alice, at Baldwyn's Farm, Newent with four children – Sheila, Harold, Muriel and Oswald. They also had a 19-year-old worker, Reginald Bird, living at the farm.

John and Alice moved to Hilter's Farm after he bought it when it failed to sell at the 1913 auction. Here they had two more children, Noel and Dennis. Sheila died in the influenza outbreak of 1918. The acreage and mixed use of the land stayed the same throughout this time.

LOT 13   Oxenhall Court Farm

TENANTS	Amos Scott and wife Eliza
CHILDREN	Cecil, Annie. Three grandchildren: Edgar, Alice and Sidney
ACREAGE	77 Acres
LAND	Oats, Corn, Root crops
LIVESTOCK	Sheep and Beef cattle
RENT	£91 per annum
SOLD	George Gurney (tenant at Little Pound Farm)
PRICE	£1,250

LOT 13

OXENHALL COURT FARM

A COMPACT HOLDING

situate in the Parish of Oxenhall, and comprising a Dwelling House known as Oxenhall Court, agricultural buildings, and **77a. 1r. 30p.** of pasture and arable land, and arable orcharding, of which the following is a particular:—

No. on Ordnance Map	Description	Quantity A. R. P.
	PARISH OF OXENHALL	
	Mr AMOS SCOTT, Tenant	
192	Pasture	2 3 18
195	Do.	6 2 19
238	Do.	5 0 19
239	Arable	2 3 20
240	Do.	36 0 36
245	Yards and Buildings	0 1 4
246	Arable	6 1 34
252	Pasture	2 0 10
297	Do.	0 1 38
298	Do.	2 0 21
299	House, Garden, &c.	0 3 22
300	Pasture	5 3 27
301	Do.	5 1 10
	Mr ROBERT SAVIDGE, Tenant	
251	Garden	0 0 32
		A 77 1 30

Oxenhall Court, which is a double gabled house, stone or brick-built, with tiled roof, contains dining and drawing-rooms, kitchen, back-kitchen with furnace, dairy, 5 bedrooms, box-room, and underground cellar.

The Farm Buildings comprise two piggeries, cart stable for three with loft over, mill-house, with mill and press, with granary over, barn with stone driving way, cart shed, and open and enclosed sheds, the latter in two yards.

With the exception of one shed, which is timber-built with tiled roof, all the above-mentioned buildings are brick-built and tiled.

The Gloucester Corporation water is laid on to the back-kitchen (tenant paying at the rate of 1/- per 1000 gals.), and under a lean-to at back of the house is a large soft-water tank.

This Lot, with the exception of No. 251, the garden is in the occupation of Mr Amos Scott, on a Candlemas tenancy, at the yearly rent of £91.

Possession may be had at Candlemas, 1914.

It is subject to a Tithe rent charge of £20 2s 10d, the value thereof on the 1st January last being £14 12s 10½d, and also to a fixed rent charge of £1 9s 4d payable to the Vicar of Oxenhall.

The Timber has been valued at the sum of £49.

The tenants at the time of the 1913 sale were Amos Scott and his wife, Eliza. In 1901 Amos was the bailiff at Yew Tree Farm, Huntley. They had seven children but by 1913 all but two had left home. On the night of the census they also had three grandchildren staying with them and a man who looked after the horses, William Griffin. They did not buy the farm at the auction but Amos died in Newent in 1927 so he clearly stayed in the area. Instead the farm was bought by Mr George Gurney for £1,250; he allegedly paid in gold sovereigns! He had been the tenant at Pound Farm and was a bachelor who lived with his sister. He grew oats, corn and root crops on the land and kept sheep and beef cattle.

LOT 14 Holder's Farm

HOLDER'S FARM
A DESIRABLE COMPACT HOLDING

situate in the Parish of Newent, comprising an excellent commodious Dwelling House, cottage, agricultural buildings, and about **139 a. 2r. 11p.** of pasture and arable land, of which the following is a particular :—

No. on Ordnance Map	Description	Quantity A.	R.	P.
	PARISH OF OXENHALL			
	Messrs D. and G. GOULDING, Tenants			
103	Arable	11	1	32
104	Do.	18	0	8
105	Pasture	3	1	31
106	Pasture (laid down by tenant)	11	1	20
122	Pasture	15	1	15
123	Arable	8	2	29
124	Old House and Garden	0	0	37
125	Pasture, with a few trees	5	1	5
126	Pasture	4	0	37
128	Holder's Farmhouse, Yards, Buildings, etc.	1	0	14
129	Lane	0	1	15
130	Old Canal	0	0	15
131	Do.	0	0	20
132	Withy Bed	0	0	33
133	Arable	10	3	0
147	Arable	24	1	35
148	Pasture	11	1	33
149	Do.	12	0	38
	IN HAND			
136	Roadway	0	0	7
Pt. 154	Old Canal	0	1	15
155	Old Tow Path	0	1	12
	A.	139	2	11

The Dwelling House, which is brick-built with tiled roof, contains dining and drawing-rooms, kitchen, dairy, two pantries, 5 bedrooms, dressing room, and 2 attics, together with underground cellar and wash-house with two furnaces.

A range of brick, timber, and tiled buildings near thereto includes cider-house with granary over, cider mill-house with mill and press, and poultry-house.

The divided yards are supplied with Gloucester Corporation water, tenant paying at the rate of 1/- per 1000 gals.

In No. 1 yard are nag stable for 2, and loose box, open shed with cow-house attached, barn with stone driving way, shed for tying up 6, with loft adjoining barn; a wagon-house at either end of barn, and in a second yard, open shed, chaff-house, cart stable for 6 trap-house, and 4 piggeries.

All the above buildings, with the exception of the chaff-house, which is brick, timber, and tiled, are brick-built and tiled.

The Cottage, formerly occupied as a farmhouse, on No. 124, is brick-built and tiled, and contains kitchen, back-kitchen, dairy, two bedrooms and an attic. There is a good well of water here, and in the large garden is a piggery.

In No. 125 is a stone, timber, and thatched open and enclosed shed.

The Farm is in the occupation of Messrs Daniel and George Goulding, on a Candlemas tenancy, at £94 8s 0d a year.

Possession may be had at Candlemas, 1914.

It is subject to a Tithe rent charge of £36 2s 4d, the value thereof on the 1st January last being £26 5s 2¼d, and to a Land Tax of £4 15s 10d.

The Timber has been valued at the sum of £128.

TENANTS	Daniel Goulding and his son George and wife Annie
CHILDREN	10 Children – 4 boys, 6 girls
ACREAGE	139 Acres 2 Roods 12 Perches
LAND	80 acres Arable, 50 acres Pasture. Cereals for feed, Cider Orchards
LIVESTOCK	Cattle and Sheep. Trained colts as working horses, broke in ponies
RENT	£94 8s per annum
SOLD	George Goulding
PRICE	£1,850 (£2,073 with lot 15)

The tenants in 1913 were Daniel Goulding and his son, George. Daniel and his wife Jane had farmed at Kews for over 20 years and had seven children still living at the time of the 1911 census. George was the eldest and had married Annie in 1897. They were the family living at Holder's in 1913. They had nine children (Kenneth was born in August 1913) and a servant, Elizabeth Watkins, living in the house. George bought Holder's at the auction for £1,850. Two more children were born in the following years but died in early childhood.

The lot also included a cottage known as **Waterlocks**, which became Waterdines, a brick-built and tiled dwelling containing a kitchen, dairy, two bedrooms and an attic. There was a good well of water and, in the large garden, a piggery.

Also included was a stone, timber and thatched shed, part open fronted and part enclosed.

The Oxenhall Tunnel, constructed as part of the Gloucester and Hereford canal, ran close to this property and mounds of earth from this enterprise were still visible in 1913.

In 1911 Bill Griffin, aged 63, a carter on the farm, lived here with his wife Harriet aged 65, 26-year-old son Alec, also a carter, and step-daughter Edith Williams, aged 15, originally from Neath in south Wales.

George Goulding with his stock bull at Holder's

George Goulding also bought lot 15, two labourers' cottages. He paid a 10% deposit, took out a loan and had paid it off within five years. In 1916 he bought Kews and Halls Barn Farm, a total of 100 acres tenanted by his father Daniel, from Major Tennant. So some farmers did extremely well out of the First World War!

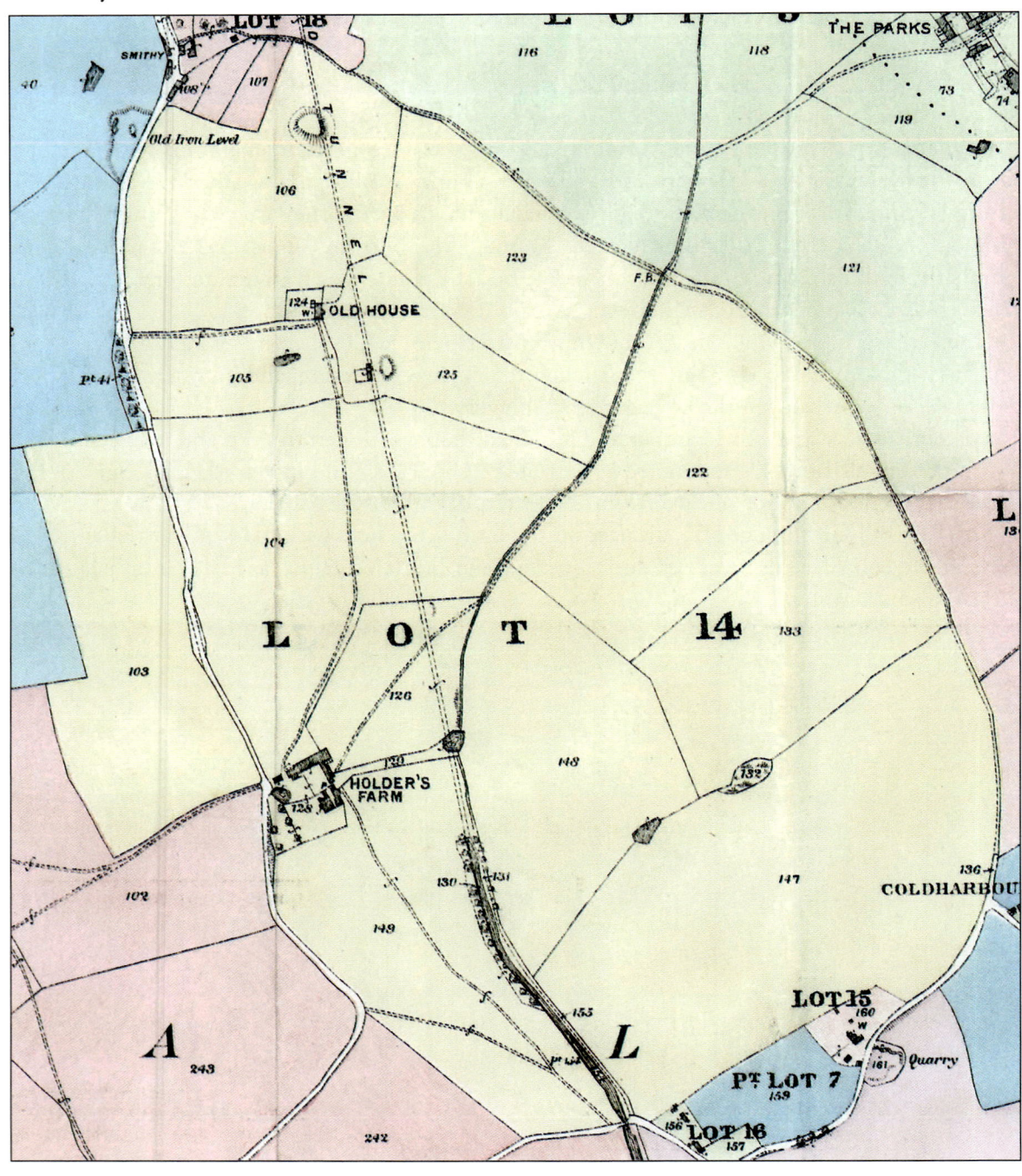

George Goulding with his eldest daughter Mabel, who married Alfred Cracknell, in Holders Meadow, next to the canal

George and Annie Goulding's family at Holder's in 1912
Standing L-R: Gertrude, Lillie, Reginald, Mabel, Dorothy, Harold,
Seated L-R: Leslie, Millicent and Florence (Flossie)

LOT 24   Pella Farm

TENANTS	Henry Charles Jones and Harriet, his second wife
CHILDREN	George, Reginald, Elsie and Albert (with first wife Jane); Ivy, Carey, Edith May and Raymond (with Harriet)
ACREAGE	187 acres
LAND	Crops: Beans, Wheat, Oats, Mangolds and Root crops (feed for livestock)
LIVESTOCK	Sheep, Beef cattle
RENT	£116 per annum
SOLD	Henry Charles Jones
PRICE	£2,100

Daniel Goulding (tenant at Kews) and Henry Charles Jones (his son-in-law) were joint incoming tenants at Pella in February 1896.

Henry married Jane Goulding in 1895 and they had four children – George, Reginald, Elsie and Albert. Following Jane's death in 1901, Henry married Harriet Goulding (Jane's sister) and they had four more children – Ivy, Carey, Edith May and Raymond Oliver. At the time of the 1911 census they had six children still living at home and a servant, a girl of 18, to help with the running of the household.

Henry bought Pella Farm at the auction for £2,100. On its 187 acres he grew beans, wheat and oats as protein feed for sheep and beef cattle. He also grew mangolds and other root crops for winter feed, along with hay.

Henry Charles Jones at Pella with L-R back row: George, Elsie, Reginald and Albert
L-R front row: Ivy, Carey and Edith May with their mother Harriet

PELLA FARM

A desirable compact estate, known as Pella, comprising dwelling house, agricultural buildings, cottage, arable and pasture land, pasture orcharding, and woodland, the whole being about **187a. 3r. 20p.** in extent, of which the following is a particular:—

No. on Ordnance Map	Description	Quantity A. R. P.	Total A. R. P.
	PARISH OF OXENHALL		
	Mr HENRY JONES, Tenant		
26	Pasture	1 2 37	
27	Roughet	0 0 38	
29	Pasture, with a few trees	8 0 12	
31	Arable	22 3 0	
35	Pasture (laid down by tenant)	16 1 6	
36	Pasture	10 2 11	
37	Pasture (laid down by tenant)	7 1 16	
40	Pasture	11 1 14	
42	Pasture, with a few trees	10 2 34	
43	Arable	9 3 29	
44	Pasture	2 2 10	
45	House, Garden, Buildings and Plum Orchard	0 2 26	
46	Pasture	7 2 14	
47	Do.	12 3 33	
48	Roughet	0 0 32	
49	Pasture	16 3 25	
98	Pasture (laid down by tenant)	10 0 27	
99	Pasture	2 0 0	
100	Do.	9 3 34	
249	Do.	0 3 8	162 3 6
	Mr WM. BOULTER, Tenant		
33	Pasture Orchard	2 0 22	
38	Pasture	0 1 12	2 1 34
	Mr DANL. HOWLEY, Tenant		
34	Cottage, Garden, etc.		0 2 12
	IN HAND		
32	Wetherlock's Grove	21 3 1	
Pt. 41	Plantation	0 1 7	22 0 8
		A.	187 3 20

The modern dwelling house, brick-built with tiled roof, occupies a most pleasant position and contains dining and drawing-rooms, kitchen, dairy, wash-house with furnace and oven, coal-house, 4 bedrooms and box-room.

There is a good well of water.

The Farm Buildings comprise cider-house with granary over, trap-house, calves'-house, cart stable for 3, cow-house adjoining, two tie-up houses for 4, root-house, barn (stone, timber and tiled), with stone driving way, open and enclosed cattle-sheds, wagon-house, implement-shed, and 4 piggeries. The Farm is in the occupation of Mr Henry Jones, on a Candlemas tenancy, at the annual rent of £116, and possession may be had at Candlemas, 1914.

The brick and tiled Cottage containing kitchen, back-kitchen, and 2 bedrooms, together with pump, good garden, in which are two piggeries and lean-to shed, is in the occupation of Mr Daniel Howley, at the yearly rent of £6, the Orchard (No. 38) is in the occupation of Mr W. Boulter, at an apportioned rent of 10s., and No. 33, the Pasture Orchard in his occupation to 1st November, 1913, at £3 12s 0d.

The Rental of the Lot is as follows:—

Mr Henry Jones		£116	0 0
,, W. Boulter		4	2 0
,, D. Howley		6	0 0
		126	2 0
Wetherlock's Grove, &c., in hand			Income derived from Wetherlock's Grove, etc., (22a. 0r. 8p. in hand) not estimated.

The lot is sold subject to a right of road from Colonel's Grove Wood, over the north corner of No. 26, and a right of road over Nos. 101 and 243 on Lot 12 is reserved for the owner of this Lot.

It is subject to a Tithe rent charge of £45 17s 6d, the value thereof on the 1st January last being £33 7s 1¼d, and to a Land Tax of £4 11s 0½d.

The Timber on this Lot has been valued at the sum of £270.

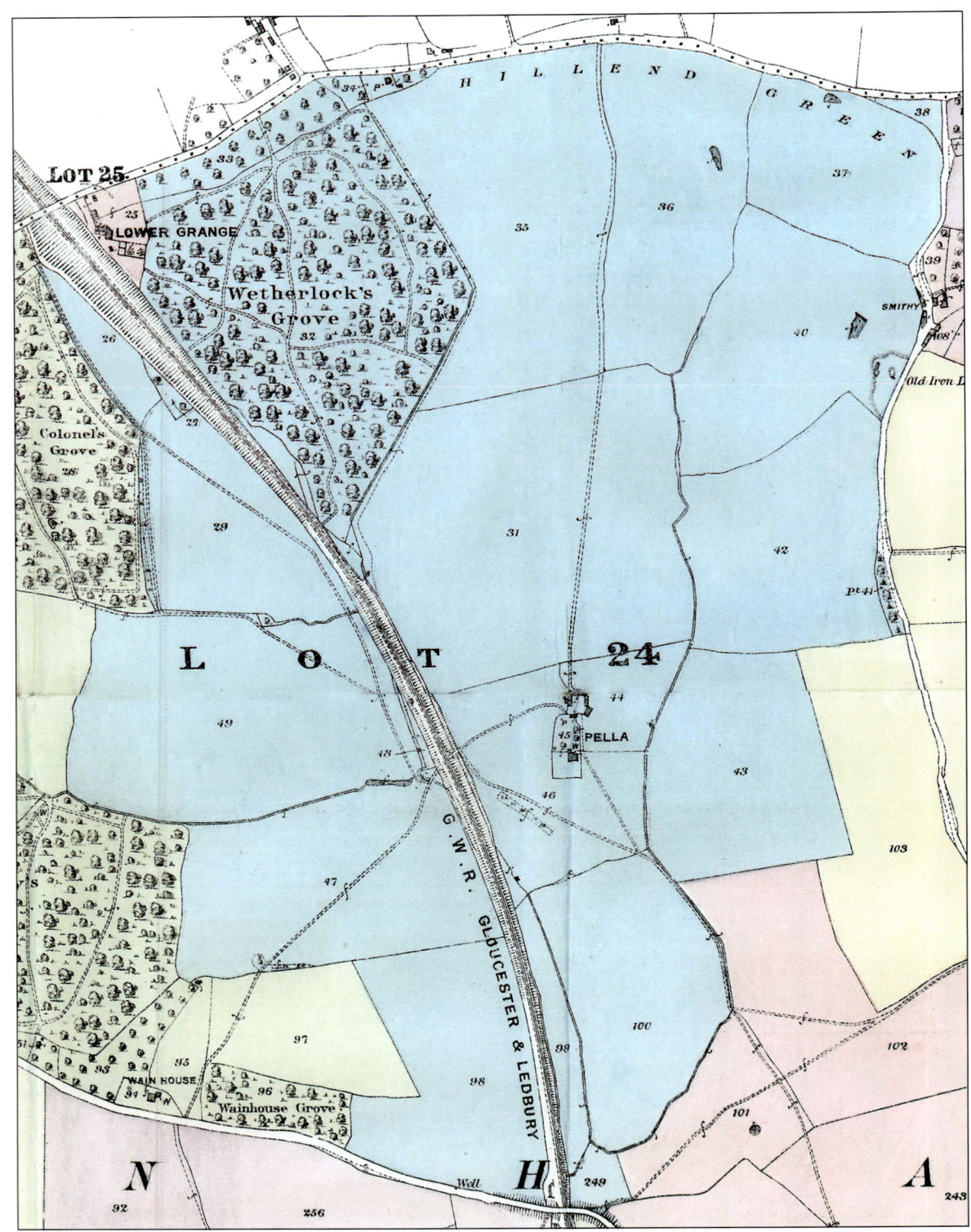

LOT 26   Peters Farm

PETERS FARM
A COMPACT DESIRABLE FARM

Situate in the Parish of Oxenhall, comprising a good dwelling house, ample agricultural buildings and about **112a. 3r. 4p.** of pasture and arable land, of which the following is a particular:—

No. on Ordnance Map	Description	Quantity A. R. P.	Total A. R. P.
	PARISH OF OXENHALL		
	Representatives of the late Mr JOHN NIBLETT, Tenants		
92	Pasture (laid down by tenant)	7 2 38	
253	Pasture	4 1 0	
254	Do.	3 3 18	
255	Arable	8 1 6	
256	Pasture, with a few trees (laid down by tenant)	7 1 21	
257	Pasture (laid down by tenant)	7 1 11	
258	Pasture Orchard	2 1 17	
280	Pasture	6 1 19	
284	Arable	10 1 21	
286	Pasture, with a few trees	3 2 16	
287	Pasture	3 0 34	
288	Do.	3 2 0	
289	Peter's Farmhouse, Yards, Buildings, &c.	1 1 14	
290	Pasture Orchard	1 3 6	
291	Arable	6 3 17	
292	Road	0 2 4	
294	Arable	8 3 17	
296	Do.	5 1 18	
302	Pasture	0 3 24	
303	Arable	10 1 19	
304	Pasture	3 1 15	
306	Do.	4 1 18	
			111 3 33
	IN HAND		
285	Old Quarry, etc.	0 1 0	
293	Spruce Plantation	0 1 21	
305	Bank	0 0 30	
			0 3 11
			112 3 4

The Dwelling House, which is brick-built with tiled roof, contains 2 sitting-rooms, kitchen, back-kitchen with furnace and baking oven, pantry, dairy, 4 bedrooms, 2 attics, and cellar.

The Buildings around the fold-yard comprise 2 calves-houses, enclosed cow-houses, barn with stone driving way, one bay pitched and with chaff-cutting floor above, cow-houses, calves house, cart stable for 4, and loose box with loft over, tie-up shed for 10, mill-house with mill and press, and with fruit store in the rear, enclosed shed adjoining, and poultry house, wagon-house and piggery, with wash-house adjoining.

Nearly the whole of the buildings are brick or stone-built with tiled roofs.

There are two good pools of water in the yards, and a good supply of water at the dwelling house.

The Farm, with the exception of **0a. 3r. 11p.**, which is in hand, is in the occupation of the representatives of the late Mr John Niblett, on a Candlemas tenancy, at an annual rent of £95. Possession may be had at Candlemas, 1914.

It is subject to a Tithe rent charge of £30 10s 8d, the value thereof on the 1st January last being £22 4s 0d, and to a Land Tax of £4 3s 4½d.

The Timber on this Lot has been valued at the sum of £53.

TENANTS	Fred, Albert, and Mary Niblett
ACREAGE	112 Acres 3 Roods 4 Perches
LAND	Approximately 47 acres Pasture, 47 Arable and some Orchard
RENT	£95 per annum
SOLD	Fred Niblett
PRICE	Not known

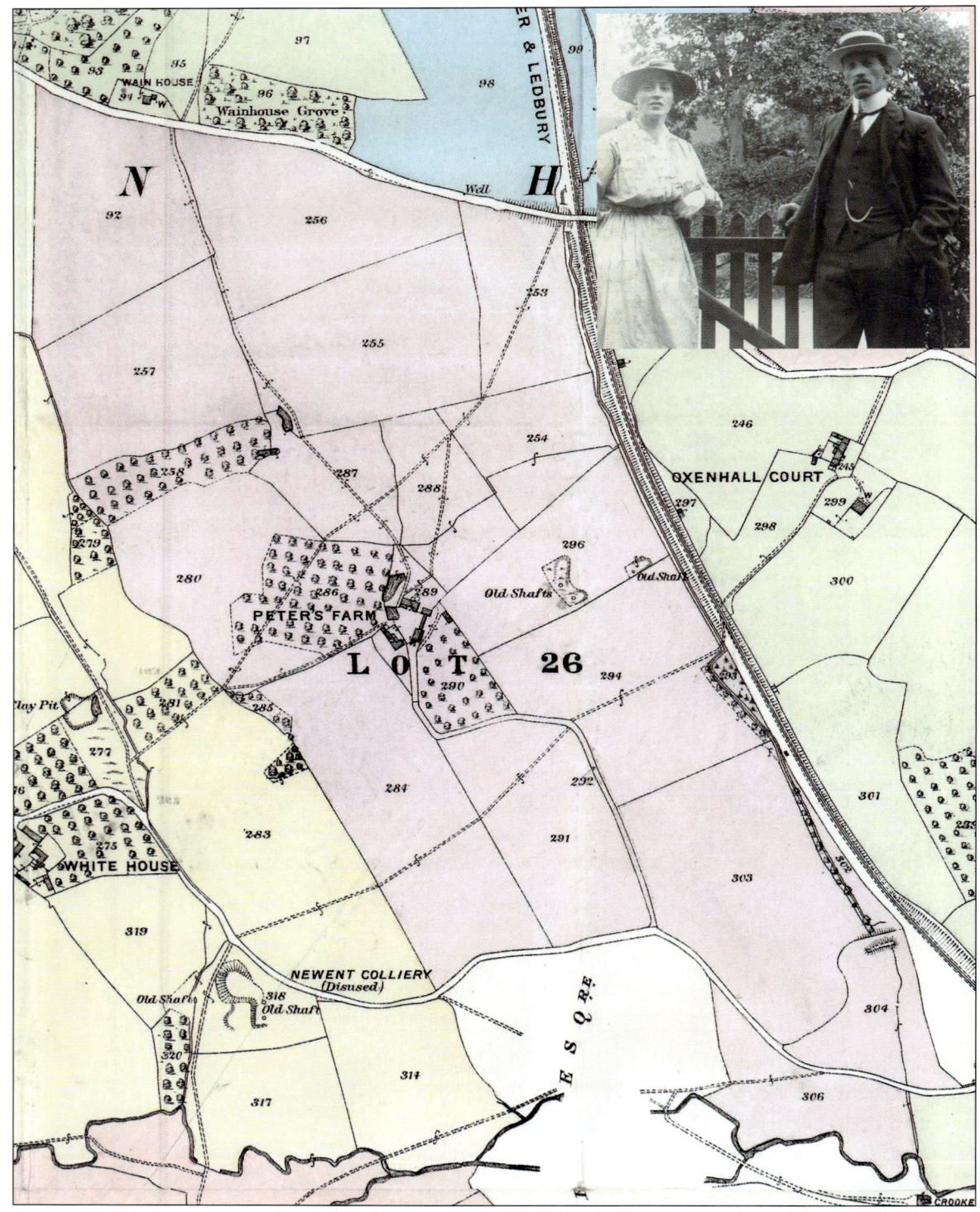

Lot 26, Peters Farm with, inset, Mr and Mrs Fred Niblett

In 1913 Peters Farm was occupied by the Niblett family. The 1901 census shows John Niblett and his wife Jane living at Oxenhall Court Farm with four children – Mary, Frederick, Albert and Florence.

Jane died in 1901 aged 57 (after the census) and John in 1907 aged 62. By the 1911 census Frederick, Mary and Albert were tenants at Peters with a farm labourer, William Morris, as a lodger. Mary married Samuel Jones, the tenant at Whitehouse Farm, that same year.

Frederick Niblett, who was then a bachelor, bought Peters Farm at the 1913 auction for £1,350. His younger brother Albert bought Gorsley Court Farm for £700 at the second day of the Onslow sale.

LOT 27   Whitehouse Farm

WHITEHOUSE FARM
A VALUABLE COMPACT FARM

Comprising a good Farmhouse, brick-built and tiled, capital set of farm buildings, and about **129a. 3r. 37p.** of pasture, pasture orcharding, and arable land, of which the following is a particular:—

No. on Ordnance Map	Description	Quantity A.	R.	P.
	PARISH OF OXENHALL			
259	Pasture	11	2	12
260	Arable	10	0	27
270	Pasture	9	1	14
271	Brake	0	1	9
272	Pasture	10	0	34
273	Arable	7	0	18
274	House, Yards, Buildings, &c.	1	0	21
275	Pasture, with a few trees	2	0	7
276	Pasture, with a few trees	2	2	2
277	Pasture	1	1	20
278	Arable	5	1	14
279	Pasture Orchard	0	2	8
281	Pasture, with a few trees	1	0	32
283	Arable	11	3	3
314	Arable, part Pasture	5	2	24
317	Pasture (laid down by tenant)	4	1	26
318	Pasture	2	2	21
319	Do.	3	3	19
320	Pasture Orchard	0	2	35
322	Arable	18	2	23
323	Pasture	4	0	3
324	Arable	3	3	20
325	Pasture	4	2	17
327	Do.	6	3	28
		129	3	37

The Dwelling House contains sitting-room, kitchen, large back-kitchen with furnace and baking oven, and to which the Gloucester Corporation water is laid on, pantry, dairy, two bedrooms, and two attics.

The Farm Buildings include nag stable, tie-up shed for 6, mill-house with mill and press, 2 poultry houses, and around a yard, open shed, cart stable for 5, with loft over; harness-room, tie-up shed for 6, root-house, wagon-house, barn with stone driving way, and one bay having a cemented floor, with chaff-cutting floor above, and 2 piggeries.

Nearly the whole of the buildings are brick-built with tiled roofs.

No. 270 is sold subject to the reservation of a right of road out of Hay Wood. A right of road is also reserved over Nos. 317 and 318 for the purchaser of Lot 29.

The Farm, together with Nos. 269, 326, and 330, in Lot 20, is in the occupation of Mr Samuel Jones, on a Candlemas tenancy, at an apportioned annual rent of £117 0s 0d, (Landlord paying rates). Possession may be had at Candlemas, 1914.

It is subject to a Tithe rent charge of £33 7s 1d, the value thereof on the 1st January last being £24 5s 0¼d, and to a Land Tax of £8 6s 3½d.

The Timber on this Lot has been valued at the sum of £63

TENANTS	Samuel and Mary Jones (second wife)
CHILDREN	Reginald, Florence and Wilfred
ACREAGE	129 acres 3 Roods 37 Perches
LAND	Approximately 55 acres of Pasture, 57 acres Arable, 18 acres Orchard (for cider)
LIVESTOCK	Horses, Cattle, Poultry and Pigs
RENT	£117 per annum
SOLD	Samuel Jones
PRICE	£1,500

Samuel Jones took over the tenancy of Whitehouse Farm in 1895 following his parents Edwin and Anne who had farmed there for ten years. Samuel married Alice Addis of Gorsley in 1887 and they became tenants at Marshall's where their son Reginald Edwin was born. Samuel was born in Linton, the younger brother of William Charles Jones, the tenant of Winter's Farm. At the time of the 1911 census his first wife had died and he was living at the farm with his son, Reginald, and his niece, Ethel Parry, who was his housekeeper. There were also two servants living in the house, Matilda Sysum, a general domestic and Joseph Bowkitt, who worked on the farm. Samuel married Mary Niblett of Peters Farm later that year and they went on to have two children, Florence, born in 1912 and Wilfred, born in 1915.

At the auction in 1913 Samuel bought Whitehouse for £1,500.

Mary Jones with Florence (Flossie), Wilfred and Lydia, Samuel's sister

Mr Samuel Jones, 1861-1932

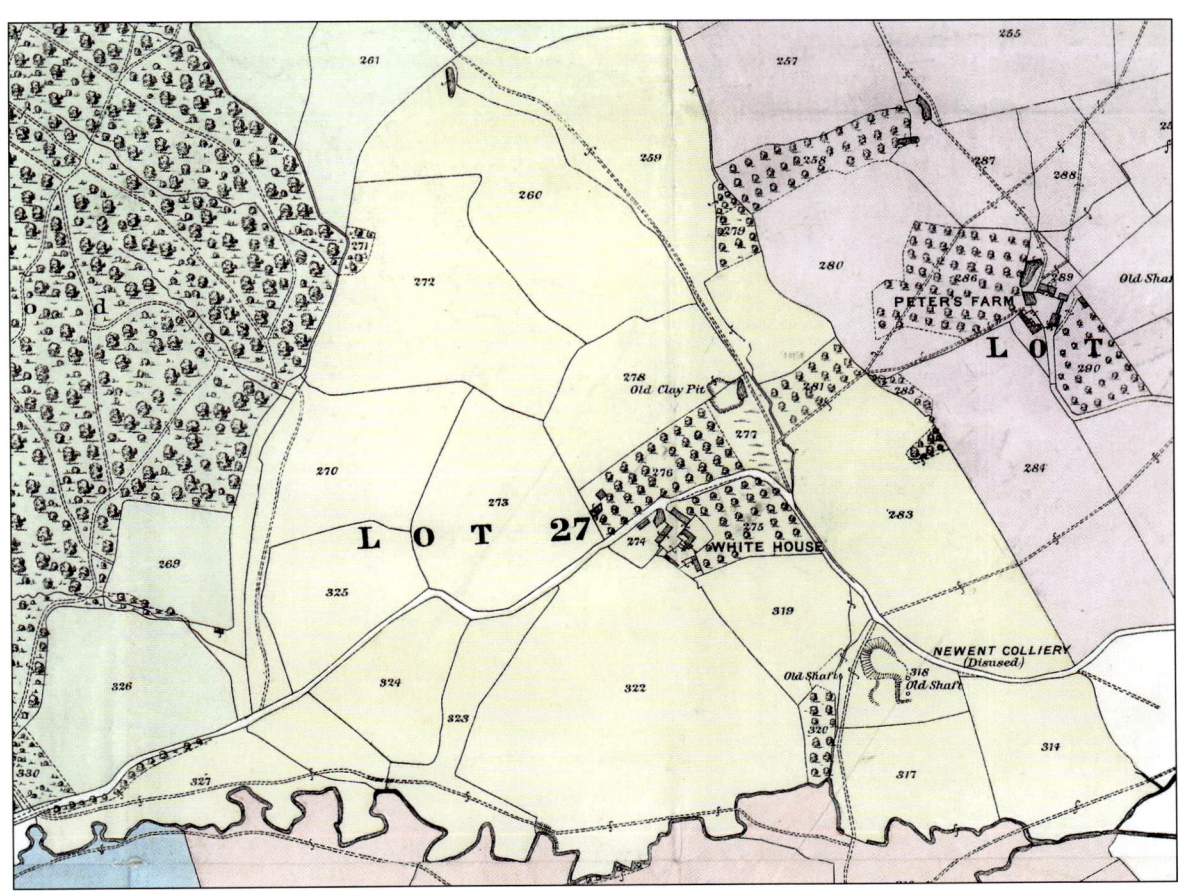

LOT 28   Brassfield's Farm

TENANTS	R.J.C. Honeyfield (92 acres) and Daniel Dowdeswell (8 acres)
CHILDREN	Jack and Agnes Honeyfield had no children
ACREAGE	157 acres
LAND	Pasture 66 acres, Arable 17 acres, woods 57 acres, Orchards 15 acres
RENT	£82 10s per annum
SOLD	Unsold at auction but bought by R.J.C. Honeyfield in 1914
PRICE	£1,653

Robert J.C. Honeyfield (known as Jack) married Agnes of Ross-on-Wye in 1908 when he was 32. Two years later they became tenants at Brassfield's, renting arable and pasture in Newent and pasture in Oxenhall that lay between Hill House Grove and a brook, a total of 92 acres for an annual rent of £76. Jack ran a mixed farm and kept a bull.

The Honeyfield family were successful Wiltshire dairy farmers who marketed milk, cheese and butter in London, where Jack was born. In 1871 the Honeyfields took up a tenancy at Knappers Farm on the Onslow Estate and soon afterwards they bought the farm from Richard Onslow. Jack's father, James, spent some years farming Knappers before moving to Bridges Farm, Kempley, leaving his siblings to farm Knappers.

BRASSFIELD'S FARM

Comprising an excellent Dwelling House, set of agricultural buildings, and about **157a. 2r. 27p.** of pasture and arable land and arable orcharding, of which the following is a particular:—

No. on Ordnance Map	Description	Quantity A. R. P.	Total A. R. P.
	PARISH OF OXENHALL		
	Mr R. J. C. HONEYFIELD, Tenant		
337	Pasture	3 0 9	
338	Do.	6 1 37	
339	Do.	7 0 10	
370	Do.	8 0 13	
382	Pasture Orchard	2 0 39	
	PARISH OF NEWENT		
570	Pasture	2 1 18	
575	Arable Orchard	9 3 26	
576	Arable	3 2 19	
578	Pasture	0 0 21	
579	Do.	0 1 5	
583	House, Garden, Yards, Buildings and Orchard	1 1 6	
584	Pasture	1 1 22	
585	Pasture Orchard	1 0 17	
587	Pasture	8 0 30	
588	Do.	1 0 36	
665	Do.	6 0 32	
666	Do.	8 1 7	
679	Do.	2 3 17	
680	Pasture Orchard	1 2 28	
681	Dingle	0 2 22	
682	Pasture, with a few trees	2 3 14	
683	Arable	13 0 22	92 0 10
	Mr D. DOWDESWELL, Tenant		
	PARISH OF OXENHALL		
329	Pasture		7 3 30
	IN HAND		
340	Road	0 1 27	
368	Hill House Grove	25 0 13	
369	Do.	27 3 6	
383	Road	0 3 24	
384	Wood	0 2 33	
	PARISH OF NEWENT		
581	Wood	2 0 12	
586	Wood	0 2 32	57 2 27
			157 2 27

The Dwelling House occupies a very pleasant position near to Christ Church, Gorsley, and to the main road leading from Newent to Ross, is stone or brick-built and tiled, and contains hall, dining and drawing-rooms, kitchen with furnace and baking oven, china pantry, dairy, 4 bedrooms, and 2 attics, together with underground cellar and mill-house with mill and press with loft over.

The buildings around the yard comprise loose box, shed for tying up 5, cow-shed, cart stable for 3 with loft over, barn with stone driving way, and cider-house or cow-shed with granary over, 4 piggeries and cart shed.

Nearly all the above buildings are brick-built with tiled roofs.

The Farm, together with No. 448, **0a. 1r. 17p.** in Lot 13 of the second day's Sale, is in the occupation of Mr R. J. C. Honeyfield, on a yearly tenancy commencing 15th May, at the annual rent of £76. No. 329 on the Map, **7a. 3r. 30p.**, is let with Hill House and Lower House, to Mr Daniel Dowdeswell, on a Candlemas tenancy. Possession may be had at Candlemas, 1914. Hill House Grove, about **57 a. 2 r. 27 p.** in extent, is in hand.

The rents apportioned to this Lot are as follows:—

Brassfields Farm	..	£75 10 0
No. 329 (D. Dowdeswell, Tenant)	..	7 0 0
		82 10 0
Hill House Grove, Roads, &c. in hand	..	*Income derived from Hill House Grove, etc., (57a. 2r. 27p. in extent) not estimated.*

This lot is subject to Tithe rent charges, that of Newent being £12 18s 9d, that of Pauntley, £8 13s 3d, the total value on the 1st January last being £15 14s 1d, and to a Land Tax of £3 3s 4d.

The Timber on this Lot has been valued at the sum of £91.

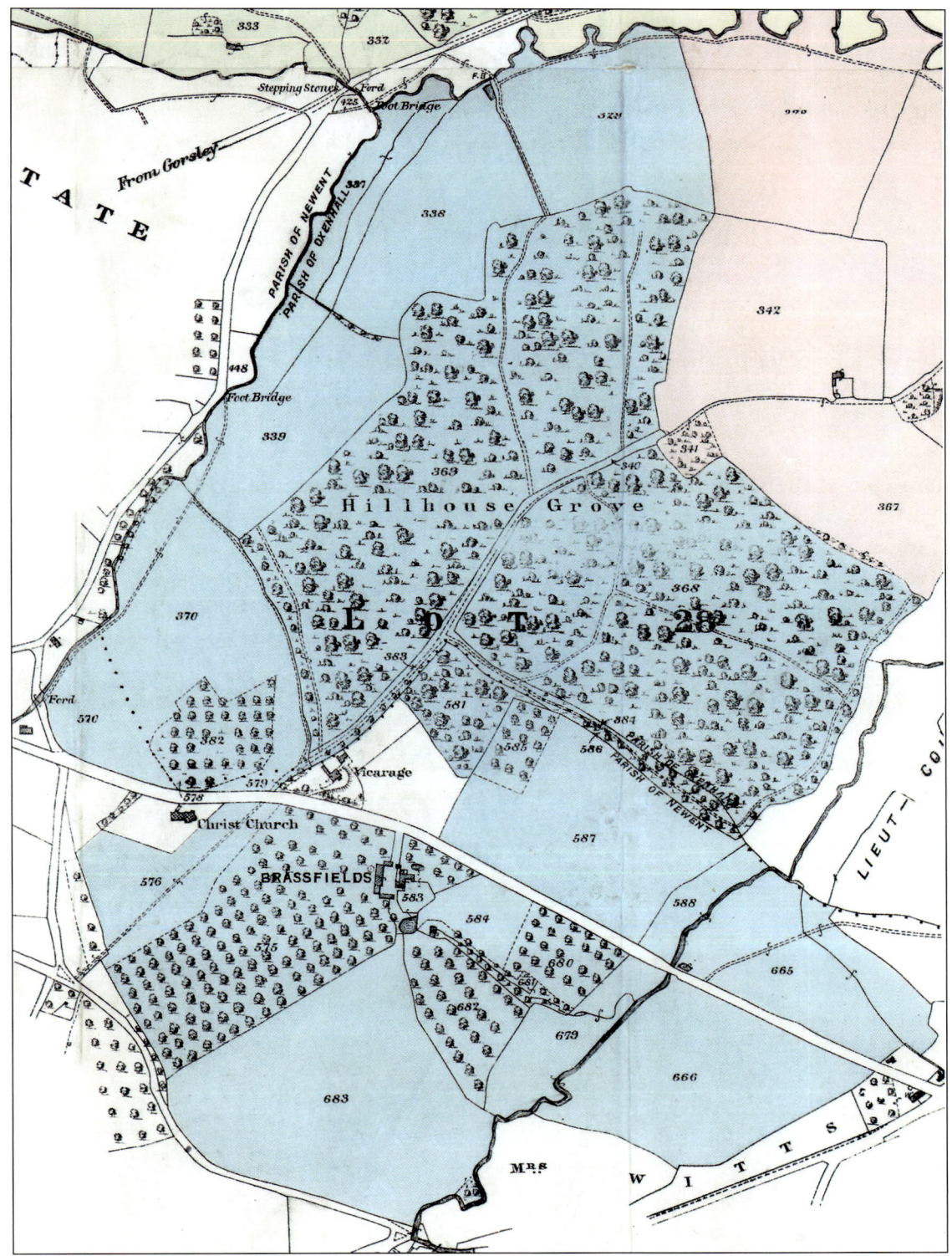

Lot 28 in the 1913 sale included Brassfield's, 7 acres of land that had been rented by the Dowdeswell family and about 50 acres of woodland that had been managed by the Onslow estate. The Lot remained unsold at the sale but in March 1914 Jack Honeyfield bought the enlarged farm from Andrew Richard Onslow for £1,653. He borrowed money from his father James and the bank, but had difficulty in repaying. Hill House Grove that had been mainly oak coppice proved to be of little value.

LOT 29   Lower House and Hill House Farms

TENANTS	Daniel Dowdeswell (Lower House)
ACREAGE	139 Acres 3 Roods 30 Perches
LAND	79 acres Pasture, 56 acres Arable
LIVESTOCK	Sheep, Pigs, Cattle Poultry and Horses
RENT	£143 per annum
SOLD	Samuel Goulding (wife Ada and five children)
PRICE	£2,800

The tenant in 1913 was Daniel Dowdeswell but his father Thomas had been the tenant from 1891. The census of that year shows him living at the farm with his wife, Emma, and four sons – Thomas (a student at Oxford University), Samuel (a student at Durham), Daniel and Joseph. His sister-in law was also living with them and as she was still there on the 1911 census she probably lived with them all that time. It seems very unusual for the 1890s to have two sons of a tenant farmer studying away from home; perhaps a family member helped with funding their education? Thomas and Samuel were both blind. By 1911 Thomas was a clergyman in Rotherham and Samuel was married and working in Stroud as a braille transcriber. Their father died in 1901 and the younger sons Daniel and Joseph must have taken over running the farm for their mother. They lived at Lower House while Hill House was used by the carter, William Day, and his large family.

Sam and Ada Goulding with Arthur, Reginald, Ethel, Violet and Lily in 1911

The Villa, another house included in this lot, was occupied by the Trigg family, three of whom were well sinkers. Cows were milked and cider made at Lower House, while at Hill House poultry were reared and seven horses were stabled. There was a 'good supply' of water though it would not be for another 50 years that the owners paid to lay on mains water.

At the auction Daniel Dowdeswell did not buy Lot 29, although his family had lived there for

THE LOWER HOUSE AND HILL HOUSE FARMS

Comprising a superior Farmhouse known as Lower House, a second homestead known as Hill House, and now occupied as a cottage, a dwelling house, two sets of agricultural buildings, and about **139a. 3r. 30p.** of pasture and arable land, of which the following is a particular:—

Mr D. DOWDESWELL, Tenant

PARISH OF OXENHALL

No. on Ordnance Map	Description	Quantity A.	R.	P.
315	Pasture	3	1	19
316	Do.	6	3	31
321	Arable	8	1	27
328	Pasture	10	1	15
341	Rough Pasture	0	2	20
342	Pasture	8	3	39
343	Do.	13	0	15
344	Do.	10	2	3
345	Hill House, Yards, Buildings, etc.	0	3	7
346	Pasture	3	1	5
347	Roughet	1	0	20
349	Pasture Orchard	0	0	30
350	Lower House, Garden, Yards, Buildings, etc.	0	1	38
351	Pasture Orchard	0	3	5
352	Arable	12	0	32
362	Pasture	3	0	22
363	Do.	6	2	22
366	Do.	5	1	21
367	Arable	8	1	19
Pt. 398	Road	0	0	10
399	Arable	1	2	21

PARISH OF NEWENT

450	Pasture	0	3	23
451	Arable	1	2	9
452	Pond and Buildings	0	0	15
453	Road	0	1	13
454	Pasture	4	2	9
Pt. 455	Arable	3	1	2
Pt.455 & pt.456	Arable	10	1	22
Pt. 456	Arable	10	2	27
457	Cottage and Garden	0	0	18
458	Pasture Orchard	1	2	23
602	Road	0	0	8
		139	3	30

LOWER HOUSE

Is a picturesque building, brick, timber and tile, occupying a pleasant position, and containing dining and drawing rooms, kitchen, dairy, back-kitchen with furnace and baking oven, large lean-to scullery, and 5 bedrooms. Near thereto are coal and wood sheds. Good supply of water.

The Farm Buildings, nearly all of which are around a warm enclosed yard, comprise wagon-house, two piggeries, cow-shed for tying up 4, mill-house with mill and press, with granary over the last two named buildings, cider house, barn with stone driving way, and chaff-machine floor, capital milking sheds for 14, with manger and feeding passage, open shed for tying up 4, and hay and root-house at end of stalls.

All the above buildings are stone or brick-built, with slate or tile roofs.

HILL HOUSE

(No. 345), formerly a Farm-house, but now occupied as a cottage, is brick-built and tiled, and contains kitchen, back-kitchen, dairy, and 3 bedrooms, together with detached second kitchen with furnace and baking oven, and a room over.

The Buildings comprise barn with stone driving way, one bay having a stone floor with chaff floor above, stable for 4 with loft over, poultry house and granary, and in an enclosed yard tie-up shed for 8, 2 enclosed sheds each for 4, with root-house at end; in a second yard, open shed with manger, poultry house, a second stable for 3.

All the foregoing are brick or stone-built and tiled. Wagon-house of stone with thatch roof. There is a good pool near these buildings.

In No. 342 is a stone-built and stone-tiled open shed, and a barn, brick-built with corrugated iron roof.

The dwelling house on No. 447 is brick-built and tiled, and contains two sitting-rooms, kitchen, back-kitchen, and 3 bedrooms, with large landing.

There is a good supply of water.

> This Lot, together with No. 329, on Lot 28, is let to Mr Daniel Dowdeswell, on a Candlemas tenancy, at £150 a year, and the rent apportioned to this Lot is £143. Possession may be had at Candlemas, 1914.
>
> The Farms are exceptionally well watered, and there is a good pool close to each of the two homesteads.
>
> A right of road over Nos. 317 and 318 on the White House Farm (lot 27) is reserved for the purchaser of this Lot.
>
> *The lot is subject to Tithe rent charges, that of Pauntley being £23 0s 3d, that of Oxenhall, 3s 0d, and that of Newent, £6 19s 2d, the total value thereof on the 1st January last being £21 18s 0d, and to a Land Tax of £5 12s 2d.*
>
> The Timber on this Lot has been valued at the sum of £49.

over 22 years. Instead it was bought by Samuel Goulding, whose father Daniel farmed Kews Farm which had the land adjacent to Lower House. Sam and Ada and their five children – Arthur, Reginald, Ethel, Violet and Lily – moved with their possessions by horse and wagon at Candlemas 1914. Samuel farmed Lower House himself (92 acres) and rented out Hill House (48 acres). Both farms were mixed, with sheep, pigs, cattle, dairying and poultry. Horses were used for haulage, transport, cultivation and as a power source for driving machinery and the cider mill. A 'horse works' situated in the centre of the yard at Hill House drove the chaff cutter and the corn mill.

The Villa was rented out to family or friends. From 1914 to 1923, Sam's in-laws, the Fowlers, lived there.

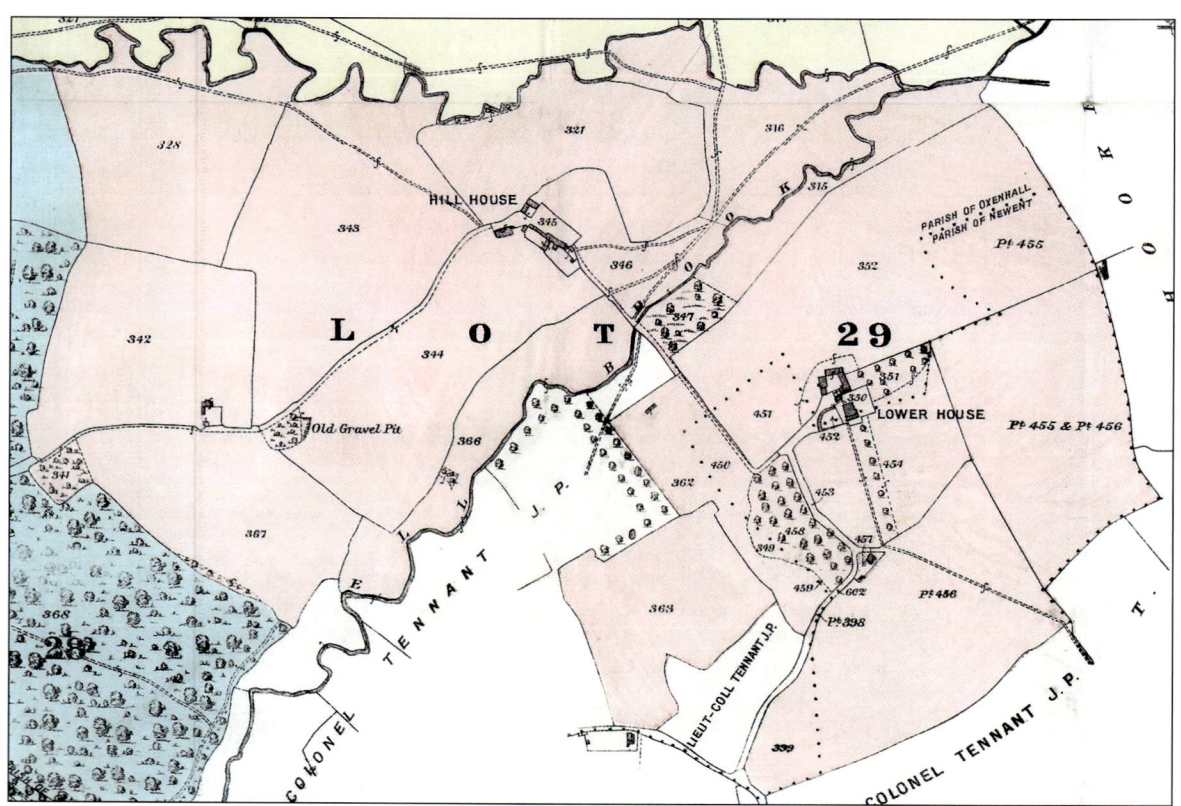

5   Cottages in 1913

Particulars of the cottages show us how craftsmen and labourers on the estate would have lived. Like the farms, they had been improved after 1750 and were built of brick and tile though they were smaller, having no more than two or three bedrooms. They usually had a garden and a piggery, so tenants could supplement their diet with home grown and home reared produce. The cottages were also near or on farmland, so labourers were near their workplace, or near a road if the tenant was a craftsman, such as a blacksmith or wheelwright, for the agricultural industry.

The 1913 sale book provide details of who lived in each of the cottages. The 1911 census provides additional information about the occupants and their families and in some cases there are photographs kept by descendants.

In 1913, with the exception of a few who lived close to Newent and went there to work (including a postman, three teachers, two sawmill workers and a baker), most people living in Oxenhall worked in the parish, and most of the men worked on the land. Seven worked on the larger farms, living in. There were three farmers who worked their own small farms, seeking help at busy times. Six men were estate workers, including a woodman, a gamekeeper, two bricklayers and a carpenter. The railway running through the parish employed two men and the Waterworks three. Plying their trade in the parish were a blacksmith and a wheelwright.

Only two female members of the parish were employed on farms: Eliza Griffin was an agricultural worker and Jane Goulding a farming administrator. The majority of the women were in domestic service and often employed as housekeepers, frequently by relatives who were widowers or bachelors, and 18 lived in the house where they worked as cook, nurse, nanny, housemaid or general domestic servant. Clara Little was the local seamstress.

Retired members of the community included the Hunt brothers, who had worked on the Argentinian railways. Others had retired from trades including a platelayer, a bricklayer, a china dealer and a blacksmith – the oldest male member of the parish.

Although the lives of the employers and the employed were inextricably linked, life at home would have been very different in the cottages. They would have been very cramped, especially for large families. Every cottage would have had a hearth, as without electricity the fire was essential for warming the cottage, cooking family meals, heating water for personal use and, at least once a week, doing the family wash. Every item had to be washed by hand, possibly using a 'dolly' and removing excess water in a wringer, all the time hoping that the weather would be suitable for drying garments on the washing line in the garden. Another use for the fire was heating the flat irons ready to use when the clothes were dry. Light was provided by candles and Tilley lamps.

In their fairly large gardens the cottagers would grow vegetables and fruit, keep pigs and chickens. Fruit would be packed into 'Kilner Jars' when ripe, apples and pears taken to local farms and made into cider. Vegetables were stored in the coolest part of the cottage ready for the winter, and once the pig had been slaughtered and 'salt cured', the sides of bacon, covered in muslin, would hang from large hooks attached to the beams.

Neighbouring woodland provided kindling for the fire which children could collect. There was also the opportunity to catch a rabbit or pigeon for the cooking pot. Bread and cakes were baked either in bread ovens or in small ovens, the latter part of the grates. Men going to work and children off to school would take slices of bread with bacon or cheese for their midday meal.

Imagine the dust the fires caused and how difficult it must have been to keep the house clean! In the spring, interior walls were distempered, paintwork washed down, rugs and carpets hung over the washing line and beaten to remove the dust, and blankets aired. The local chimney sweep would have been very busy too.

ELLBRIDGE

In the 16th and early 17th century there was a corn mill on the Ell Brook and by the 1630s the lord of the manor was using water power to make iron in the blast furnace. As well as ashes from the furnace still visible in local gardens, some buildings remain as evidence of the old Newent or Elmbridge ironworks. One, situated next to the furnace, housed the bellows and behind the furnace a very substantial sandstone building, with huge buttresses, stored charcoal, cinders and iron. The blocks of sandstone for this building

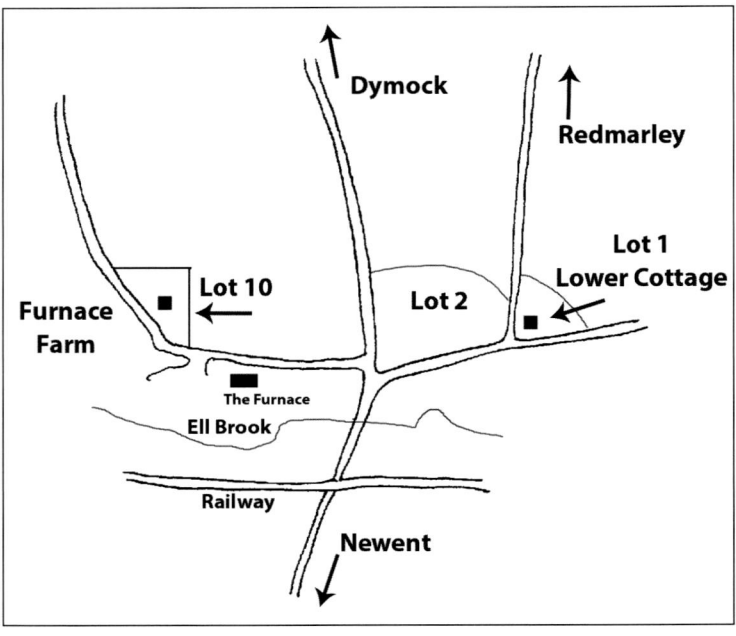

Ellbridge

would have been hewn locally, from cuttings in the roads leading to Ledbury and Redmarley, or from Coldharbour Lane and Winters Lane.

Furnace House, once the home of the manager of the ironworks, with its adjoining land, was not included in the 1913 sale as it was the home of Andrew Richard Onslow, who had the use of the Onslow Estate for his lifetime.

In 1861 Richard Foley Onslow and his wife were living at the Furnace while Stardens was being renovated and rebuilt. As soon as the alterations were finished they moved to Stardens and rented out Furnace House. In 1871 it was occupied by Henry and Ann West. They were farming 100 acres and employing four men and one boy. In 1881 Captain Byron and his family lived at the house.

By 1891 Captain Andrew George Onslow was living at Furnace House with his wife Mary, his niece Mary Frances Owen and servants Sydonia Powis, a 42-year-old nurse, Elizabeth Evans, the cook, Rhoda Trilloe, a housemaid, Frederick Jones, the butler and a groom, William Little, the son of the blacksmith Harry Little, who lived in Furnace cottages.

In 1913, at the time of the sale, Andrew Richard Onslow was living at the Furnace with his 59-year-old aunt, Emma Onslow, and his cousin, Mary Frances Owen. Interestingly, their 65-year-old housekeeper, Sydonia Jones, was still working for them. The cook, aged 22, came from Hartpury and the 15-year-old housemaid, Agnes Spiers, was local. Andrew Richard Onslow continued to occupy the Furnace until 1941/2, when he sold it to R.H. Goulding.

A notebook, written in pencil and now held in Gloucester Record Office, contains the survey of trees in 1912/13 for the whole estate. Though the Furnace was not up for sale, its trees were included in the survey: 37 Scotch pine plus 35 young pines, 20 poplar, 16 oaks, 10 beech, 5 spruce, 5 ash, 4 lime, 4 birch, 3 wych elm, 2 elm, 2 plane and 1 larch. The oaks were valued at £20 15s, the beech trees at £8 18s, a total of £63 4s 3d.

LOT 1   The Lower Cottage

In 1913 the Estate Foreman, William Phillips, lived at Lower Cottage with his wife, Julia, and their five children. Lower Cottage, occupying a corner position close to Stardens and Newent Railway Station, was one of the largest cottages on the estate and a very suitable dwelling for somebody holding the post of Estate Foreman.

The cottage contained a drawing room, dining room, kitchen with range, scullery with range, furnace and baking oven, four bedrooms, an attic and an underground cellar. In the excellent garden surrounding the cottage, as well as the usual pigs' cot there was also a WC and brick-built stable.

The tenants in the smaller cottage behind Lower Cottage but part of the same Lot were Mr and Mrs Charles Preedy.

In the 1913 sale O.T. Price bought Lower Cottage for £460. He also purchased Lot 2, a three-acre enclosure of pastureland known as Hillyfield, having a frontage to three roads and close to the railway station, for £200.

LOT 10   Two Newly-Built Brick and Tiled Cottages

One of these two cottages, built close to the Furnace, was occupied by Harry Little, his wife Lucy and daughter Clara – described as a dressmaker in 1911. Harry Little's premises, for which he paid a yearly rent of £11, contained a cider-house and workshops in which he plied his trade as wheelwright and blacksmith.

Hubert Jones rented the other cottage. As well as being the local postman, Hubert also worked for Mr Onslow at the Furnace. His yearly rent of £7 was reduced to £6 10s as part of his garden was not being sold with the property. Each cottage had a garden and piggery and was supplied with Gloucester Corporation water, for which each tenant paid 10s a year. Hubert's daughter, Ada, aged 25, looked after the house and on 1 June 1914 she married Cornelius Kingham in Oxenhall Church.

Wedding of Ada Jones and Cornelius Kingham

In the 1913 sale, Lot 10 was bought by Mr Grimes on behalf of Mr Little, for £260. Mr Little's daughter, Clara, was a teacher at Oxenhall School in 1913.

THREE ASHES

The area of Oxenhall known as Three Ashes is bisected by the road that links Newent and Dymock. From 1769 until 1874 this was a turnpike road, greatly improved by the trust in 1832. Various lanes, running westwards, give access to the farmsteads and cottages in this part of the parish.

In the late 16th and early 17th centuries a small group of cottages were built on freehold land alongside Three Ashes Lane which ran eastwards from the main road. One of these cottages was certainly erected before 1733 and in 1841 Richard Peters, the local wheelwright,

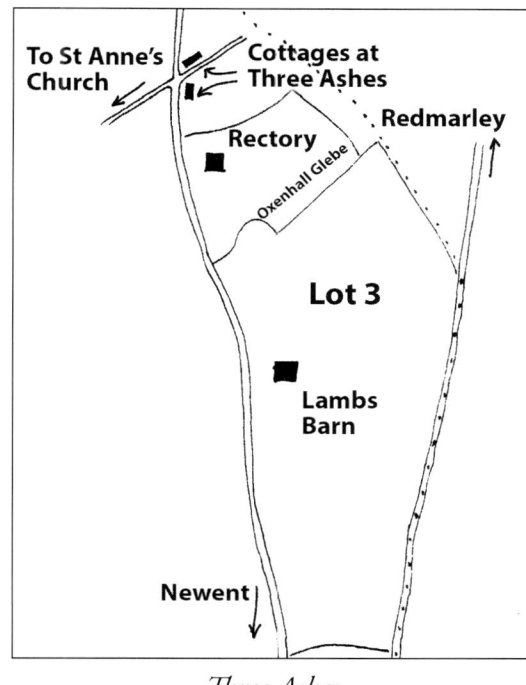

Three Ashes

purchased an adjoining plot, on which four other cottages were built.

As these were not included in the sale it is not certain who lived here in 1913, but the 1911 census tells us who occupied them then. It appears that they were occupied by farm labourers and retired people except for the one where Walter Spragg, a 'small farmer', lived with his wife Eliza and teenage sons Albert and Arthur.

Farm labourers living in this group were Albert and Sarah Wells, whose grandson, Oliver J. Holman, aged 7, was staying at the time. William Gorin, his daughter Kate and granddaughter Lily, lived in another cottage, and in two separate cottages lived bachelors Matthew Phillips and Joseph Green.

Ralph Bridgetts, a retired china dealer, and his sister Rose lived in another of these cottages while Thomas Grimmett, a retired bricklayer, and sister Neah Tranter occupied a further one.

In 1855 Oxenhall Rectory was built on glebe land. Reverend Irving lived here for many years before the church sold the house in the 1950s.

The Rectory built on glebe land in 1855

COLDHARBOUR LANE

Coldharbour Lane, a steep and winding single track, links the main road from the nearby market town of Newent to Kempley, crossing a valley which carries the disused Herefordshire and Gloucestershire canal. The age of the lane can be judged from the depth to which it has been worn.

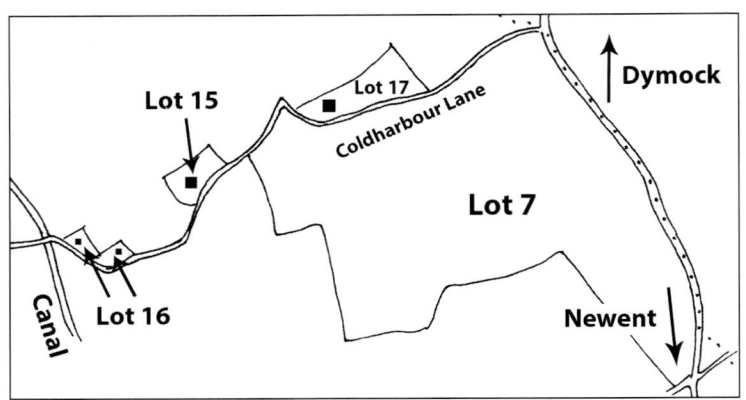

Coldharbour Lane

LOT 17 A Brick and Tiled Cottage – Known as Coldharbour Cottage

According to the 1913 sale details, Mr R. Baldwin junior rented Coldharbour, paying an annual rent of £6, free of rates, to live in this three-bedroomed cottage with sitting room, kitchen, box-room and cellar. The wash-house contained a furnace. The whole plot measured 1 rood and 4 perches and in the large garden there were two piggeries, a shed and coal-house together with a good well of water.

Richard Baldwin was a carpenter on the Onslow Estate and lived here with his wife Martha and twin daughters Edith and Margaret, born in 1907, and Gertrude born in 1911. Two sons were born later, William in 1913 and Arthur in 1916.

The earliest reference to the name 'Coldharbour' is 1779, soon after it was purchased by Elizabeth Hope and rebuilt whilst retaining features from an earlier dwelling.

William Charles Jones, of Winter's Farm, bought Coldharbour for £70 in the 1913 sale.

LOT 15 A Block of Two Brick-Built and Tiled Cottages – Known as Sandpit Cottages

This plot measured 3 roods and 16 perches. Both of these two-bedroomed cottages contained a kitchen and back-kitchen, with a garden in which there was a shed and piggery. A well and wash-house were shared between the tenants: Mr Richard Baldwin senior and his wife Louisa in one cottage and their son Fred in the other. Each tenant paid an annual rent of £10, free of rates. Both Richard and Fred worked on the Onslow Estate, Richard as a bricklayer and Fred as a bricklayer's labourer.

In the 1913 sale George Goulding bought both cottages for £95. He also purchased nearby Holder's Farm.

LOT 16 Two Brick- and Timber-Built Cottages – Known as The Cottage and Brook Cottage

This plot measured 2 roods and 4 perches. Both the cottages had tiled roofs and contained four rooms. The one known as 'The Cottage', with a good garden and shed, was occupied by Mrs Boto with, as her sub-tenant, Eliza Griffin, an unmarried farmworker who was employed on local farms. Although many women in 1913 helped out on local farms when required, it was unusual for 'farmworker' to be recorded on census returns. However, as a single person and head of the household, it seems appropriate that in 1911 Elizabeth Griffin should use the term 'general farm worker on farms' on her census form.

Matthew Elliott and his family lived in Brook Cottage, which had a large garden, piggery and shed. Matthew, an army pensioner and farm labourer, was married to Ruth and three of their children lived in the cottage in 1913. James, aged 16, was a farm labourer; Andrew, aged 9, was still at school; and Frederick was just a year old.

The rents of the two cottages amounted to £7 18s 0d. George Goulding bought both these cottages at the sale for £70.

Brook Cottage close to the canal in Coldharbour Lane

HOLDERS LANE

In 1913 Holders Lane linked Coldharbour Lane and Four Oaks Road, meeting Coldharbour Lane opposite the old entrance to Hilter's Farm. It was a very steep and narrow lane, formed in the gap between layers of rock, and two very sharp corners made it extremely hazardous for vehicles and travellers.

LOT 18   A Brick-Built Cottage with Slate Roof

This cottage contained a kitchen, back-kitchen and four bedrooms. Outside there were two sheds, piggery, trap-house and a good garden. Peter Trigg, the sub-tenant, was a 74-year-old farm labourer who lived here with his wife Emma, also aged 74.

A brick, timber and tiled dwelling included in this lot, had a sitting-room, kitchen, cider-house, back-kitchen with furnace and three bedrooms. Outside was a brick and tiled blacksmith's shop and enclosures of arable and pasture land. Mr Alfred Jones paid an annual rent of £23 as tenant of this whole plot measuring just over 4 acres.

Alfred had been a tenant at the smithy at Holders Lane. His father, Charles Jones, was recorded as renting the smithy and 2.5 acres for £14 in 1892. Charles Jones died in 1913 aged 85, his wife, Mary Ann, had died in 1891 aged 57.

Alfred Edward Jones was born at the smithy in 1870, and in 1911 he lived at the smithy with his wife Ellen Sarah and children, Ellen Mary, aged 5 and one-year-old Alfred Charles. His father, the retired blacksmith, lived there too.

As horses provided the basic power for farm-work and were used for many tasks, their hooves had to be kept in good condition by the blacksmith. He also repaired farm equipment such as ploughs and harrows damaged by stones or rocks. It is interesting to note that iron deposits had been mined, in the past, to the west of the smithy.

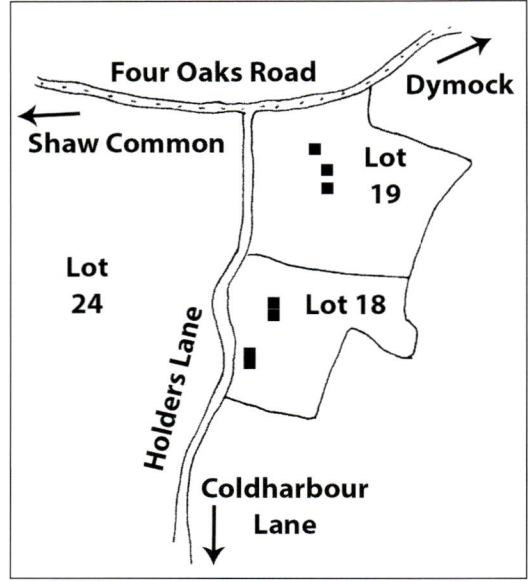

Holders Lane

Charles Jones, the blacksmith, outside the old smithy in Holders Lane

In the 1913 sale Alfred Jones paid £300 for Lot 18, and he lived here until his death in 1949.

LOT 19   A Brick-Built and Tiled Cottage – Hill View

William Boulter, a small farmer, lived in this cottage with his nephew. The cottage contained a kitchen, back-kitchen and three bedrooms with and was offered for sale along with a good garden, buildings and enclosures of pasture and arable land, with the addition of a field rented from Pella Farm. William Boulter paid an annual rent of £14.

On this plot of land measuring about 6 acres and 28 perches there were many outbuildings including a lean-to shed, a poultry-house, a piggery, a small barn, a stable with piggery attached and a cider shed with mill and press. The property benefited from access to two roads.

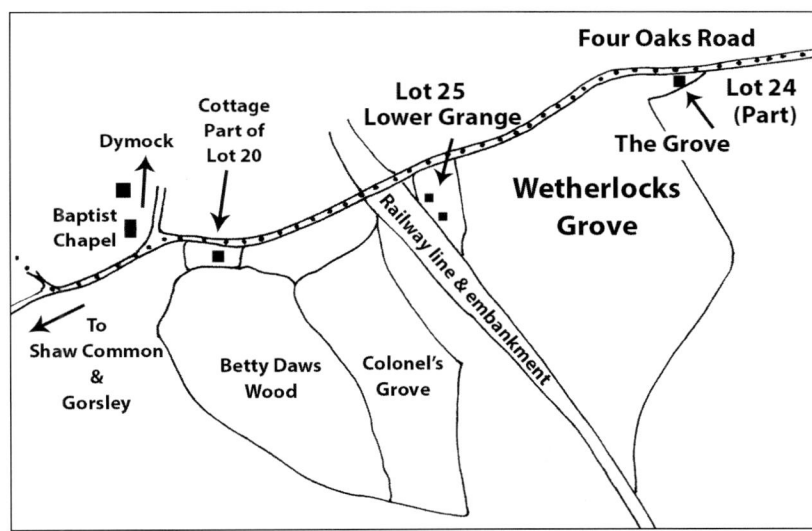

Four Oaks

FOUR OAKS

The area of Four Oaks is in the north of the parish, bordering the parish of Dymock. Cottages were built here alongside one of the lanes that led eastwards, linking dwellings in the west of the parish with the main Newent to Dymock road.

LOT 24   The Grove

Daniel Howley was paying an annual rent of £6 to live in this brick and tiled cottage, containing kitchen, back-kitchen and two bedrooms. He obtained his water from an outside pump. In the very substantial garden there was a lean-to shed and two piggeries.

Daniel was a boiler stoker at the Waterworks and in 1911 he lived at The Grove with his wife, Rose, daughters May, aged 10, Winifred, aged 9, and son Cyril, aged 7, together with his father John, the local woodman.

William Boulter, who lived at the top of Holder's Lane, paid an apportioned rent of 10s for use of a nearby orchard. He also occupied pasture orchard in Four Oaks until November 1913 at £3 12s pa.

In the 1913 sale Henry Jones purchased Pella, The Grove, Wetherlock's Grove (see below) and Pasture Orchard for £2,100.

LOT 25   A Modern Brick-Built and Tiled Cottage

For one of the two cottages included in lot 25, Joseph Gladwin, a shepherd, paid an annual rent of £2. This cottage, close to Four Oaks Bridge, had four rooms plus a wash-house, pig's cot and garden.

The other, larger cottage made of stone and brick, **Lower Grange,** had previously been occupied by the Under Gamekeeper. This house contained a sitting-room, kitchen, scullery, pantry and three bedrooms. Outside was a brick, timber and thatch barn, a paddock and a dog kennel which, according to the sale details, could easily be converted into piggeries. The estimated rent of Lower Grange was £8pa.

Lower Grange had been rented to Mr Campbell of The Parks along with shooting rights to the woods. An indenture dated 25 April 1902 states:

> all that right of fowling and sporting in Oxenhall, Pauntley, Dymock, Gorsley, Aston Ingham, Linton and Newent over Onslow land. And two keeper's houses.
> Except ground game and except the right of the lessor to dispose of rabbits in February and March and in the woods (unless the lessee has killed at least 750 rabbits in the preceding year).
> For SIX YEARS; £100 for two years and £120 for four years.
> Keeper's house, garden, outbuildings and pheasantry at Shaw Common.
> Under keeper's house, garden, barn and pheasantry at Hill End Green in Four Oaks.
> 26 wood coops   6 alarm springs   2 tin troughs
> Mincing knife and board   1 game bag, 2 nets and a dozen steel vermin traps.

In the sale Alfred Edward Jones of the Smithy paid £120 for each property.

PART OF LOT 20   A Cottage by Betty Daw's wood

In 1913 Richard Howley, a farm labourer, was paying £4 19s 2d to live in this brick and timber-built cottage with his wife, Fanny. According to the 1911 census another farm labourer, 50-year-old Thomas Wood lived there too. This four-roomed cottage had a well of water, a good well-planted garden and a pasture paddock.

There is a description of the cottage in an article written by Cathryn Abbott for *The Oxenhall Anthology* in 1999. Cathryn lived at Lower Grange in the 1960s and as children she, her brothers and other local lads enjoyed many happy hours playing in Betty Daw's wood:

> There used to be an old cottage at the entrance to Betty Daw's wood. It was small, two rooms up and down and a back door in the middle at the rear. In the right-hand room there were some rickety stairs leading up to bedrooms. This derelict cottage was the focus of our adventures even if it was really out of bounds. The gang went off to investigate, slowly filing up the overgrown garden to the broken back door. Creeping inside we had a look around the almost empty rooms with odd old junky bits of furniture, old tin cans, newspapers and bits of wood littering the two rooms and an old fireplace along the end

wall. Then somebody spotted the stairs which enticed us upwards. There was an old bed and chair but little else and the cottage was in a state of collapse.

So who was Betty Daw? From various parish records we can assume that Betty Daw lived all her life in Oxenhall. Elizabeth (Betty), daughter of William and Hannah Brooks was baptised in Oxenhall Church on 5 January 1759. The record of marriages records that she and Edward Daw 'made their mark' on the occasion of their marriage in Oxenhall Church on 8 June 1781, following publication of their banns. Edward is probably the son of Robert and Mary Daw, baptised in Huntley on 14 June 1761.

According to the 1840 Tithe Map and Apportionment an Elizabeth Daw lived in a cottage which stood on rough ground to the right of the entrance to what is now Betty Daw's wood. Her husband, Edward, had died in 1830 aged 69. There is no mention of an Elizabeth Daw in the 1851 census returns and it appears that the cottage was empty. Her death, in 1842, aged 85 is recorded in an entry in Oxenhall Church burial records, but her grave in the churchyard could not be identified in the record of memorial inscriptions undertaken by Derek Pearce and Frances Penney in 1998.

According to the baptism records of Oxenhall Church, this couple had nine children. The eldest, Edward, born in 1782, had a very short life, dying in 1783. As was the custom at the time, a later addition to the family was given the same name and also baptised Edward.

PART OF LOT 24   Wetherlock's Grove

Wetherlock's Grove, a woodland area of just over 21 acres and part of Pella Farm, was bought by Henry Jones. In the 17th century Henry Wetherlock owned land in Oxenhall by copyhold (see p.17), whilst living at Waterdynes. He was illiterate and apparently rode all the way to Stoke Edith to deliver a letter of complaint about himself from the estate steward to the Foley family.

SHAW COMMON

In the post-mediaeval period, Shaw Common was the only part of the woods where tenants were allowed to exercise rights of common, resulting in encroachment and settlement by cottagers from the mid 17th century onwards. In 1775, 24 acres remained commonland but by the middle of the 19th century most of the land had been absorbed by further encroachment.

Many of the cottages in Shaw Common sprang up alongside a lane from Newent which gave access to scattered farmsteads and continued through the woods to neighbouring parishes.

During the building of the canal and sometime before 1812, a horse tramroad was built across Shaw Common, probably to allow materials to be carried from nearby quarries.

LOT 20   Wain Cottage

Wain Cottage is very old, apparently built in the 1680s. In 1913 it was built of brick and timber with a thatched roof and comprised four rooms with a lean-to shed outside in the

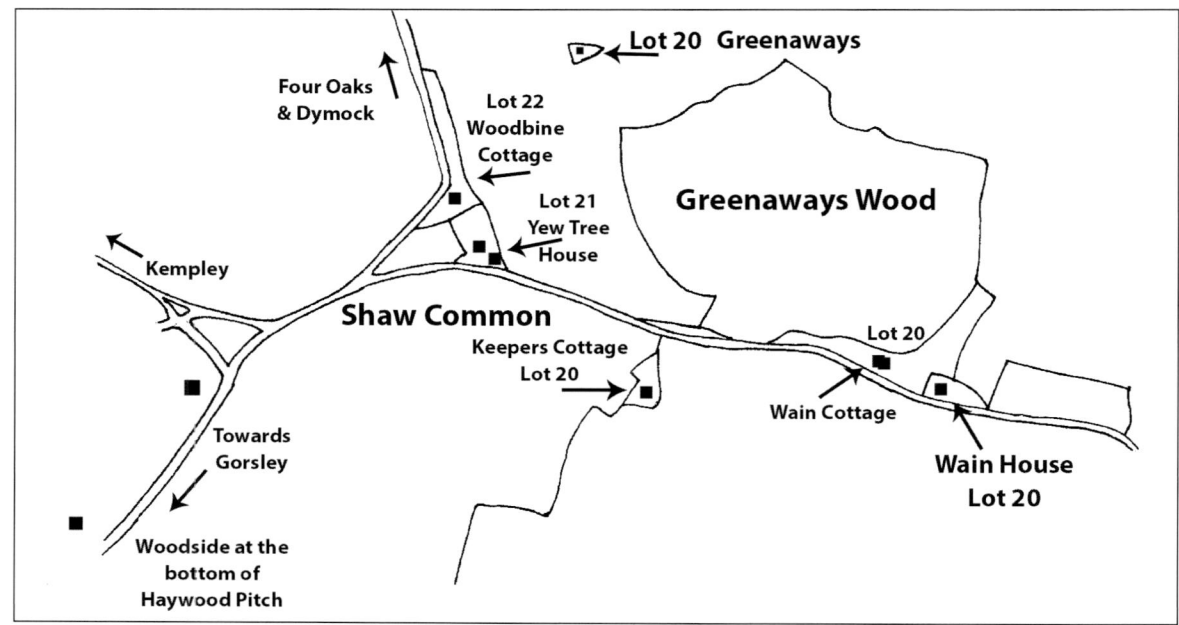

Shaw Common

pasture orchard. John Griffin rented this plot of 1 acre 27 perches for £6 a year. Aged 54 in 1911, John Griffin was an estate labourer who lived here with his wife, Mehetable, and three of their ten children – Rose, Amos and Sidney Albert.

In the 1913 sale Mr Archibald Weller bought Wain Cottage as part of Murrell's estate (see sale particulars on p.50).

LOT 20   Wain House

Wain House was a brick, stone and timber-built cottage with a tiled roof, containing five rooms and a cellar. In the garden was a piggery, a well of 'good water' and a lean-to shed. Henry Loade was a driver at the sawmills in Horsefair Lane, Newent and he lived here with his wife Naomi, two daughters Nora and Jane, and sons Percy, a carter at the Sawmills, and John, a farm labourer.

In the 1913 sale Archibald Weller bought this house as part of Murrell's estate.

LOT 20   Woodside, the bottom of Hay Wood Pitch

Woodside was a stone-built, newly thatched cottage containing four rooms. Outside there was a small barn, a stable for two horses, a trap-house and two piggeries. Mr Edmund Sysum paid £9 5s 4d a year to live on this 3-acre plot. According to the 1911 census, living in the cottage with Edmund was his cousin and housekeeper, Georgina Sysum, his son, Wallace Henry, and a boarder, Alice Maud Sysum, aged 13. Wallace went away to fight in the Great War and never returned.

LOT 20   Cottage in The Field (Greenaways)

In 1913 Mrs Keyse paid a rent of £3 18s to live in this stone-built, thatched cottage which contained four rooms. There was a pigs' cot in the garden and they drew their water from a well.

In 1911 Mrs Keyse was a widow aged 67 sharing her cottage with son Thomas, aged 29, and daughter Fanny, aged 26, 'feeble minded from birth'.

LOT 20   Keeper's Cottage

Keeper's Cottage contained three bedrooms, a sitting room, a kitchen with range, a scullery with furnace and oven and a pantry. In 1913 it was unoccupied but previously Arthur Williams had lived here. Outside, a brick and tiled shed adjoined the cottage and the plot included a pheasant house, a timber and tiled divided shed and a piggery.

Archibald Weller bought this property in 1913 and Mr A.E. Walker, a forester, moved in. He was living here when, soon after the sale, the woods were bought by the Crown. During the First World War much timber was lost in ships crossing the Atlantic due to submarine warfare, and in order to avoid a similar situation in the event of another war, consideration was given to the need to provide home-grown timber. In 1919 the Forestry Commission was established to protect local woods and ensure an ample supply of timber for national use, particularly pit props for the mines, and the following year the Crown passed the woodlands over to the Commission.

Workmen cutting ash used in the production of wooden wheel spokes

LOT 21   A Block of Two Brick-Built and Tiled Cottages

The 1913 sale details tell us that one of these cottages was 'void' and the other dilapidated. Both cottages had 'good gardens'. The one labelled as 'void' had a kitchen, back-kitchen, pantry, two bedrooms and a loft.

Also included in Lot 21 was a brick-built and tiled cottage, occupied by John Griffin junior, containing four rooms, a wash-house and an adjoining shed. John Griffin was a carter on a local farm and he lived here with his wife, Emily, and three children – Lilian Louise, Richard Frederick and Phyllis May – paying £5 a year rent.

Both the Howley and Griffin families continued to live at Shaw Common after the sale.

The cottage occupied by John Griffin at the time of the 1913 sale was not renovated until the 1990s, giving local historians the opportunity to see exactly how this old building was constructed. The two living rooms were each 10 foot square. The ground floor consisted of bricks laid straight on the earth. There were narrow doors, small windows and low ceilings. Upstairs the ceilings sloped parallel with the roof.

John Jones was born here in 1798. In 1836 John left Shaw Common and became a successful tenant farmer of two local cider farms – Farmers and Knaphead. His descendants were among the tenants who became owners in 1913.

LOT 22   A Stone-Built and Tiled Cottage – Known as Woodbine Cottage

This cottage had a small sitting-room, a kitchen, a back-kitchen, a larder and three bedrooms. Under the lean-to stable attached to the cottage was a cider-mill and press. Water was drawn from a well in the garden and fruit was grown in the large pasture orchard.

Charles Merrick, the occupant, paid an annual rent of £9. The 1911 census records that Charles, aged 50, was a Great Western Railway platelayer. He lived at Woodbine Cottage with his wife Maria and children Arthur, George and Ethel.

In the sale Alfred Edward Jones of the Smithy bought this property for £110 but the Merrick family continued as tenants until 1925.

CENTRE OF THE PARISH

Down the ages the area surrounding St Anne's Church, standing on a small hill in the south of the parish, has always been considered 'the centre of the parish'. In 1841 a small school was built across the lane from the church and in 1913 these two buildings would have played an important role in the lives of parishioners.

People going to Newent from the west of the parish would

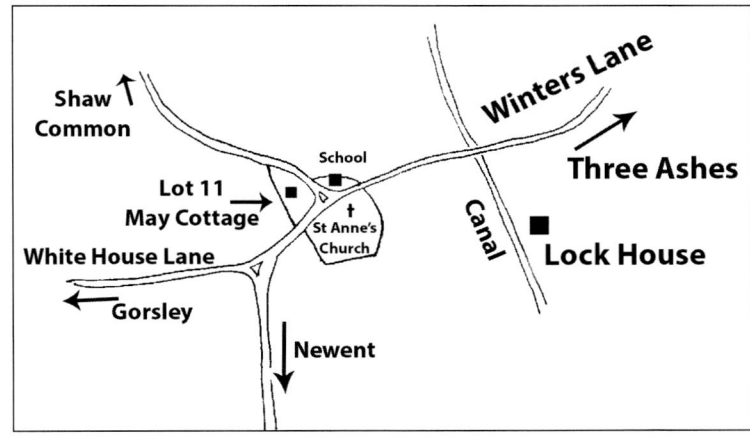

Centre of the parish

have travelled through this area, perhaps choosing to walk along the route of the old canal.

LOT 11   A Brick and Tiled Gabled House – Known as May Cottage

May Cottage, built in a very pleasant position close to St Anne's Church, was one of the larger cottages on the estate. It contained both a dining room and a drawing room plus three bedrooms, a kitchen, a scullery with a furnace, a baking oven and a soft water pump, and an underground cellar. Outside in the large garden was a piggery.

1913 sale details photograph of May Cottage

The 1911 census tells us that May Cottage was occupied by Caleb Hunt, a retired signal fitter with the Argentinian Railways, his wife Annie, sister Sarah and brother Joseph, who had also worked for the Argentinian Railways as a clerk. Caleb died in 1912 and at the time of the sale it is assumed that the occupants of May Cottage were the rest of his family.

The cottage was not sold at the auction and was bought in December 1913 by Miss Niblett. She later married Mr Tarbarth, a farmer from Upleadon.

The remainder of the buildings in this area were not included in the 1913 sale as they had been built on land not owned by the Onslow Estate.

Just below St Anne's Church stands **Lock Cottage**, which was built in 1838 on land belonging to the company which built the Herefordshire and Gloucestershire Canal. In 1911 John Preece, a 75-year-old widower, lived at Lock Cottage with his servant, Mary Trigg. He received a pension from the railway, having worked for many years as a platelayer.

Further along the canal towards Newent was **The Willows**. In 1911 this house was occupied by a 44-year-old single lady, Maud Bigland, originally from Birkenhead, and her servant Edith Ethel Higginbottom, aged 18, originally from London. Miss Bigland taught in a local private school.

Another building in this area is the waterworks. In 1913 the engineer in charge of the waterworks, Stanley Murrell Reece, lived at **Waterworks Cottage** with his wife, Adah Lavinia, baby daughter Muriel Lucy and servant Anna Maria Sysum, a local girl from Aston Ingham.

6 OXENHALL IN 1913

In 1913 the people living and working in Oxenhall would have been concerned for the future, wondering what difference the sale of the Onslow Estate would make to their lives. Many farmers would have relished the opportunity to become owners rather than tenants. However, uncertainty of ownership would have caused concern amongst the workers – concern not only for their jobs (many of them would have been employed by the same family for several years) but also about retaining their homes.

Everyday life in Oxenhall would have continued throughout the weeks leading up to the sale – farm work can never stop – but there must have been keen interest in who was expected to bid for which property.

After the sale the new owners would be planning for the future. For those who worked and lived in cottages and farms with new landlords perhaps there was some apprehension about the future, a future that would soon be affected by a much greater concern, the threat of war.

Perhaps there was comfort in the thought that two buildings, St Anne's Church and the Parish School, very much part of parish life for many years, would remain unchanged.

St Anne's Church
In 1913, Revd William Swain Irving was appointed as Rector of Oxenhall and Pauntley, replacing Revd Griffin. Revd Irving had been ordained in the London diocese in 1898 and served in several Gloucestershire parishes before coming to live at The Vicarage in Oxenhall. He was very interested in music and many of his compositions were recorded by the BBC.

Mr Fred Baldwin, a churchwarden at St Anne's for many years, remembered Revd Irving as a 'devout high churchman'. During his incumbency, from 1913 to 1953, many 'high-church' trappings were used, including blue curtains and poles around the altar, tall candlesticks, gongs, bells and incense. Pictures depicting scenes in Jesus's life, were placed around the walls of the nave. Another thing Fred remembered were green interior walls and black pews!

In a report of 1914, the Rural Dean mentioned that the church was kept locked 'on account of suffragettes' and in a visitation of 1917 he referred to the window in the coal hole under the vestry as 'the only part of the former church now left'. It is possible that this was an

Oxenhall Church in 1905

old window thrown out at the rebuilding and used to illuminate the cellar where wood and coal was kept to provide the fires to heat the church.

Dave Preece remembered being let out of school at 3pm in order to attend Revd Irving's confirmation classes at the rectory on the Ledbury Road. He recalled that Revd Irving rode a tricycle, on which he would visit almost every parishioner throughout the year. 'He was welcome. He was quite a decent old boy really but we weren't religious in those days … like … we were all living a bit wild … kids did as they liked … we were free.' However Dave did attend church occasionally and was in the choir for a spell 'but it got too much of a bore'. In those days the church was always open in the daytime and Dave Preece unlocked it every morning and locked it up again after school.

Revd Irving took a great interest in the local children as he had no children of his own, his wife having died in 1918, a victim of the influenza epidemic. Every Christmas he gave a party for the schoolchildren with a tree and games and, in the summer, a party at the rectory. At the end of every school term he would hold a special service in the church when he talked to the children about the stained glass windows and explained the story behind the pictures on the wall.

Oxenhall School

The pupils of the parish school received Religious Instruction from Revd Irving, who visited the school regularly. His teaching was obviously very effective as, from an entry in Oxenhall School Log Book for 1913, we learn that many pupils received certificates for excellent written and oral work in a recent scripture exam. In the 1990s Oxenhall Parish History Group interviewed a number of local people who had attended Oxenhall School in the early part of the century. Using their memories, together with information obtained from school log books and registers, we are able to paint a picture of school life in 1913.

Mrs Berkley was headmistress of Oxenhall School from 1894 until 1922. According to an ex-pupil 'she was a "big one" for manners and when you came up the school steps if you didn't touch your cap and say "Good Morning ma'am" you would be in trouble! She didn't use the cane but she would give you such a look – you had to respect her.' Her assistant was Clara Little, whose family lived in Oxenhall at Furnace Cottage.

Infants were taught in the small room, which was heated by a small coal fire, and juniors in the larger room, which had a stove. The school day started at 9am and finished at 3.30pm. Each day began with hymns and prayers, followed by lessons which included 'sums', reading, and handwriting. The children sat on forms and wrote on slates. In sewing lessons the girls made petticoats and pillow cases, often embroidered. The older girls went to Picklenash School in Newent for basic cookery and household lessons.

Oxenhall School in 1913, teachers and pupils

Name of Child	D.O.B.	Father	Living at:	Name of Child	D.O.B	Father	Living at:
Edith Baldwin	06.06.07	Richard	Coldharbour	Beatrice May Howley	28.07.00	Daniel	Rose Cott., Hillend Green
Margaret Baldwin	06.06.07	Richard	Coldharbour	Cyril Howley	13.02.04	Daniel	Rose Cott., Hillend Green
Ernest Beale	21.01.01	Henry	Botloe Green	Winifred Violet Howley	21.11.01	Daniel	Rose. Cott., Hillend Green
Florence Beale	13.09.99	Wm Henry	New Barn	Grace Hyett	06.11.04	George	Shaw Common
Ernest Beard	02.03.00	Charles	Hillend Green	Raymond Hyett	23.03.06	George	Hillend Green
Florence Beard	14.08.03	Charles	Four Oaks	Clara Jenkins	29.10.02	Frank	Station Road
Gladys Beard	20.12.01	Charles	Hillend Green	Albert Jones	21.01.00	Henry	Pella
Herbert Beard	26.05.05	Charles	Hillend Green	Alfred Jones	11.07.08	Alfred	Hillend Green
William Henry Beard	20.05.08	Charles	Four Oaks	Edgar Carey Jones	29.09.08	Henry	Pella
Ethel Cox	21.01.99	William	Conigree	Ellen Mary Jones	23.10.05	Alfred	Lime House
Caroline Davies	11.07.05	Albert	High Street, Newent	Elsie Jones	06.10.99	Wm. Charles	Winter's
Ernest Davies	12.05.01	Albert	Three Ashes	Ivy Jones	13.07.07	Henry	Pella
Byron Davis	28.06.03	William	Lime Tree	Charles Keyse	11.12.00	Charles	Sysum's Pitch
Eva Davis	15.02.03	Albert	Three Ashes	Edith Keyse	01.11.99	Richard	Wyatt's Gorsley
John Davis	20.03.06	William	Botloe Green	Ellen Keyse	19.12.08	Charles	Botloe Green
Dorothy Day	23.11.03	William	Lower House Cottage	Richard Keyse	11.07.03	Charles	Sysum's Pitch
Ellen Day	10.05.06	William	Lower House Cottage	William Keyse	11.08.08	Charles	Botloe Green
Gladys Day	13.02.02	William	Lower House Cottage	Albert James Kirby	09.10.07	Oliver	High Street, Newent
Thomas Day	09.05.08	William	Lower House Cottage	Ethel Merrick	07.09.08	Charles	Haines Oak
Dorothy Goulding	02.05.04	George	Holder's	Beatrice Palmer	05.08.99	Arthur	Four Oaks
Gertrude Goulding	02.07.01	George	Holder's	Ernest Palmer	12.04.07	Arthur	Four Oaks
Harold Goulding	10.05.06	George	Holder's	Harold Robinson	07.01.07	John	Baldwins, Newent
Horace Goulding	07.04.06	John	Line House	William Selwyn	28.01.97	Amos	Botloe Green
Olive Annie Goulding	05.06.07	John	Line House	Albert Winters	07.07.04	George	Lamb's Barn
Reginald Goulding	23.05.07	George	Holders	Elsie Winters	02.08.00	George	Lamb's Barn
Gilbert Green	15.10.00	Charles	High Street, Newent	Lyndon Samuel Williams	15.07.08	Percy	Botloe Green
Amos Griffin	02.07.01	John	Shaw Common				
Lilian Griffin	30.09.01	John	Four Oaks				
May Griffin	24.05.09	John	Shaw Common				
Sidney Griffin	16.09.05	John	Shaw Common				

Children who attended Oxenhall School in 1913

At break times the boys played in the front yard while the girls used the yard behind the school. Apparently the teachers were not responsible for the children at lunch time. Once they had eaten their packed lunches, they played games in their separate playgrounds. The girls played marbles, ring-a-ring a roses and jumping games. The boys either played with hoops, tops or 'obbleyonkers' from the conker tree across the road, or went off looking for birds' nests. Sometimes the older Oxenhall boys, the Oxpuddings, would challenge Picklenash (Newent) boys, the Pickled Onions, to fights near Lock Cottage.

In March 1913 there were 53 children on the register, a figure that fluctuated throughout the year and from day to day. In March only 36 children were in school as several 'were away flower picking', probably wild daffodils, which were sent to the big cities. In September it was noted that 'several children absent, hop picking and picking blackberries'.

The weather, too, had an impact on attendance figures. On a very wet day in April, 14 infants were absent and on a similar day in June only 26 children were present out of 56. Illness was another cause of absenteeism. On 24 June 1913, the vicar ordered the closure of the school as many children were still unwell following absences caused by contracting measles and mumps.

Schools were regularly inspected by His Majesty's Inspectors. In the summer of 1913 the HMI report stated that 'Schemes of lessons are arranged carefully and the work is carried out in an efficient manner. Children are trained fairly well in habits of thought and individual expression and they are interested in their work, but they are still too shy in answering questions.'

Four Oaks Chapel

The hamlet of Four Oaks was quite far from the parish churches of Oxenhall and Dymock and the inhabitants rarely attended church. The architect and builders employed to build Linton Hall in Gorsley in the 1880s, by the name of Cracknell, started open air services at Four Oaks that were well attended. In 1887 they constructed a 17ft x 17ft wooden building in Gorsley at a cost of £17. It was then transported by two teams of horses to Four Oaks and placed on rented ground next to Mr Wood's barn. One hundred people squeezed into the building for the opening and two hundred sat down to tea in a tent set up for the occasion. In 1919 this chapel was moved, on rollers, across the road to a new site on land given by George Chapman. Additional land was later given by his son Howard for the burial ground. Every week local people led services and ran the Sunday School.

Four Oaks Chapel built in 1887

The interior of the canal tunnel

The Canal
Although the Gloucester to Hereford canal had closed in 1881, the section of the canal close to the church and school was not affected by the construction of the railway. Many of the schoolchildren walked to and from school along the towpath. Lilian Chamberlain remembers being scared when she had to walk under Coldharbour Bridge. Someone had told her that the reddish rusty drips from old iron brackets were, in fact, blood from someone who had been killed! Many local residents would have chosen this route to get to Newent, passing Lock Cottage and the old lock which, in 1913, was gradually becoming covered in trees and vegetation.

The Railway
The railway running through Oxenhall became known as The Daffodil Line. From the windows of the train passengers were amazed to see fields and woods carpeted with these beautiful wild spring flowers. Local people seized the opportunity of making some extra

money by picking the daffodils while still in bud (it was allowed in those days). They were put in the family copper under which a fire was lit and kept alight all night in order to gradually warm the water. By the morning the bud had turned into a pale flower which could be sold for a good price.

These bunches of daffodils were put on trains and delivered to hospitals and churches in London and the Midlands. Special trains brought daffodil pickers from many parts of the country. Passengers on excursion trains from Paddington to Gloucester were given a choice, either alighting at Gloucester for sightseeing or continuing their journeys to pick daffodils in Oxenhall!

Hop pickers brought to the area in special trains disembarked between Barber's Bridge and Ledbury where they set up camps on various farms.

Freight trains carried cattle to market in Gloucester, and seasonal fruit and sugar beet to markets in the North and Midlands. An essential requirement for all households was coal, which was brought by freight trains from coalmines in south Wales. Eventually the Great Western Railway developed a country lorry service for the consignment and delivery of goods from outlying farms.

Newent Station laid on a facility whereby luggage was collected from local people ahead of departure and on return delivered back to their homes. At this time, before telephones were in general use, letters and postcards were the only means of communication with family and friends living in other parts of the country or world. This correspondence, together with parcels, arrived at Newent Station, and was then taken to the local post office sorting office in Broad Street, run by Mary Ann Bisco and her son Robert. Hubert Jones, a postman who

Steam train passing through Four Oaks Halt

Postcards posted one day arrived the next!

lived in Oxenhall, collected and delivered the mail destined for parish households. This postal service was very reliable, with letters delivered the day after they had been posted.

News and events happening in other parts of the country and the rest of the world could be read in newspapers and magazines, brought by rail and delivered to newsagents.

Whatever shoppers were unable to purchase locally could probably be obtained in Gloucester, easily accessible by train, where there were larger and more specialised stores.

Excursion trains which stopped at local stations on the journey from the Midlands to south Wales offered the opportunity to travel further and faster for pleasure. Employment outside the local area was now accessible via the rail network, allowing young people more choice in their careers. Manning and maintaining the rail track and signals were jobs undertaken by many local people.

Travel and Shopping

Oxenhall people walked along the many paths and lanes that criss-crossed the parish to visit friends and family, to go to church, to school and to shop in Newent. Here John Meates and Sons Ltd stocked a vast selection of goods and materials, and indeed it was possible to find most items required for everyday life in Newent, as evidenced by invoices in the possession of the Jones family who lived at Whitehouse. Others travelled the lanes and roads on horseback or by horse and trap and, increasingly, by car. An article in the *Gloucester Journal* in 1910 mentioned a proposal to erect two signs warning about motorised vehicles, one in Newent and one opposite the sawmills in Horse Fair Lane, Oxenhall.

Water

The pumping station that supplied water to Gloucester as well as the local area continued to function. By the time the Onslow Estate farms were auctioned off in 1913 some of their wells had run dry, as the level of the water table had dropped. The sale details suggest that in 1913 most properties in Oxenhall, without a mains supply, continued to have an adequate or good supply of water from ponds, wells, pumps, soft-water tanks and underground cisterns. Winter's Farm had additional rights to draw water from the old canal. Water for grazing stock was sourced from natural springs, which in some fields never ran dry, and from Ell Brook and its tributaries in others. These small streams were the arteries and veins of the local landscape.

The Onslow Agreement, originally sealed by an Act of Parliament was terminated at the end of the 20th century when the water industry was privatised and locally became part of Severn Trent. The reasons given for the termination have been the subject of debate in the community ever since.

Newent Pumping Station with Oxenhall church in the background

Woodlands

All the Onslow Estate woodlands were located in Gloucestershire and records indicate that, at this time, the woodland was not in the best condition. It appears that timber had been sold for cash and not replaced by new trees.

Hazel coppice, widely spaced, grew under much older oak. Older oak coppice was a remnant from the charcoal making period when the oaks had been singled out to create a high forest. Twenty-two acres of larch had been planted in the early 1890s but never thinned. The roads through the forest were in good condition, however, but there were areas with no trees. The boundary fence was constructed using six strands of plain wire with cleft oak stakes.

Each year standing hardwood trees, usually oak, were auctioned by Bruton, Knowles and Company. Prior to the auction the trees would have been selected and numbered by the woodward and roving gangs of 'fellers'. In 1913 the woodward was Richard Baldwin, who lived in Aston Ingham. The standing trees were put into 'lots' according to the land and parish on which they grew.

The local gentry held shooting parties when friends and acquaintances would pay to shoot birds in the woods. Cottagers supplemented their diet with rabbits caught in the woods; records tell us that 750 rabbits were killed in one year.

Advertising the annual timber sale in 1912

In 1913, 648 acres of Oxenhall woodland belonging to the Onslow Estate were sold to the Crown for £7,500 15s. In 1920 this woodland passed to the Forestry Commission, which had been formed in 1919 to provide employment for rural areas and manage the woodland. There was an urgent need for pit props and the Forestry Commission's plan included the planting of conifers in areas with the poorest soil.

7 Timelines 1914-2013

As a way of showing what happened around the world, around Britain, and around Oxenhall between these dates we decided to use timelines of roughly each decade to remind readers of important historical events and more local concerns. We hope that these timelines will provide a quick reference to Oxenhall events (some details may be followed up in later chapters) and tell some interesting stories. The accompanying photos capture something of that particular decade in Oxenhall.

1914	First World War	1919
1914-18	World War 1	**Around the world**
1917	Russian Revolution	
1919	Treaty of Versailles	
1919	First Atlantic flight – Alcock and Brown	
Herbert Asquith 1915		**David Lloyd George 1915 – Coalition**
1916	Sinn Fein uprising in Ireland	**Around Britain**
1918	Spanish flu	
Revd Irving		**Local Ministers**
Around Oxenhall		
1914	2nd February, Candlemas – The day that outgoing and incoming owners and tenants moved following the Onslow Sale	
1914	The woods sold by Mr Archibald Weller became Crown Property. Keepers Cottage occupied by Head Forester, A.E. Walker, renamed Crown Lodge	
1914	5th August Inspection and sale of horses at Newent for use in the war	
1914-18	Revd Stanley Cox, Minister at Four Oaks and Gorsley Baptist Chapels served in the Royal Army Medical Corps and suffered ill health thereafter	
	Seven Oxenhall men died in the war	
	Howard Chapman and Albert S. Jones returned from service in the army	
	Wallace Sysum of Haywood Pitch was 'lost'	
1915	Experimental plot planted in the Crown woodland	

1916	Lt-Col Tennant sold Kews Farm to George Goulding but retained ownership of Oxenhall tithes
1917	Farmers began building Dutch barns
1918	The vicar's wife, Dora Irving (41) and Sheila Robinson (13) of Hilter's died of Spanish flu
1919	Henry Jones of Pella purchased Hillbrook Farm, Kempley at the Beauchamp Estate Sale
1919	War Memorial at Oxenhall Church given by Mrs Brooks Knowles commemorating the death of her son and Oxenhall men who died in the Great War:
	Andrew Brooks Knowles
	Frederick H. Bayliss
	William Henry Cox
	Arthur John Little
	John Loade
	Arthur E. Merrick
	Thomas James Merrick, DSO, MC, Croix de guerre
	Alick Williams
1919	Baptist Chapel at Four Oaks re-sited on land given by George Chapman Howard Chapman gave an additional ¼ acre for use as a burial ground
1919	The Forestry Commission took over the Crown Property woodland
1912-19	Four people emigrated to New Zealand: Emily and Edith Goulding from Kews, Carey Parry and his sister Edith Parry, servants on their uncles' farms at Winters and White House

The day after war was declared a sale of horses took place in Newent Market Square. Farmers were urged to sell any horses that they could spare to the War Office.

Dave Preece, aged nine, was at school when the war ended on 11 November 1918:

> We were out playing and all at once the church bells started ringing down in Newent and Lancaster's hooter at the saw mills was a-going all the time. A young girl came up the hill pushing a bicycle and we asked her what was happening and she said, 'The war is over'. Mrs Berkley came out wanting to know what the noise was. After speaking with the girl she lined us up and said, 'Now I'm not supposed to do this, but I'm going to send you all home', – so we were away up that road like greyhounds.

Daniel and Jane Goulding helped their children to take up farming

John Anderson, Chief Forester, recalls:

> An under-planting experiment was established in Woodground, near Four Oaks on Crown property in 1915. Young trees tolerant of shade were planted under European Larch including Douglas Fir, Western Hemlock, Red Cedar (thuya), beech and sweet chestnut. The larch trees planted in 1892 were about 30 feet high. The aim was to produce mixed woodland and to avoid clear felling. In 1960 large areas of 30 year old larch in Dymock Woods were under-planted with Douglas Fir but this method proved difficult to manage in a commercial way and was abandoned.

Albert Jones of Pella, a soldier, visiting Parks Farm at harvest time c.1918

1920	The Roaring Twenties	1929
1920	League of Nations founded in Paris	
1921	Einstein awarded Nobel Prize	
1924	Lenin died	
1924	World population reaches 2 billion	
1927	Lindbergh's solo flight across the Atlantic	
1928	First talking film, *The Jazz Singer*	
1929	Wall Street Crash	

Andrew Bonar Law 1922-23	Stanley Baldwin 1923	Ramsay Macdonald 1924
	Stanley Baldwin 1925-28	Ramsay Macdonald 1928 -

1925	Summertime became permanent
1926	General Strike
1928	Universal suffrage (equal votes for women aged 21 and over)
	Farm subsidies removed

Revd W.S. Irving

1920s	Semi-detached houses Windyridge and Penease built
1921	The Cottage and Brook Cottage in Coldharbour, purchased by Richard Baldwin
1922	Arthur and Lavinia Yates bought Marshalls Farm. Daughter Margaret born (now Hinds) Former tenants Philip and Beryl Fowler moved out
1922	Milking began at Pound Farm and the following year at Holders
1923	Lillie and Gertie Goulding, sisters training to be teachers, died of TB at Holders
1923	Sugar beet grown as a cash crop at White House, followed by other farms Sugar beet transported by rail from Newent station to Kidderminster factory
1924	Opening of new chapel building at Four Oaks
1925	Opening of Newent Grammar School on the site of the former Workhouse
1925	Mr Selwyn moved into Bridge Cottage (now Grange Cottage) and former tenant Mr Gladwin moved along the road to The Moors, Dymock, also owned by A.E. Jones
1926	Revd Stanley Cox died and Revd Schofield became minister of Gorsley and Four Oaks
1926	90 yards new road built privately, connecting Holders Lane to Kempley Road
1926	Deridene built
1928	Diamond Wedding anniversary – Daniel and Jane Goulding of Kews
1928	Marjorie Goulding of Lyne House died aged 21 of TB
1929	Greystones built for Albert Stanley Jones of Pella and his family

'One of the first cars owned in Oxenhall was a Napier. If a car passed whilst you were walking or cycling you were enveloped in dust or spattered with mud. The roads were not all tarred and piles of stones were left beside the road to fill pot holes.'

Farmers drove their animals to the weekly market in Newent where fat cattle were sold, often to local butchers such as Mr Akerman.

Left: Ledbury Hunt at Pound Farm

Below: Newent Grammar School

Local butchers bought sheep and fat cattle at Newent's weekly market

Reaping at White House

Christening of Elsie Savidge at St Anne's Oxenhall in 1921

1930	**The Depression**	**1939**

1930	Television introduced and Gandhi's Salt march
1931	Mao Zedong proclaimed the Chinese Republic
1936	Jesse Owens won four gold medals at the Berlin Summer Olympics
1938	Germany annexed Austria
1939	Germany invaded Poland forcing Britain to declare war on Germany
1936-39	Spanish Civil War
1939	Francisco Franco became dictator in Spain

1931-35 Ramsay McDonald   1936-37 Stanley Baldwin   1938-39 Neville Chamberlain

1936	Edward VIII abdicated as he decided to marry Wallace Simpson, an American divorcee
1937	King George VI was crowned
1939	Double summer time began

Revd W.S. Irving

Changes in ownership and tenancy

1930	The Parks – William Fender and his daughter Kathleen
	The Grove – Mary Hyett opened a tobacconist's shop
	Winters Farm – When William Charles Jones died his daughter Kate and her husband Charles Frank Savidge bought the farm
	Pella Farm – George and Edith Annie Jones married and became tenants at Hill View, part of Pella
	Holly Bush cottage built on Peters Farm for Jane Niblett
	Peters Farm – Nibletts sold farm to Harold Monkley and he sold to William and Hilda Evans. Their son Eric was born in 1932
	White House Farm – Samuel Jones died and his widow Mary took over the farm
1933	The new Crown Lodge built for Head forester – A.E. Walker
	Old Crown Lodge – Webbs and three sons moved in
	18-year-old Wilfred Jones died in gun accident at White House
1934	Kews Farm and Holders Farm – Mrs George Goulding took over on death of her husband
	Oxenhall Court – George Gurney sold to William John and Beatrice Cummins (parents of Lyndon)
1935	Hilters – The Robinsons left: Arthur and Ruby Griffiths and their children Jean, Brian and John moved in as tenants
1937	Nellie Jones, daughter of blacksmith in Holders Lane, married William Huff and they farmed in Dymock
1937	Sandpit Cottages (now Studley House) – Ernest and Gertrude Hale moved into the first dwelling and William Rogers moved into the second dwelling
1938	Parks Farm – Charles Hulme died. Hannah Mary Hulme continued farming
1939	Deridene – William and Ivy Price moved in
	May Cottage – Herbert and Jessie Calvert became tenants, after Henry and Mildred Cornall
	Waterdines – Bert and Alice Wood moved in as tenants after Reg and Madge Jones moved to Gorsley. Mr Wood was employed at the Parks

Other events
1930s	Five hauliers set up in business:
	R.H. Goulding (milk, livestock and vegetables) – telephone Gorsley 8
	A.S. Jones (gravel, timber, sugar beet) – telephone Newent 256
	Elliott of Cold Harbour
	Merrick of Shaw Common and Selwyn of Shaw Common
1931	Revd Havelock Roderick appointed Minister at Gorsley and Four Oaks Chapels
1936	Foot and mouth outbreak near Newent
1937	Oxenhall celebrated Coronation of George VI on 12 May
	Oxenhall School closed
	Four Oaks Halt opened
	First set of MEB power lines crossed Oxenhall
	Telegraph poles along the roadside carried lines to farms
1938	Oxenhall Fellowship Guild formed for young people
	First tractors purchased by Oxenhall farmers
1939	Oxenhall School re-opened for evacuees

Farmworkers' daily programme:

We started work at 7am and had a break at 10.30am for bread, cheese and cider. We walked home for lunch 1pm–2pm. Then we continued working until 5.30pm. At haymaking and reaping time we worked until dark and at these times the farmer's wife provided a picnic tea but cider was the staple drink for farmworkers.

Ron Chapman:

Every member of the family had set jobs that they had to do daily or weekly before or after school – milking certain cows, feeding the chickens or the pigs, grooming the horses, baking the bread, sewing and mending clothes, cleaning certain rooms or areas outside, scrubbing floors, washing clothes, or ironing.

A member of the Neville family who lived at Greenaways cottage:

We five got up in the morning, and whatever the weather, in summer or winter, we went outside to the pump, stripped off to the waist and washed in the cold water from the well.

Albert Heath on the hay rick at Furnace Farm

From the Farnham Collection:
In 1933 the Milk Marketing Board agreed for Mary Jones to keep 12 Milking cows at White House. Cadbury Bros Ltd agreed to pay her for 'pure new milk, sweet, clean and marketable with all its cream and without any preservative' that was sent to the depot at Newent on time. The rates varied according to the month of the year. In March Mary received 10½ pence per gallon whilst in May the rate was reduced to 6½ pence per gallon.

Betty Jones:
Home was a friendly place with the kettle on the hob, the brown teapot, the willow pattern china on the dresser and the pinch of bicarb to make the tea go further. Father had a bicycle, then a motorbike – a Cotton made in Gloucester and then he had a three wheeled car – a Morgan. At Waterdines the toilet was at the bottom of the garden under the yew tree. Squares of newspaper were hung up neatly: newspaper print did not come off so easily then!

John Griffiths of Hilters:
Frank Stephens was the cowman and Chris Stephens the carter. Mrs Stephens used to help with the washing on Mondays (there was a big copper for laundry) and ironing on Tuesdays. Three of their relatives helped at haymaking time.

We boys were mischievous. One day we found a snake near the bridge on Peters Farm. When the train went under the bridge we dropped it on the driver. The next time the driver saw us he threw coal at us.

Howard Chapman checking his crop at Pound Farm.
Corn was left to dry in stooks before being gathered into the barn

R.H. Goulding with the first livestock lorry of his company that continued for 60 years

*Feeding poultry and pigs
– everyone on the farm was expected to help*

*A lavatory situated
down the garden path*

1940	**Second World War**	**1949**

1940	8 January. Food ration books introduced for every man, woman and child
1941	Holocaust begins and Pearl Harbour is bombed
1943	Parachutes first used as means of attack. Radar developed
1944	D-Day landings. First computer, Colossus, comes online
1945	Creation of the Atom Bomb. Bombing of Hiroshima and Nagasaki
1945	Germany surrendered unconditionally to Allied powers
1947	Independence of India and Pakistan
1948	Start of Arab-Israeli War. Gandhi assassinated. Start of Apartheid in South Africa
1948	NHS introduced in Britain
1949	Creation of NATO and partition of Germany

Winston Churchill 1940-1945   **Clement Attlee 1945-**

1940	Petrol Rationing introduced
1940	Children evacuated to rural areas
1941	Farm surveys for WARAG
1943	Blue adult identity cards introduced
1947	One of the most severe winters on record

Revd W.S. Irving

1940	Fred Baldwin joined the Fleet Air Arm as a mechanic
1940	Albert and Dorothy Heath bought Furnace Farm from R.E. Hooper. Roy Heath was born there
1940	John and Herbert Pritchard became tenants at Hilters
1941	R.H. Goulding bought 'The Furnace' from the Onslow family and renamed it Oakdale. His son Stanley took over the farm at Hill House aged 14
1942	Jim Bates joined Special Boat Services and made 60 sorties into enemy territory. Awarded DSO and Croix de Guerre
1942/3	Howard Chapman bought Knapp Farm, Kempley (56 acres). Chapmans now farming 159 acres
1943	Mixed farming at White House for the war effort following the order to plough up land
1944	Michael Beaman of Lyne House was awarded the Military Cross for action in France, medal presented by Field Marshal Montgomery.
1944	Electricity installed at Holders for agriculture and household
1944	Joy and Will Goldring took over farming at Brassfields
1945	May Cottage sold to Mrs G.F. Powell
1945/6	New dairy for bottling milk built at Pound Farm. For coolness the dairy roof was eight inches thick
1946	Edwin and Elsa Dawkins bought The Parks. Elsa, born in Sweden, ran an antique shop in Newent
1946	Margaret Yates (Marshalls) married David Hinds at Oxenhall Church
1946	Richard Baldwin sold The Cottage and Brook Cottage (Coldharbour Lane) to his son, Arthur, with two pieces of land

1946	Leonard Smith, Joy Tyler's father, bought Furnace Cottages
1947	David Goulding returned from National Service. Became a Partner in R.H. Goulding and son Ltd, transport company
1947	KEM Transport took over collection of milk churns from R.H. Goulding
1947	Fred Herrick bought Hilters from John Robinson, at auction
1947	Robert and Martha Onslow bought Lamb's Barn Farm
1948	Michael and Geraldine Beaman bought Lyne House. They were dairy farmers until the 1990s
1948	Stan and Joan Goulding set up a dairy herd at Hill House
1948	Les and Lily Millard lived at Woodbine Cottage. Les worked at Moor Farm and Lily was the caretaker at Four Oaks Chapel
1949	A.E. Jones (blacksmith) died at Wisteria Cottage, where he was born
1949	Sarah Parsons (Wisteria Cottage), mother of Ellen Sarah Jones, celebrated her 100th birthday
1940s	Cadbury's sold two semi-detached houses and the depot to R.H. Goulding
	The Pearman family lived at Yew Tree Cottage

Second World War

Men who took an active part in the war:
    Soldiers: Arthur Baldwin, Michael Beaman and William Smart
    Navy: Commander Hooke and Lieutenant Commander James Bates
    Fleet Air Arm: Fred Baldwin in Australia
    Airmen: Bert Arthur, Joe Gladwin, Thomas Hedworth and Graham Webb

A tea party in the front garden at Church House.
Left to right: Mabel Strutt, Caroline Bendle, Jessie Calvert, Celia Bendle and Francis Bendle

Evacuees in Oxenhall
Albert Shotton, evacuated from Birmingham, recalled:

> We arrived at Newent Station, in the late evening. With gas mask round my neck, name tag pinned to my coat and carrying a brown paper bag with all my belongings, a shirt and a pair of short trousers, we were taken to the Grammar School to spend the night. The next morning I was taken by Reverend Irving to Vine Cottage where Mrs Rosa Howley welcomed me with open arms, a warm loving smile and a peck on the cheek.

Severe Winter 1947
All roads in Oxenhall were closed for weeks. The biggest problem for farmers was to get milk to Newent; eventually they took the churns by tractor across the fields. Some workers walked on top of the hedges to get to work.

Clearing rabbits from Pella during the war:
Ron Chapman and his brothers used to clear rabbits from Pella Farm. Wilf Gladwyn, living in Birmingham but a regular visitor to his father in Kempley, heard about these five boys catching rabbits. He offered to buy them to take back to the city for extra meat during rationing. Ron reminisced 'On a dark night, with the wind a-blowing, we used to take long nets, wires and ferrets to catch them. It was like a bit of sport as well as a way of earning money.'

An early electric washing machine

In the very severe winter of 1947 all roads in Oxenhall were closed for weeks

1950	Post-war Britain	**1959**

1953	Korean War; Discovery of DNA; Everest conquered
1955	Signing of the Warsaw Pact
1956	Suez Crisis
1957	Launch of Sputnik 1
1957	Common Market established
	World Population 3 billion

Clement Attlee -1951	Winston Churchill 1951-55	Anthony Eden 1955-57
	Harold Macmillan 1957-	

1950	Petrol de-rationed
1953	Coronation of Queen Elizabeth II
1952-54	The rationing of many commodities including tea, sugar, sweets, butter, cheese, meat and eggs ended
1958	Campaign for Nuclear Disarmament founded

Revd W.S. Irving -1953	Canon D. Gethyn-Jones (Oxenhall and Kempley) 1955-59

1950	Golden wedding of Sam and Ada Goulding, Lower House
	Harry and Florence Beesly were tenants at Lyne Cottage
1951	The owners at Wisteria Cottage dug a bore hole to the canal
1952	Newent Grammar School and Picklenash Secondary School combined to create Newent Bilateral School
1953	Parish celebrated coronation of Queen Elizabeth II
1953	Six new council houses, named Woodview, built at Four Oaks for local workers. Les and Doreen Selwyn moved in first, closely followed by Boyce, Gardner and Brown families
1953	Henry Innes and family moved to Waterdines. Bert Wood (as Farm Manager) and family moved to Kempley
1953	Average wage for a forestry worker was £533 per annum, 20% of which was earned by piece work
1953	Church House (May Cottage) sold to E.I. Allen who, in 1954, sold it to M. and C. Allen, probably relations
1954	Revd L.G. Stapleton, minister at Four Oaks Chapel
1954	Ron Chapman completed his National Service and returned home to work at Pound Farm
1955	Howard Chapman died. Sons George, John and Ron took over Pound Farm and changed to milking by machine
1955	Miss Eva Dyer, formerly of Church House, moved to Coldharbour Cottage with her father and brother. She sold twine to farmers
1956	Chimney at waterworks demolished
1957	Water mains – 6 inch pipe laid from Newent to Gorsley. Replaced in 2013/4
1957	Church House sold to C.E. Allen, who sold to F.W. Woodbridge
1958	Work began on M50
1958	Florence Farnham (née Jones) inherited White House from her mother, Mary Jones
1958	19 acres of Wetherlock's Grove sold to Reg Eversham

1958	Whitehall Cottage, on Pound Farm, demolished when M50 was built and land sold nearby
1959	Last passenger train on Daffodil line
1959	Michael Smith bought White House
1959	Jim Bates and Marjorie Adamson bought Church House. Marjorie's parents, Catherine and Thomas Adamson, lived at Church House for the rest of their lives
1959	17% of Gloucester's water supplied by the waterworks at Newent and Ketford
1950s	The Grove was occupied by the Mann family
	First combine harvesters in Gloucestershire purchased by Pella Farm
	Working farm horses disappeared. Challoners/Kem transport collected milk from farms
	Indoor toilets and electricity extended to most homes
	Hillcrest bungalow built for Mr and Mrs Cummins following the marriage of son Lyndon
	Market days in Gloucester were important social events for farmers. They could meet friends and visit trade stands

Winters Farm

Stuart Savidge, Ken and Edna Savidge's nephew, remembers fun days at the farm:

> The antics we got up to … In the Dutch barn we made the most elaborate dens in the bales, with tunnels and secret passages to escape from. As the bales got used up, up went the trapezes. I think Dick and I had been to a circus in Gloucester, either Chipperfield's or Billy Smart's, had seen this gorgeous girl riding astride a pair of 'dapple greys' and had decided it might be a good idea to join a circus! We were both good at PE at school and so it came naturally. We ended up with what is now called 'a six pack' each from all the exercise.

Michael Howley, living at Oakdale, spent all his spare time at Newent Station:

He played in the signal box, watched the passengers coming and going and the goods trains being loaded and unloaded. Sometimes he helped to unload trucks of coal in the evenings. He travelled in the engine and photographed the last passenger and last goods train.

Children playing at Winters Farm

Celebrating the Coronation

Rowley Beaman recalled:

> We went to the Coronation celebrations in the field behind the old Oxenhall School where all the children were presented with a Bible. In the evening went to the Parks farm to watch the ceremony on television. It was the first thing we ever saw on television.

The last passenger train on the Daffodil Line

Above: The kitchen at The Parks; Below: Cyril Farnham topping sugar beet at White House Farm

1960	**Space Travel**	**1969**

1961	Yuri Gagarin became first man to go into outer space
1961	Berlin Wall erected
1963	John F. Kennedy assassinated
1964	Civil Rights Act passed in USA
1968	Robert Kennedy and Martin Luther King assassinated
1967	Christian Barnard successfully conducted first heart transplant
1969	Neil Armstrong became the first man to walk on the moon

Harold Macmillan -1963   Alex Douglas-Hulme 1963-64   Harold Wilson 1964

1965	Death of Winston Churchill
1966	England win Football World Cup
1967	Troubles in Northern Ireland started

Revd J. Thackwell 1960-63   Revd J. Barton 1963-66   Revd T. Madoc Jones 1966-

1960	Junction 1 to Junction 4 of M50 opened
1960	A milking parlour was built in the cowshed at Furnace Farm and the farm went from using churns to bulk collection
1960	New woodland plan introduced to fell older oaks and replace with conifers
1961	Revd Mervyn Evans became minister at Four Oaks Baptist Chapel
1961	Mr Jeffers bought Lower Grange Cottage
1961	William Goldring purchased Brassfields where he had been a tenant
1961	Geoff and Shirley Goulding married
1961	Mains water to Lower House from Hall's Barn on main road
1961	Electricity to Hilters and Shaw Common
1962	Telephone connected to Coldharbour Cottage
1962	Electricity to Lower House
1962	John Anderson posted to Dymock Forest and the family moved into Crown Lodge
1963	Geoff and Shirley Goulding moved to 'The Villa' from a caravan
1963	55 acres of woodland cleared at Brassfields
1963	Joyce Smith married Ken Tyler and they took over funeral services
1963	Ken Savidge died. His wife, Edna, continued farming with the help of her brother Lionel Phelps and Ken Goulding (Holders)
1963	Brian Smith, the county archivist, and his wife, Alison bought Coldharbour Cottage, mains water obtained from Marshalls – septic tank dug and modern kitchen and bathroom installed
1964	Last commercial freight train on Daffodil line
1964	Roy and Margaret Batchelor bought Yew Tree Cottage and named it 'Wenryl' after their two daughters Wendy and Cheryl
1964	Stan and Joan Goulding became owners of Hill House and laid on mains water from White House Lane
1964	Newent Community School moved to new buildings in Watery Lane
1965	Electricity to Coldharbour Cottage

1965	Newent Cricket Club moved to Three Ashes with Hockey Club
1967	Ken and Joan Abbott and family moved into Lower Grange Cottage
1967	Brassfields first farm to be divided, sold in two parts. Stan and Joan Goulding bought 105 acres and the Taylor family bought 49 acres
1967	Foot and mouth disease struck at Winters and all stock at Winters and Holders was destroyed
1967	Hillview House built by Colin Jones
1969	Open View, a bungalow between Oxen Hall and Lamb's Barn, was built for Mrs Martha Onslow, widow of Robert Onslow
1960s	Fred Ellis lived at Greenaways. He had a passion for steam engines
	Amos Griffin and family lived at Wain Cottage owned by the Forestry Commission
	Cottage by Betty Daw's wood demolished
	When pasteurisation became compulsory Pound Farm changed from bottling the milk to collection in 10 gallon churns
	Roy Heath took over the running of Furnace Farm aged 18/19. When he married Rae they lived in the farmhouse and became tenants to his father
	Dutch Elm disease changed the rural landscape when trees died
	Chemicals increased farms' output

These elm trees were destroyed by Dutch Elm Disease in the 1960s

Memories of Betty Daw's wood by Cathryn Abbott who lived at Lower Grange, with her parents and brothers, from 1967:

Nest boxes in Betty Daw's wood

Much of our childhood revolved around Betty Daw's wood. Dad (Ken) has always done the bird box survey with John (Anderson) or Edna (Riley), walking up the road with a ladder on one arm and record cards and pen in the other hand, checking 60 boxes or more. Up the ladder, lid carefully taken off and a quick peep inside. Sometimes we would get a shock – a field mouse shooting out, a mother great tit spitting at us, a dormouse curled up asleep at the bottom, or a brave blue tit who would only leave the nest at the very last moment. Eggs would be counted and recorded and then, later, if all was successful, the cluster of open beaks stretching to the sky would be recorded.

Mr Ken Goulding of Holders Farm remembers a visit by the Ministry of Agriculture during the 1967 Foot and Mouth outbreak:

At about 12 o'clock the ministry man put in his first appearance on the farm accompanied by the valuers, so we proceeded with the valuation. As we walked down the straggled line of 41 condemned cows contentedly munching their daily ration of sugar beet tops, there were times when I had to turn away from the valuers to hide my emotions – especially when we came to one or another cow which had an above average milk yield and a good family history, every cow having been born on the farm and recorded under the National Milk Records Service.

The herd of Friesian cows soon to be slaughtered in 1967

1970	**Industrial unrest, political change**	**1979**

1970	Ratification of Nuclear Non-Proliferation Treaty
1974	World population reaches 4 billion
1975	End of the Vietnam War

Edward Heath 1970-74   Harold Wilson 1974-6   James Callaghan 1976-79

1971	Decimalisation
1972	Direct Rule in Northern Ireland
1973	Miners' Strike
	Britain joins the European Economic Community
1977	The Queen's Silver Jubilee
	Winter of discontent and three day week

Revd W.G. Jeffrey 1971-1974   Revd J.B. Hall 1977-

1970	The first trail in the woods opened
1970	No more chickens at Furnace Farm – 3 large chicken sheds demolished
1970	Arthur Baldwin sold Brook Cottage and The Cottage to his son Christopher. Michael Baldwin and his wife Cheryl lived in Brook Cottage for some time
1971	The Cottage was renamed Doublet Cottage and Christopher sold it to D.P. Rose who bought a piece of land from Ken Goulding to extend the garden
1971	Lamb's Bungalow (re-named Lark's Rise) and a nearby barn were renovated and joined by builder Roger Cook to create a new dwelling
1971	Geoff Goulding took over Lower House Farm
1970s	Richard, Peter, John and Mary Savidge joined their mother in running Winters Farm. They diversified into soft fruit, cereals, cauliflowers, sprouts, cabbages and early potatoes.
1973	Celia and David John moved into Studley House
1973	Mr and Mrs W.J.D. Leeke bought White House Farm
1974	Revd Mervyn Evans left Four Oaks and Gorsley chapels
1974	Hilters Farm was split and sold by Fred Herrick. He and Doris built Ashfield for their retirement. The land was sold to neighbouring farmers and Forest Products, who planted fruit trees
1974	Hugh Vickery (Canadian) and Martine (French) bought Hilters from Fred Herrick to run as a pig farm. Martine taught French at Newent School
1975	Forage maize introduced as a new crop at Furnace Farm
1975	Janet and Mike Manns inherited Lamb's Barn from her father, Richard Robert Onslow
1976	Revd Patrick Goodland became minister at Four Oaks Chapel
1977	Bob and Liz Taylor moved into Parks Farm and started Parks Farm Nurseries
1977	Nancy and David Jones moved into Church House to look after Mrs Adamson
1977	Ron Chapman at Pound Farm bought 22 acres of land from Little Pound
1978	Wakefield family bought Little Pound Farm with 13 acres
1978	Andrew Bennett bought Hilters Farm from Hugh and Martine Vickery. They went to Canada
1978 Dec	A lorry crashed into and demolished part of the bridge over the M50 motorway

1979	Doug and Diana Birks bought Hilters house and garden from Andrew Bennett. He kept the remaining land and outbuildings
1979	Brian and Ann Edwards bought Wain House and planted a vineyard called St Anne's

Land Rovers and trailers were used to carry stock
Central heating became the norm in most homes
The top of the spire of St Anne's Church was taken down

Sue Gayther, daughter of Dot and Dave Rogers, remembers growing up at Waterdines:

Our groceries were delivered to the top of the drive, not that we needed much, as we were living 'The Good Life' long before the TV programme. All our veg came from the garden, Dad grew everything, and all our vegetables were seasonal. Potatoes were kept in the cellar, apples in the attic, but then Mum and Dad bought a freezer and we could freeze our excess fruit and veg, though it was a bit hit and miss at the beginning. Dad brought the milk home every day from the farm. I thought milk from a bottle tasted very strange. The milk was brought over in a small carry churn, sometimes warm and frothy, sometimes icy cold. I could tell when the cows had new salt licks in the field or even better when they were eating sugar beet!

Sometimes the whole of the parish would get together. One such occasion was 1977, the Queen's Silver Jubilee. Street parties were the vogue, but we didn't have a street, we had Mrs Savidge's barn. There was bunting and music, tables of food and drink, games for the children, a party fit for a Queen. At the end every child in Oxenhall had a commemorative mug and certificate given to them by Mr Goulding. What a fantastic day!

The vegetable garden at Waterdines

Albert Heath with grandchildren Philip, Stuart and Georgina in fancy dress for the Queen's Silver Jubilee, 1977

Inside a barn at Peters Farm

Mill at White House Farm

Roof timbers

1980	**The Thatcher Years**	**1989**

1981	First flight of the Space Shuttle
1984	Famine in Ethiopia
1986	Chernobyl disaster
1987	Global stock market crash
1989	Fall of the Berlin Wall

Margaret Thatcher 1979-1990 First British woman Prime Minister – 'The Iron Lady'

1980	Housing Act introduces Right to Buy council houses
1981	Rupert Murdoch buys *The Times*
1982	Riots in Toxteth (Liverpool), Handsworth (Birmingham) and Brixton (London)
1982	Falklands War starts with Argentina
1984	Brighton bombings at the Conservative Party Conference
1984	Live Aid concerts in response to the Ethiopian famine
1980s	Trade Union power limited and reformed
	Financial sector deregulated
	Denationalisation – state-owned assets sold to the private sector
	Move towards a market economy in the public sector

Revd R.W. Martin 1984-91

1980	Bridge over M50 reopened after two years
1980	The first Site of Special Scientific Interest opened in the woods
1980	John Anderson became Head Forester in the Forest of Dean
1980	The Webbs bought Old Crown Lodge from The Forestry Commission
1980s	Rose, daughter of Amos Griffin, bought Wain Cottage from The Forestry Commission
1981	Mrs De'ath bought Lark's Rise
1981-3	The land at Winters Farm (4 fields of well over 20 acres) was sold to neighbouring farmers
1982	Theo Cracknell bought 33.5 acres of land from Mr Barter
1982	Eifion and Kath Rees bought Coldharbour Cottage
1982	Lyndon and Barbara Cummins moved to Hillcroft from Oxenhall Court
1982	Paul and Christine Wright bought Oxenhall Court Farm. They sold 47 acres and used the remaining land for sheep farming
1983	Rosemary Rimmer bought Doublet Cottage
1983	Roger and Gwen Tutt moved into White House Farm
1983	Oxenhall Festival event – 12 places of interest opened for fundraising
1984	Andy and Penny Heaysman bought Wisteria Cottage
1984	Richard and Jenni Elgie bought Hilter Fruit Farm with 50 acres from K. & J. Lewis. Richard was previously Manager of Hilter and three other farms
1985	John and Sue Teire bought Winters Farm with outbuildings and 2.5 acres
1985	Gwyn and Doreen Davies bought a range of outbuildings and 32 acres of Winters land
1986	Brian and Megan Goulding moved to Hill House Farm
1988	Richard and Lyn Martin bought Hilters Farmhouse

1988	Terry and Laverne Williams bought Lyne Cottage. Terry was Headmaster at Dean Magna School and became Vicar of Oxenhall in 1991
1989	Andrew Bennett took down the grain silo and demolished the big threshing barn and some stables at Hilters Farm.
1989	Richard Elgie sold 6 acres to St Anne's Vineyard for wine production. He bought 20 acres from Winters Farm and planted it with apple trees.
1980s	New owners renovated farms, buildings and cottages
	Farm buildings extended – covered yards introduced
	Milk quotas were introduced for dairy farmers
	Water pipes laid through Oxenhall
	The Sports Union bought the old Grammar School playing fields from the council for £7,000
	A campaign was started to prevent a new road through the Ell Brook valley
	Plans were made to restore the Herefordshire and Gloucestershire Canal through Oxenhall, including the lock keeper's cottage, a rare example and the only original unaltered lock cottage on the canal
	Leisure activities increased, especially equestrian

Cold winters

In Jan 1982 Eifion and Kath Rees should have moved from Tibberton to Coldharbour Cottage but snow fell heavily on the day of the move. The removal van failed to reach Tibberton and as the oil had run out, the family stayed with friends for ten days. In the meantime, there was great concern about the cottage as it had no central heating, only two open fires. The council advised them that clearing Coldharbour Lane was low on their list of priorities. So, with no transport able to get through, Eifion and a friend walked from Tibberton to inspect the property. On their way they stopped off at the Kings Arms for a pint. It was quite a relief to find the cottage undamaged. The header tank had frozen and they took a block of ice 3-4 inches thick out of it, but no burst pipes!

When the family did move in, the work to improve the cottage began. Treatment to the roof timbers, oil central heating and double glazed windows meant the cottage was much easier to keep warm.

John and Sue Teire moved into Winters Farm in Dec 1985, another long, cold winter period.

> We started the task of updating the house and making Winters our home. John Williams of Eldersfield was engaged to do most of the building work and we acted as builder's labourers. We fetched and carried, cleaned bricks, stacked roof tiles and made endless cups of tea and coffee.
>
> The first job was to stabilise the old outbuilding (now lovingly called 'the barn'), but the removal of an elder tree dislodged a corner stone and almost in slow motion the whole of the end bay collapsed.

Renovating Winters Farm.
Top left: The collapsed 'barn'
Above: Removing tiles
Left: Moving mountains of soil

During the stripping of the roof, when all the old timbers were exposed, we discovered the words 'William Herbert 1860' written in beautiful copperplate handwriting on one of the old rafters.

The other noticeable change was that we created a garden. Tons of earth were shifted from the steep bank at one side of the house to the fold yard at the other.

In 1984 Richard and Jenni Elgie started Hilter Fruit Farm, in 1989 buying more land on which to plant apple trees.

Richard and Lyn Martin moved to Hilters Farmhouse, next to the Fruit Farm, in 1988.

Lyn remembers:

> the year we made cider with Richard Elgie (he had the press, we had the cellar and we both contributed apples, pears and barrels). The cellar is under our dining room and Richard was instructed how to top up the barrels and skim off the 'mothers' every day. The smell that came up through the floorboards was intoxicating and the barrels bubbled loudly for weeks. It was probably beginner's luck, but that cider and perry were superb. We never managed to make anything close to it again.

Richard Elgie picking apples at Hilter Fruit Farm

David, Josie and John Anderson collecting acorns in Shaw Common wood

1990	**War and Peace**	**1999**

1990	Gulf War – the invasion of Iraq
1990	Sir Tim Berners-Lee invented the World Wide Web
1994	End of Apartheid in South Africa
1994	The Channel Tunnel opened

John Major 1990-97   Tony Blair 1997-2007

1991	The Poll Tax was abolished
1992	Sterling Crisis – Britain left ERM
1997	Dolly the sheep – first cloned mammal
1996	Prince Charles and Princess Diana divorced
1997	Princess Diana killed in car accident in Paris
1998	Good Friday Peace Agreement in Northern Ireland

Revd Dr T. Williams 1991-2000 (Oxenhall/Redmarley/Bromesberrow/Pauntley/Upleadon)

1990	Lands End farmhouse built
1990	Coldharbour Cottage – E. and K. Rees bought half acre field from the Hinds family
1990s	Kim and Susan Benniman, Ron Chapman's niece and husband, bought Greenaways and several acres of land, originally part of Pound Farm
1990s	Alan and Pam Graham bought Yew Tree Cottage
1990s	Hilter Fruit Farm – apples picked into bulk bins and cold stored off the farm. Started to diversify by pressing apple juice and growing strawberries, raspberries, plums, pears, apricots and asparagus
1990s	Joan Harcombe, Christine Wright's mother, lived in The Apple Mill at Oxenhall Court Farm
1990s	Furnace Farm – lake in field bordering Three Ashes Lane was dug out and stocked with fish
1991	Restoration started on the canal.
1991	The Yeates family bought 61 acres of land, originally part of White House Farm, from the Leeke family
1991	Miss Head, a nurse, lived at Woodside, Haywood's Pitch
1991-	Chris Greenwood and Domenico Traversari bought two properties and 8 acres of land, formerly glebe land. They set up the Poultry Park
1991	Richard and Jenni Elgie built a new farmhouse at Hilter Fruit Farm after their bungalow was damaged by fire
1991-7	Coldharbour Cottage had a new driveway and garage, and was then further extended
1992	Philip and Carrol Gough bought the outbuildings and land, formerly part of Hilters, from Andrew Bennett. They extended the brick barn and outbuildings and called the property Overton Farm
1992	Gerald Jones, grandson of Henry Jones, took over farming 126 acres at Pella Farm
1993	Roger and Bronwen Carless bought Woodbine Cottage
1993	Tom and Susan Brown and Susan's mother, Bobbie, bought Marshalls Farm to turn into a golf course
1994	The opening of Newent Golf Course
1994	South portal of the canal tunnel at Oxenhall repaired

1994	Land at White House Farm, owned by Roger and Gwen Tutt, became part of the Countryside Stewardship Scheme
1994	Alan Smith and family moved into Wain Cottage
1994	Revd Patrick Goodland retired from Gorsley Chapel
1995	David and Paula Jenkins bought Wain House (St Anne's Vineyard)
1995	Newent Cricket Club bought the pitch at Three Ashes from the Hockey Club
1996	Canal dredged and work started on the lock
1995	Oxenhall Parish History Group put on an Exhibition commemorating 50 years since the end of the Second World War: War Memories
1996	Raymond and Patricia Hill bought The Parks
1996	Joseph and Helen Taylor bought 49 acres at Brassfields. Beef replaced dairy and 1997 saw the last visit of R.H. Goulding's stock lorry – to take away the dairy herd
1997	Parish Hall Trust established and hall refurbished
1998	Fred and Peggy Baldwin moved into Old Crown Lodge
1999	Severn Trent now charged Oxenhall properties the full rate for water
	Four Oaks Chapel closed
	TB in cattle increased. Some dairy herds were sold
	Big sheds built to keep stock in all year round
	Maize grown for fodder

Anna and Lucy Teire remember playing outdoors at Winters:

Anna: Trees were another favourite. We climbed anything we could, trees at the front of the house, the big old oak tree along from Lock Cottage and the trees at the hockey and cricket field which had really bendy branches, great for sliding down. We also used the hockey pitch to train our rather small hockey team, the Shooting Stars.

Lucy: Our two favourite slides were the badger banks and the grass slides. The badger setts are on the steep banks of the lane that lead down to the lake and when the badgers dug them, they excavated huge piles of red earth. It turned out that a small child is light enough to sit at the top of one of these piles, push off and ride the loose soil right down to the bottom of the bank. There was the occasional mishap – like losing control, flying off the side and landing bang in the middle of a large patch of nettles. We would come home filthy, with the seats of our shorts and the backs of our t-shirts brick-red, but it was a fantastic game. The other natural slides were in the garden. The steep slopes at the back of the house were covered with long grass and during a hot summer the grass became parched and slippy. With large pieces of cardboard as mats, we found that we could nudge ourselves over the lip of the bank and then go flying down to the bottom, taking off occasionally if we hit bumps on the way down!

Laura Davies of Winters Farm Lodge remembers lambing:

I remember our annual lambing and I often had to bottle feed the orphan lambs. In 1994 Rambo was born on the farm weighing in at 22lbs, which attracted lots of media attention and our family appeared on Central News!

The lake being dug out at Furnace Farm, in the field behind Lock Cottage

Orchid at White House Farm

Coldharbour Cottage before and after the new extension

Wild daffodils at White House

| 2000 | The 21st century and the recession | 2013 |

2001	9/11 Terrorists crash planes into New York Trade Centre and Pentagon
2001	War in Afghanistan
2002	Euro currency introduced but not in UK
2003	War in Iraq
2006	Saddam Hussein executed
2007/8	Global financial crash
2008	Barack Obama elected President of USA

Tony Blair 1997-2007   Gordon Brown 2007-10   David Cameron 2010- Coalition with LibDems

2000	Millennium celebrations
2002	Queen's Golden Jubilee
2005	Suicide bombers attack London
2007/8	Start of the recession; MPs' expenses scandal
2008	Troops out of Iraq
2012	Queen's Diamond Jubilee
2012	Olympic Games held in London

Revd Pat Phillips 2000-10   Revd Tony Lomas 2011-   Leadon Vale group of 9 parishes

2000	Winters Farm Lodge – the Davies family move into their new farmhouse
2000	Ian and Karen Crispe bought Greystones
2000s	Nick and Nicole Yeates built a new farmhouse – Hawthorne Hill Farm
2001	David and Susan Ellis bought Lark's Rise
2002	Brian Goulding sold dairy herd and changed to beef at Hill House Farm
2002	Hillcroft sold after Barbara Cummins died. Lyndon moved to live with his daughter
2002	Doublet Cottage bought by Anne Thompson
2003	Brook Cottage bought by Alan and Tina Hopkins
2003	Lyne Cottage bought by John Addey and Angela Humphries
2004	Tim and Beth Goulding moved into Holders Farm.
2005	Dairy herd at Lower House Farm sold. Land rented to S. and J. Goulding
2005	Goat milking started at Pella with 500 goats
2006	Wilf and Sheila Goulding moved from Kews to Waterdines
2006	Don and Lynn Meredith bought Ashfield and over 13 acres
2006	Aidan and Sue Dowle bought Church House
2007	Sam and Genevieve Wilkes bought Lyne House Farm to run as livery stables
2008	Hillcroft bought by Richard and Jane Muller
2009	Chris and Libby Drew bought Coldharbour Cottage
2009	Rick and Rosie Benson-Bunch bought The Parks
2010	Brassfields Farm became sheep only
2010	Three Ashes Care Home opened by Richard and Judith Cockcroft
2010	Peter Lea and his wife bought Yew Tree Cottage
2010	Cracknells bought Grove field and Buttersfield when Brockmore sold

2011	Proposals to sell off forest stopped after protests
2011	Herefordshire and Gloucestershire Canal Trust drew up plans to restore the canal
2012	Oliver and Bethan Hunt bought Wain House (St Anne's Vineyard)
2012	Brockmore brook ford flooded in White House Lane
2012	The Heath family started converting the old threshing barn at Furnace Farm
2013	Nigel Evans took over the running of Peters Farm after his father's death
2013	Brian and Megan Goulding became owners at Hill House
2013	Christopher and Karen Goulding reared beef at Orchard House
2013	Sam Goulding reared sheep at Sunnydale
2013	Goat milk production stopped at Pella, replaced by pig rearing
2013	Badger cull started in Gloucestershire

Other events

2000	The Millennium Arts for All project. Three textile hangings created for the Parish Hall (fabric squares crafted by residents illustrate 55 Oxenhall properties). An exhibition was held and a photographic record of all Oxenhall residents and their properties was also made
2002	Oxenhall celebration for the Queen's Golden Jubilee on the Church field
2007	Oxenhall Parish Plan produced
2007	Formation of OCRA group to raise funds for the re-roofing of the church
2010	St Anne's Church re-roofed
2011	New kitchen and roof on Oxenhall Parish Hall
2012	The Queen's Diamond Jubilee – young trees planted by the canal Oxenhall celebration for all ages at the Cricket Club field
2012	Oxenhall Parish History Group awarded Heritage Lottery Funding for 'Then and Now' project

The Oxenhall Parish Plan (2007) states:

> Horse riders and cyclists enjoy the quiet lanes, and visiting walkers make good use of the many footpaths in Oxenhall's fields and woods, with some joining the annual parish walk at Christmas. The Gloucestershire Wildlife Trust brings visitors to Gwen and Vera's Fields and to Betty Daw's wood. The Herefordshire and Gloucestershire Canal Trust is making a significant contribution to the parish's visitor amenities with its ongoing restoration of the canal, Oxenhall lock and the nearby aqueduct.

Of the things that people liked most about living in Oxenhall, the rural environment came out top with 87%, and the least liked were the state of the roads and the traffic, with 67%.

The threshing barn being converted at Furnace Farm

Happy pigs at Hawthorne Hill Farm

Holstein Friesian calves at Lands End Farm

Display of produce at Hilter Fruit Farm

8   Farms and Houses in 2013

At the time of the sale in 1913 the main farms were all tenanted mixed farms and though times had been hard, farmers and their families still worked the land with the help of full-time workers and casual labour. When tenant farmers bought the farms, their new-found freedom to run things their own way did not last long, for the First World War meant that the demand for British produced food grew and land use was regulated for crop growing. Prices rose and farmers benefited. The government paid farmers well for their surplus horses and their hay. Only two of the men from Oxenhall who went off to fight were farmer's sons as farming was a reserved occupation.

After the Depression of the '30s, the Second World War brought more government control over farming, and the Farm Survey of June 1941 was used to plan food production to beat the effect of submarine warfare. More permanent pasture had to be ploughed up for growing grain. TVO, a mixture of petrol and kerosene, was licensed for agriculture, horticulture and forestry, encouraging the use of more machines. Casual labour for gathering cider fruit and potatoes, sugar beet hoeing, hay and corn harvesting and threshing was provided by local women and prisoners of war. Many farms took in evacuees.

In a century starting with such upheaval, it is amazing that the Oxenhall farms are still so recognisable in 2013. Nearly all have the same names, and the Chapman, Goulding and Jones families still run farms bought by their ancestors in 1913. The Evans family came to Peters Farm and the Cummins to Oxenhall Court in the '30s and the Heath family to Furnace Farm in 1940. Some farms began to be split up in the '60s and '70s (Brassfields, Hilters and Winters) and some owners sold off some of their land (Oxenhall Court, White House). But new farms have been created from the bought land (Hilter Fruit Farm, Winters Farm Lodge, Lands End, Hawthorne Hill and Overton). It is more unusual for farms to have grown but Hill House, Pound, Lamb's Barn and in particular Holders are all larger than in 1913. A significant change has been that farms are now more specialised, and some have had a complete change of use, including three farms in the sandy eastern part of Oxenhall: Marshalls is now Newent Golf Course, Lyne House is a livery, and Parks Farm Nurseries grows hedging and deciduous trees.

Many orchards were lost from local farms as the cider and perry pear industry declined between the '60s and '80s but Oxenhall still has its fruit trees at Hilter Fruit Farm and the land in Oxenhall belonging to Michael and Christiana Bentley at Castle Fruit Farm. For 70 years dairying was the predominant industry. After the Second World War farmers were encouraged to increase their dairy herd because electricity was available for milking, for cooling milk and sterilising equipment. In the 1970s ten-gallon milk churns were replaced by bulk tankers visiting farms. Farmers had to invest in refrigerated bulk tanks and new milking parlours. Dairy cattle are no longer seen in the fields as local farmers gave up dairy after milk quotas came in and the Milk Marketing Board closed in 1993, allowing milk prices to fall. In the 1990s the number of reactors to TB testing increased and more cattle had to be slaughtered. In 2013 this area of Gloucestershire is part of a pilot cull of badgers to try and reduce the spread of TB to cattle. The cull has sparked protests and divided opinion. The fight against TB continues to be vital and a source of stress for farmers.

Animal healthcare has greatly improved and animals are now protected from many diseases by immunisation. However, the memory of the BSE outbreak in the late '80s and '90s, commonly known as 'mad cow disease', and the link to human deaths from variant CJD (Creutzfeldt-Jakob disease), shows the importance of regulations governing how food is produced. Now people are more concerned to know what their food contains and its effect on their health, meaning, for example, that farmers rear and breed animals to produce meat with less fat.

In 2013 arable land is used for growing animal feed, with crops like maize and oilseed rape replacing sugar beet, which was a popular cash crop until the closure of the sugar beet factories in Kidderminster and Shrewsbury. New fertilisers and insecticides have improved land and yields. Pasture is mainly used for sheep and beef cattle, with only some rare breed pigs and a few poultry, which contrasts with 1913 when most farms kept pigs and poultry. Animals are often kept inside for at least part of the year, meaning that large stock sheds have become common on farms, requiring a big investment. Older farm buildings are often used for storage and stables may still be in use as horses are popular for leisure. Some traditional barns have been converted into houses.

Farmers work mainly on their own and they use contractors who have expensive machines for specialised tasks such as the maize harvest and making large bales of hay, silage or straw. Eastern Europeans and New Age travellers are employed on the fruit farms. Several farmers' wives are partners on the farm but others have careers of their own. Families are smaller than in 1913 and most children have gone on to higher education and may have moved out of the area. The decline of local livestock markets and agricultural shows caused by foot and mouth outbreaks have meant fewer opportunities for farming families to socialise with other farmers and to show their livestock. Computers are used for accounting, sales and farm management and increasingly to access government and EU regulations and subsidies. The question of how and when to retire or even take a holiday has become a more pressing problem for the farmers of 2013 whose children have not chosen farming as a career. (Farmers in 1913 never thought of having a holiday!) Farmers who need a bigger holding are renting more land, whilst those who want to scale down, but don't wish to move away from their home, gain an income from renting out their land. The value of farmhouses has greatly increased in comparison to 1913 when the house was just part of the tenanted farm. Farmhouses have been renovated, restored and modernised by their owners and in 2013 are often surrounded by lovely gardens as well as garages to house that essential of life in the country – the car!

The Parks
The house continued to be rented out by the Hulme family, the owners since the 1913 sale, until 1946, when it was bought by Edwin and Elsa Dawkins. The Dawkins family brought up their children Peter and Anne there and Mrs Dawkins continued to live in the house after her husband died. After living at The Parks for 50 years she sold the house in 1996, moving to Newent. The new owners, Raymond and Patricia Hill, who had worked in publishing, concentrated on the garden, opening their organic Millennium Garden in 2000.

Rick and Rosie Benson-Bunch and their three children moved to The Parks in 2009 from Cheltenham. They also bought a 17-acre wood near Redmarley and use the wood for heating the house with a biomass boiler. Rick keeps chickens and grows all the family's vegetables, and he has also planted a 'forest garden' with edible crops from canopy to ground level. He has a moth trap in the garden and the data he collects is submitted to a national database, which contributes to a picture of environmental change over the years.

The large house has not been altered upstairs, where there are six bedrooms and a Victorian bathroom and WC. Four of the bedrooms still have working fireplaces. Downstairs, Rick's

father lived in the old butler's and housekeeper's rooms, with a kitchen in the maid's room, until he passed away. The scullery has been incorporated into one large kitchen with a modern wood-fired range and the original servants' bells. The larder is still in use. A 1950s conservatory off the kitchen has been replaced by an orangery and a double garage added with a games room above.

Parks Farm – Parks Farm Nurseries
Charles and Hannah Hulme bought Parks Farm and The Parks at the 1913 sale, but always lived and farmed at Parks Farm. After Charles died in 1938, Hannah and Billy, their son, continued to run the farm. When his mother died in 1960, Billy ran the farm with the help of farmworkers. In later years he had a housekeeper, Rene Matthews, who lived in one of the downstairs rooms and kept many cats. She seems to have been a bit of a local character as many people remember her riding a moped with permanent L-plates, with the chin strap of her helmet undone! Billy died in 1977, Rene went to live in Dymock and the farm was sold at auction in 1978 to John Nicholson of Castle Farm, a neighbour. He kept 60 acres of the land.

Bob and Liz Taylor bought the farmhouse, buildings and 33 acres of land from John Nicholson in 1978, having previously started their business on The Scarr. Bob has lived in the area all his life and met Liz at Pershore College. They have two daughters, Clare, who is a vet, and Catherine, who is a police officer.

They have added a two-storey extension to the house so it became L-shaped and has extra rooms – an office, a utility and shower room, and a new bedroom and bathroom. The kitchen has been modernised (the outside door to this room, not used now, was wide enough to allow a dairymaid carrying a yoke to get through). Most of the outside buildings in the sale details

are still in use, and in the 1950s the Hulme family added a Dutch barn and improved the cowshed. The Taylors have enclosed the hay barn and trebled its size. The buildings are used for storing machinery and processing the tree and hedging plants which they grow on their land to sell through their business – Parks Farm Nurseries.

Lyne House Farm
John and Charlotte Goulding owned Line House Farm and cottage from 1913 and lived at the farm with Gilbert, Gladys and their daughters until 1948 when Charlotte died. In 1948 Michael and Geraldine Beaman bought the farm at auction. Geraldine had been in the Women's Land Army in the Second World War and Michael served in Africa as an anti-tank gunner. They had five children and through their years at Lyne House kept dairy cows, chickens and turkeys, and grew blackcurrants which were made into Ribena. Michael had stopped milking by 1999 and in 2007 the farm was sold 59 years after the Beamans made it their home.

Sam and Genevieve Wilkes bought the property in 2007. They met at Hartpury College where Gen, who is from Ireland, studied Animal Behaviour. Sam plays rugby for Moseley and does not like horses! Gen wanted a property to set up in business running a livery and show jumping enterprise. It was a lengthy business to obtain planning permission for 16 stables and a menage on their 31 acres. The livery stables are now well established and Gen is a successful show jumper.

The farmhouse dates back to 1643 with later additions. The stylish veranda was built in Victorian times. The story goes that to celebrate the visit of Queen Victoria to the area, many householders upgraded their property to impress the royal party!

Lamb's Barn Farm
The farm was occupied by two tenants, William Fowler Beckett, the new owner of Newtown Farm, and George Winter, until 1919 when Arthur and Blanche James occupied it until the mid 1940s. Robert Onslow, who came to this country with his parents William and Andrewina from Nebraska in 1921, then bought the property. He lived there with his wife Martha and their two daughters, Susan and Janet, until 1975.

Janet and her husband Mike Manns now live at the farm. In 1975 the original house was extended with a two-storey extension. Of the buildings, half the hay barn, the piggeries and the saw-pit have been demolished. The hay barn is still used for hay but the root house is now a workshop. The two yards are used for storing farm machinery. A large open barn, on the site of the piggeries and saw-pit, is used for agricultural equipment.

In the 1940s the farm was run as a mixed farm but changed to dairy in 1975, with Jersey cows until rich milk went out of fashion. Then the herd was replaced by Friesians and rose to 40 cows in the 1990s. Mike started growing maize to feed the cattle at about the same time. Contractors harvested the crop. Animals were sold at Gloucester market, then Ross when Gloucester closed. In 2011 the herd was sold.

Mike and Janet have both held other jobs while running the farm on their own. From 2011 they have kept sheep and grown maize.

Marshalls Farm – Newent Golf Club
In 1922 Arthur (Joe) and Lavinia Yates bought Marshalls Farm. Two years later their daughter Margaret was born. They kept poultry, dairy cows, sheep and pigs. In the war they grew potatoes and sugar beet, and Italian and German prisoners of war from the camp in Newent

worked on the farm. Margaret married David Hinds of Waldon Court Farm, Pool Hill in 1946 at Oxenhall Church. In 1974 Joe died and the house was rented out, but the land was farmed by the Hinds family until 1993.

Tom and Susan Brown and their two children, Ian and Margaret, and Susan's mother Bobbie, bought Marshalls Farm in 1993. Tom is a professional golfer so they had been looking for a property suitable for a golf course. The ground had to drain well and the course not be too close to dwellings and main roads. The 40 acres that came with this property were ideal, although they were not allowed to use the land bordering the main road. By 1994 the course, designed by Tom, was open for business. The licensed clubhouse is on the site of an old barn. Because of the good drainage buggies can be used all year.

The family moved into the farmhouse and installed central heating, but it was not until 2007/8 that they had the time and money to extend the house itself, adding a new kitchen and bedroom. In 1998 most of the buildings around the old farmyard were converted to provide eight Bed and Breakfast units, with plans to convert the rest of the buildings in the future. Maggie, a University of Gloucester graduate, helps Susan run the B & B and oversees the website. Ian is a professional golfer and plays around the world.

The boundary of the property has not altered since 1913 apart from three acres on the other side of Coldharbour Lane, not sold with the property in 1993. There is still evidence of cider making in the cellar at the farm with the slope for rolling barrels, together with perry pear trees in the orchard.

Winters Farm

In 1930, after William Jones had died, his son-in-law Charles Savidge bought the farm and ran it with his wife Kate. They ran a mixed farm, raising store cattle and sheep and growing cereals. In time the farm was passed to Ken Savidge and his wife Edna, who introduced the growing of sugar beet. When Ken died in 1963, Edna continued farming with the help of her neighbour Ken Goulding of Holders Farm. In 1967 the two farms were hit by foot and mouth disease and lost all their stock. It was a terrible time for them and all the neighbourhood was affected.

In the early 1970s Richard, Peter, John and Mary Savidge joined their mother in running the farm and diversified into growing soft fruit, some cereals, cauliflowers, brussel sprouts, cabbages and early potatoes. They supplied the vegetable markets of Tewkesbury and Cheltenham. In the early 1980s some fields were sold to local farmers and the size of Winters was reduced to about 35 acres.

In 1985 Winters Farm was split into two lots and put up for sale. John and Sue Teire bought the house, outbuildings and 2.5 acres of land. Their daughters Anna and Lucy were 8 and 6 years old. The old outbuilding was in a state of disrepair and the removal of an elder tree dislodged a cornerstone and the whole end bay collapsed. 'The barn', as it is now called, was rebuilt and repaired to leave two bays of the original three.

The house was altered to make a bigger kitchen and the old back kitchen became a utility room. A new double garage was added, with a bedroom and shower room above. A conservatory was added to the side of the house, using the stone flags from the back kitchen for the floor. Old bricks from outbuildings at Hilters, now Overton Farm, formed the new three-storey gable end wall of the house. During the stripping of the roof, 'William Herbert 1860' in copperplate writing was discovered on one of the old rafters. All the dormers, doors, windows and floors seem to date from this Victorian modernisation. The black and white paint on the outside was removed for ease of maintenance and it was only when John and Sue looked at old photographs that they realised the house had been brick and timber in 1913.

A garden was designed with the help of local designer Julian Dowle, and hundreds of tons of earth was moved from the steep bank on one side of the house to fill the steep and potentially boggy fold yard on the other side. Now the garden has mature trees, shrubs and flower borders and a vegetable patch surrounding the house.

Winters Farm Lodge

Gwyn and Doreen Davies have lived here since 1985, when they bought a range of traditional outbuildings, a mobile home and 33 acres of Winters Farm land running down to the lake. They battled for a long time to get permission to build a new farmhouse but finally succeeded. In 2000 they moved into their new house with their two children, Craig and Laura. Gwyn was a serving soldier but retired from the military in 1996. He became a security consultant working all over the world for large oil companies. Now he concentrates on the farm. Doreen helped to run the farm while bringing up the children. She has worked at local farms and is

currently a nursery nurse at a children's nursery. Laura is a primary school teacher and Craig is site manager for a large building firm; both went to Newent Community school. They live in Gloucester now.

Gwyn has purchased another 38 acres of land so the farm now has 71 acres and he rents 154 acres. They breed sheep for meat/mutton and run a Limousin single suckler herd. No crops are grown, all the land is laid down to grass.

Hilters Farm – Hilters Farmhouse

In 1935 the Robinson family moved from Hilters Farm and Arthur and Ruby Griffiths and their children Jean, Brian and John moved in as tenants. Arthur had bad rheumatism from serving in the First World War and was advised that working a farm with light, sandy soil would be better for his health. They had four working horses and in the last year they were there, a tractor. It was a mixed farm with dairy cows, sheep, some poultry and they grew sugar beet and corn. There was an upstairs bathroom with cold water, lighting was by Tilley or paraffin lamps. When Arthur died in 1940 the family moved into Gloucester.

In 1940 John and Herbert (Bert) Pritchard took over as tenants. They kept store cattle and sold bullocks and heifers in calf. They grew wheat, oats, potatoes, mangolds, kale and sugar beet. They had 80 chickens, four ducks and two geese. There were two horses on the farm, a tractor and one full-time worker. There was no electricity supply; the roofs of the buildings needed repair, as did the fences. From 1943 they had a car, an electric dynamo, tractor and a telephone. In 1946 John Robinson gave them a year's notice to quit and there was a protracted dispute, which ended with the Pritchards being awarded compensation. Jack Pritchard's descendants now farm at Green Farm, Cliffords Mesne.

In 1947 Fred Herrick, wife Ivy and daughter Jennifer bought Hilters at auction. Fred came from Northampton and sent his cows by train to Newent and drove them up the road to the farm. He ran it as a mixed farm. In 1961 Ivy died and Fred married Doris, a teacher, in 1964.

In 1974 Fred Herrick retired and Hilters Farm and its 115 acres was split up. He built a new bungalow, Ashfield, just up the road, and kept a few acres round it. The farmhouse and buildings and some of the land was bought by Hugh and Martine Vickery to run as a pig farm. It was not successful and in 1978 they sold the farm to Andrew Bennett and went to Canada. He sold the house and garden to Douglas and Diana Birks in the following year and thus the farmhouse and garden became a private residence, no longer a farm. After nine years the Birks decided to move to Ledbury and the house was for sale again.

Richard and Lyn Martin and their three children moved to Hilters Farmhouse from north Devon in 1988. Richard ran textile businesses in Wales and Nottingham, so it was a good location. Lyn, a secondary English teacher, found a post in Ross-on-Wye.

The farmhouse has had new heating, windows, kitchen and three new bathrooms. Internally, a house of corridors was opened up to create bigger, lighter spaces. In 2004/5 the old cider mill barn was converted to provide a self-contained cottage for Lyn's parents, and new garages were built at the side of the house.

The entrance drive, terraced gardens, pond and vegetable garden have been developed over the years. In the farmhouse, the stone salting slab, hooks in the kitchen ceiling, wide elm and slate shelves, old planked doors and internal bells still remain from earlier times. Outside, a cidermill stone and trough are features in the courtyard at the side of the house, the brick-floored cellar has stone steps and a slope for barrels, and the lower barn, reached by steps down from the original cobbled courtyard, which has a very deep well, has two floors with a hayloft. Hilters' origins as a working farmhouse are still there in the fabric of the building.

Hilter Fruit Farm

In 1977 Richard Elgie was manager of four fruit farms owned by K. and J. Lewis, one of which was Hilter Fruit Farm. The land was used for growing apples. In 1984 Richard and Jenni bought Hilter Fruit Farm from Jim Lewis and moved in with their sons George, Thomas and William. At the time the farm was 50 acres surrounding the house, including three acres of canal and towpath. The canal was mostly dry and full of rubbish, timber and scrap iron. At first Richard was the only full-time worker and Jenni helped whilst the boys were at school. At certain times of the year two self-employed farm contractors helped with pruning and tractor driving. In 1989 Richard sold six acres to St Anne's Vineyard and bought 20 acres of Winters Farm, planting it with 16,000 apple trees. By 1990 the apples were cold stored off the farm and then graded and sold to major multiples.

Richard and Jenni have diversified into pressing apples and fruit for juice and growing strawberries, raspberries, plums, pears, apricots and asparagus. They have won awards for their fruit juice. The Chinese community in the Midlands come to pick their Fuji apples off

the trees before Christmas – their transparent core tastes like pineapple and is considered a delicacy.

In 1991 the Elgies built a new farmhouse after their bungalow was damaged by fire. Jenni has always been a partner in the business and worked on the farm, doing all the paperwork and accounts as well as juice production. Extra labour is provided by New Age travellers living in caravans by the canal. Most return each year; they have become part of the life of the farm. Since 1975 all the customers who stand on their yard in spring have admired the view of the fruit trees in blossom down to Oxenhall Church, and all year the vista of the rolling countryside beneath May Hill.

Overton Farm
Philip and Carrol Gough bought the outbuildings and land behind Hilters Farm in 1992. Philip is a local builder and developed the barn and outbuildings into a family home for them and their four children – Victoria, Gilly, George and James. They called their smallholding Overton Farm, created gardens and bought more land down to the canal. Over the years they have kept horses, cows, chickens, pigs and sheep. Carrol works as an inclusion officer at Newent School.

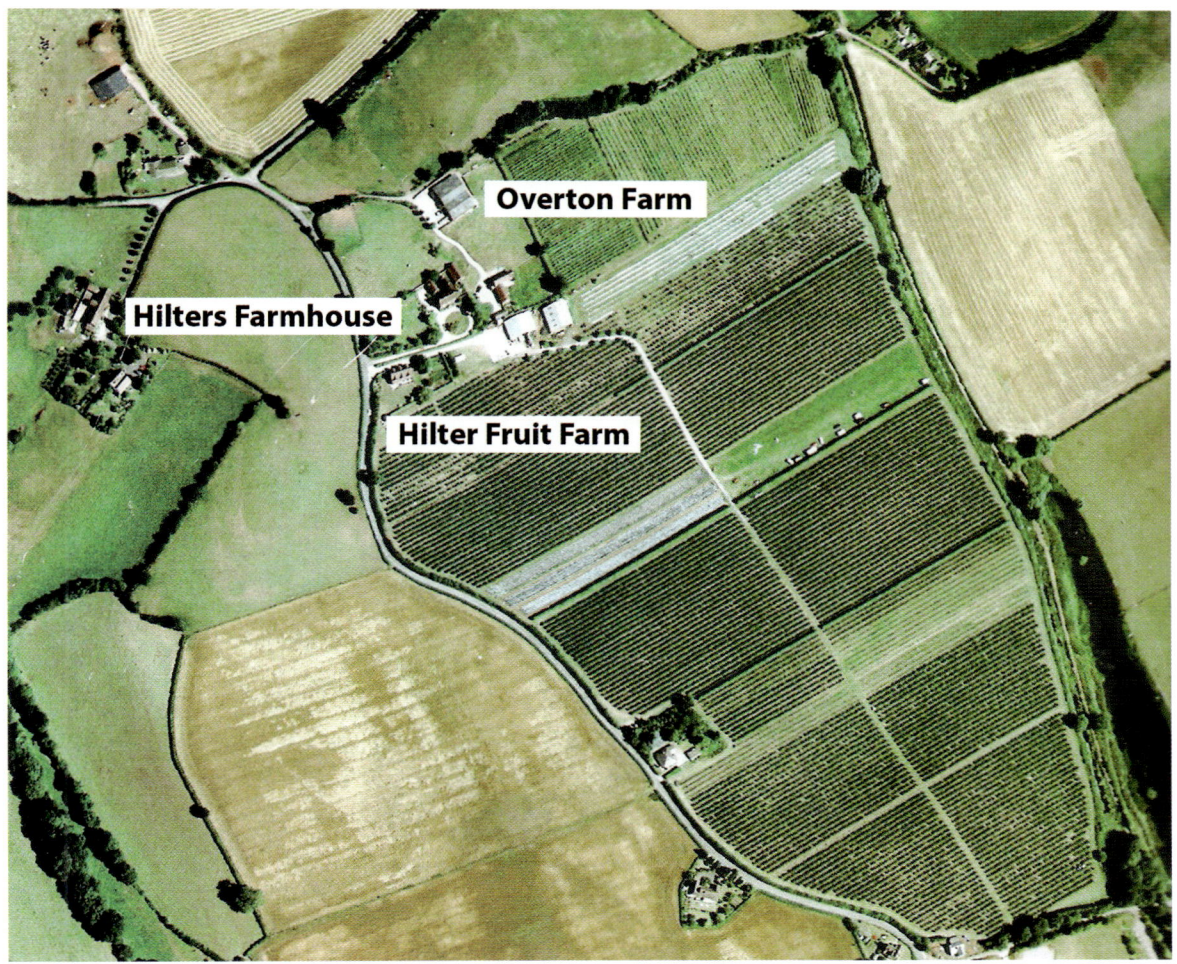

An aerial view of Overton Farm, Hilters Farmhouse and Hilter Fruit Farm

Furnace Farm

Albert and Dorothy Heath bought Furnace Farm in 1940. They had two children, Julia (known as Judy) and Royston (Roy). They had a tractor, two horses and a car. They grew potatoes, peas, mangolds, wheat and barley, all the hoeing being done by hand and the workers paid by the day. In 1942 the War Farm Survey showed that 51 acres were arable, and that store cattle and sheep were kept. In 1944 electricity poles were erected on the land. Prisoners of war worked picking peas. In 1948 a telephone was installed and a milking parlour was built. By 1966 Albert Heath was selling chickens, eggs and kale locally, had some dairy cows and was growing wheat and barley.

Roy Heath was born at Furnace Farm and when his father became ill (he had farmer's lung which enlarged his heart) he took over the farm aged 18 or 19. After he married Rae they lived in the farmhouse and became tenants to his father. At first they kept chickens but

in 1970 Roy changed to concentrate on dairy farming – new units for cows were installed in 1972. By 1995 Roy had built up the herd to 73 cows, but he later gave up dairy farming for a combination of reasons – his health was suffering, milk prices were plummeting and restrictions were increasing. Rae has always worked on the farm and run her own business. Her celebration cakes and flower arrangements have featured in many local weddings and parties. Roy and Rae are now officially retired but Roy still looks after other people's stock and grows maize for sale.

Over 40 years the Heaths have modernised the farmhouse, adding a two-storey extension, bathrooms and heating. The land around the farmhouse has been made into a beautiful setting with a lake, pond, gardens and maturing trees.

Georgina (their daughter) has been an RAF musician for 22 years but is now converting the old threshing barn so that she and Craig Schofield and their three daughters can come back to live on the farm.

Holders Farm

George Goulding and his wife Annie were very successful in expanding their landholdings and helping their children. George sent two sons and four daughters to grammar schools in Gloucester, paying their train fares and school fees. He bought Kews and helped two sons, Harold and Leslie, to buy farms in Dymock in 1927 and 1931. He and his wife were active in the Baptist Chapel and together with their in-laws, Henry and Harriet Jones, instigated the rebuilding of Four Oaks Chapel.

In 1926 when George Goulding bought his first car he gained permission to alter the route of Holders Lane to provide better access to both Holders and Pella farms. Previously horses had difficulty in pulling the threshing machinery up the steep hill.

Ken Goulding, the youngest son of George and Annie Goulding, who were tenants at the farm in 1913, was born, lived and died at Holders Farm. In 1934, after his father died, Ken ran the farm for his mother. He bought his first tractor in 1938. He also did contract work for other farmers. He and his wife May had four children – Evangeline, Celia, Wilfred and Rosemary.

In 1944 mains electricity was installed at the farm. This allowed an electric milking machine and cooling unit to be used as well as providing lighting for the buildings. A herd of Friesians was milked twice a day; their female calves were reared to follow on. During the war May had evacuees from Birmingham and London sharing the house. She also gave the prisoners of war who worked on the farm a lunchtime meal. She was one of the few women able to drive a car but petrol was rationed so she usually walked. During the war Ken had three workers – Bill Rogers, Bill Baldwin and Ernie Hale, who lived at Sandpit Cottages and worked as a cowman.

Dairy production continued, with sheep, pigs and poultry for eggs. In the 1960s the dairy herd was increased to over 40 cows, so the outbreak of foot and mouth disease in 1967 was devastating for Ken. All livestock on the farm had to be destroyed. As a result of this, dairy farming was discontinued but beef and sheep rearing continued. Ken and his son Wilf, helped by Dave Rogers who lived at Waterdines, farmed the land for many years. Wilf moved to Kews when he married Sheila in 1969 and this unit was run in conjunction with Holders. Land was purchased from Hilters, Winters and Oxenhall Court to increase the total acreage to 234 acres. Ken died in 1998 and May in 2003.

Wilf's son Tim, his wife Beth and their three children, Rosie, George and Jacob, have lived at Holders since 2004. Tim went to Hartpury Agricultural College and worked for Reg Eversham learning how to maintain and service farm equipment. Beth is also from a farming background but taught at Gorsley Goff's Primary School for several years. She helps with the farm accounts. The farm is run by Wilf, Tim and his brother Anthony. Cattle are fattened in large barn units built in the 1990s. Maize is grown for feed, provided to the cattle in a chopped mix with grain, straw and concentrates. The farm has been TB-free for many years.

Pound Farm
Ron Chapman is the grandson of George Chapman, who bought the farm after the 1913 sale. He worked for his uncle in Upleadon for two years after leaving school and then did his National Service. In 1954 he returned to the farm and found that two of his brothers had left to work on farms in Dorset and Hampshire. Ron was needed on the farm and he has stayed ever since. In 1954 all their milking was done by hand. Pound Farm then became one of the first farms in the area to move to machine milking.

His father Howard died at the age of 59, leaving two brothers plus two others to work the farm. When the M50 was built, the Chapmans had to give up 14 acres and Whitehall Cottage. Someone decided to fell some trees the weekend before the official start of building the motorway, and 12 of the Chapmans' heifers got out, ate yew and died. There was no compensation as it occurred before the official start date. In 1977 the Chapmans bought another 22 acres of land from Little Pound Farm. Ron now farms the 170 acres of land with his nephew, Stephen Oates. In 2013 Ron was 80 and believed to be the oldest inhabitant of Oxenhall. After undergoing heart and joint operations, Ron gave up working outside on the farm and took computer courses. He now does the paperwork for the farm. They have 40 suckler cows, buy in calves and also have 150 breeding ewes. They have given up arable because of the need for machines and they use a contractor for hedge-cutting.

Little Pound Farm
Ambrose Preece, his wife Margaret and their four children Adolphus, Mabel, Francis and David bought the farm from Archibald Weller some months after the 1913 sale. The children all walked to Oxenhall School. Years later David still remembered his mother's wonderful cooking – 'she had years of experience in the big houses and could cook anything'. His father taught him to take ferrets in the woods and snare rabbits and to use guns properly. They

made lots of cider at the farm and sold it at threepence or fourpence a gallon. Someone from Gorsley would take it to the pits in the Forest of Dean for the miners.

In 1978 the Wakefield family bought the farmhouse and 13 acres from the Preece family. Gary grew up on the farm with his parents and lives there now with his wife Debbie and family. They have increased their acreage by purchasing fields that lie on the western edge of Hay Wood.

Gary is a farrier with a mobile forge, working within a radius of about ten miles, on horses now kept mainly for leisure. Debbie has a hairdressing business. The family's great interest is harness racing and they have their own practice track on their land.

Gary shoeing a horse

Oxenhall Court Farm

William and Beatrice Cummins bought the farm in 1934 from George Gurney, who had owned it since the 1913 sale. They had one son, Lyndon. In 1936 they bought another four acres from Fred Niblett. They farmed beef cattle, arable and a few dairy cows. Threshing was carried out using a steam engine which moved from farm to farm and was followed by a group of labourers who would work on the ricks. When additional help was required a notice would be put up at the post office in Newent. Horace Webb, who lived with his brothers at Old Crown Lodge, worked on the farm, mainly with the horses. After the war local contractors were employed to do the more demanding arable work.

In 1950 William and Beatrice retired and moved to Hillcroft bungalow. Lyndon and his wife Barbara took ownership and continued to run the farm as a beef, sheep and arable unit until 1982.

Paul and Christine Wright bought the farm at auction in 1982. Subsequently they sold 29 acres of land to Wilf Goulding of Kews and 18 acres to Geoff Goulding of Lower House. The remaining land was used for sheep farming – Chris comes from a farming family. Paul was a GP at the Health Centre in Newent.

The farmhouse was extensively restored and renovated. In 1991 the west end of the barn was converted into a home for Christine's mother. The Apple Mill, as it is now called, is occupied by the Wrights' youngest son Martin and his wife Helen and family. The land continues to be used as permanent pasture for a self-contained flock of 70 ewes kept for fat lamb production. The original restored cidermill and press, dated 1838, have been placed along the entrance drive.

Pella Farm

The Jones family have owned Pella since the 1913 sale, when Henry Jones bought the farmhouse and 187 acres. He grew beans, wheat and oats as food for sheep and beef cattle, and root crops for winter feed with hay. When ready for sale, animals were walked to Newent Market (which was behind the Market House). Henry was still living at the farm in 1940 with his son Raymond and Raymond's wife Kathleen. They had four children – Audrey, Geoffrey, Keith and Gerald. The wartime farm survey showed that the farm had no electricity but did have a tractor and three horses. The water supply was both from catchment and a well. Cattle were kept for fattening, along with sheep, pigs and some poultry. As the land was heavy, the crops grown were mainly used for animal feed.

In the 1950s autumn wheat was planted, mostly to be sold, and the first combine harvester in the area was used at Pella. Both local and Cotswold farmers came to see it working. In 1958, 19 acres of Wetherlocks Grove woods was sold to Reg Eversham who later cut down the trees and levelled the land. This was also the year that mains electricity came to the farm and house. Poultry keeping, chickens for eggs and turkeys for Christmas, expanded in the late 1950s. In the early 1960s dairy production started and in 1992 Gerald Jones took over Pella Farm.

In 1995 Geoffrey and Gerald Jones divided the farm. Geoffrey took over Hill Brook Farm, Kempley and retained 56 acres of the original Pella Farm land, named Greenaways. Gerald continued to farm the remaining 126 acres of Pella. In 2005 it was decided to move into goat milk production, with new buildings and equipment and 500 milking goats. The unit was very efficient but required constant supervision by Gerald and his son Paul, and the production of feed was very demanding. The price of goats' milk fell sharply and milk production was discontinued from May 2013. The farm will now be used for rearing pigs.

Peters Farm

Eric Evans was one year old in 1934 when his parents moved to Peters Farm as tenants of Harold Monkley, a Hereford corn merchant. He had bought the farm from the Niblett family in the 1930s. The Evans family later bought the farm. Eric married Dilys and they brought up three children at the farm. They bought land alongside the track after the railway closed in the mid '70s, and kept cattle and sheep, producing milk until 1998. They also grew spring corn and sugar beet.

Eric died in early 2013 and his son Nigel, married to Judy, now runs the farm, keeping suckler cows and sheep on pasture, with occasional crops of winter corn. Most of the original farm buildings are still being used, with the addition of a new barn. Nigel and Judy and their three children live in Horsefair Lane and Dilys still lives at Peters Farm.

White House Farm

After purchasing White House Farm from the Onslow Estate in 1913, Samuel Jones and his second wife Mary (née Niblett) from Peters Farm continued to farm it with their descendants for more than 60 years. Early on during that period, and soon after Sam's death in 1932, their son Wilfred, aged 18, was accidentally shot dead by his cousin from Peters Farm when out shooting magpies in the moonlight. This left widowed Mary and her daughter Flossie to cope on their own. Cyril Farnham came to help them out and in due course married Flossie.

After Flossie's death in 1975, Cyril and his son Robert continued farming at White House until 1976, when they finally sold up. Robert joined the Air Force and then made a career elsewhere. His father Cyril retired to Ross-on-Wye where he wrote a fascinating record of the history of the farm as he knew it.

The Farnhams had a difficult time with the farm and sold off land progressively from 1959 to 1976 – to Michael Smith, a fruit grower, and to Mr Barter. In 1976 Mr and Mrs W.J.D. Leeke bought nearly 100 acres of the land that had once belonged to White House.

Meanwhile, in 1976 the original farmhouse, the buildings and seven acres were sold to Robin Boswell from London. Structural alterations were made to the house with many internal walls removed and some idiosyncratic features added. The former milking parlour, stables and hayloft were also remodelled, resulting in a cottage which they called the Herb House.

In 1979 Mr and Mrs Leeke bought the farmhouse, buildings and paddock from Mr Boswell to put it back together with the farmland. They planned to retire to White House from their farm elsewhere. This didn't happen and instead their daughter and son-in-law Gwen and Roger Tutt bought the house, buildings and paddock in 1983. They had spent many happy times at White House with their three children in the school holidays. Roger and Gwen then began many years of restoration and improvement to the property as it became their family home.

The remaining acres, including the hill opposite the house and the field alongside the Ell Brook, were eventually bought in 1994 by Roger and Gwen Tutt to put back with the original farmhouse and paddock and small field, making a 36.5 acre holding altogether.

By 2013 this complicated series of land transfers had resulted in three farms where in 1913 there was just the one. The major threat of a new dual-carriageway A40 slicing through

the original farm on its way through the Ell Brook Valley was eventually cancelled in 1994. An oak tree planted in the field overlooking the valley and alongside White House Lane commemorates the saving of the valley from the road.

Meanwhile the Tutts placed much of their landholding into a Countryside Stewardship Scheme where it has remained. Neighbouring farmer Ian Cracknell grazes his pedigree heifers on 24 acres and Roger Yeates grazes sheep on the remainder. Since 2004 low intensity grazing regimes to improve biodiversity have led to an increasing number of wild daffodils and there are now some orchids and wild green hellebores to be seen. Hedges have been re-laid or replanted to replace dead elm. Standard varieties of local cider apples and perry pears were planted in what had traditionally been the orchard to mark the Millennium, and a pond was created. The old mineshaft in the field where the 19th-century Newent Colliery existed was finally filled in by the Coal Authority in 2009, making safe a hazard which had existed for more than a century.

The farmhouse, though called White House, was not painted white until after the Farnhams' time. Although it doesn't look very old from the outside, it was first mentioned as White House in a document dating from 1443 now held in Westminster Abbey. It has been restored and extended by the Tutt family over the years and is now surrounded by a large garden instead of a farmyard. However the old part 17th-century, part Victorian barn and old cidermill still stand as they always have.

Hawthorne Hill Farm

Michael Smith grew fruit on 61 acres of what had been White House land until 1973. Then the Leeke family bought the land and grew cereal crops. In 1991 the Yeates family purchased the 61 acres. Nick and Nicole Yeates built their new farmhouse on the field that was called

Great Hawthorne Hill. The land includes one acre of woodland and five fields, now mainly pasture. They also rent 16 acres of land from Michael and Sandra Taylor. They raise various breeds of beef cattle, mainly Aberdeen Angus, plus free-range rare breed pigs and some sheep. Nick also works full time with plant and machinery elsewhere. The clay soil has the advantage of not allowing the grass to burn in hot summers.

Lands End Farm
In 1982 Theo Cracknell of Withymoor Farm, Gorsley bought 33.5 acres of land, formerly part of White House Farm, from Mr Barter, who had used it for growing soft fruit. One of the fields is called Strawberry Slinget, reflecting the fruit that used to be grown there, and another is called Black Goose meadow.

In 1990 a barn was put up and in 1991 a house was built for Ian and Julia Cracknell and their three children, Josh, Ruth and Naomi. In 2010 the Cracknells bought Grove field, Butters field and a small piece of land running down to the ford from Mrs Boughton of Brockmore Farm.

The Cracknell family own the Withyland herd of Holstein Friesian cattle. The cattle graze at Lands End Farm and on rented land nearby from six months old until their calves are born. They then move on to Withymoor. Most of the land is put down to grass for grazing, hay and silage, but maize or wheat are also grown for cattle feed and bedding straw.

Brassfields Farm
In 1967 the farmland was split when Will Goldring sold up. Stan and Joan Goulding bought 108 acres that adjoined Hill House Farm. The farmhouse, buildings and the remaining 49 acres lying in Newent parish on the south-western side of the Ross road were purchased by Albert Taylor and his sons Michael and Joseph. So from 1967 none of Brassfields Farm was in Oxenhall.

Lower House
In 1964, after the death of Sam Goulding and his wife Ada, their son Arthur bought Lower House Farm and their grandson Stan bought Hill House Farm. Arthur and Sophie had eight children. Their youngest son Geoffrey and his wife Shirley took over the farming at Lower House and moved into the farmhouse in 1971 where they brought up their three sons, Christopher, Mark and Richard.

Geoff and Shirley built up the dairy herd. They bought up land from Kews and Oxenhall Court Farms and rented 50 acres at Crookes. Christopher became a partner in 1990, Mark became an agricultural engineer running his own business from the farm and Richard was a general worker for 18 years. They bought the original farm in 2003 when Sophie died. In spite of hard work their overdraft was increasing and Christopher was disenchanted with farming and wanted a new career. So in 2005 Geoff decided to retire and the stock and machinery

were sold, and most of the 110 acres of land rented to cousins Stan and Joan Goulding, who use the pasture for rearing sheep. As a hobby, Christopher and Karen are building up a herd of Dexters on pasture called Crazy Field and Mark's son, Sam has started rearing sheep.

The farmhouse, where Geoff and Shirley still live, is largely unchanged from 1913. The kitchen has been modernised and windows replaced. Most of the buildings from 1913 still exist but have different uses, though some are obsolete. The wagon house became the dairy, the milking shed is now a workshop. The metal barn is used for storage and the barn turned into stables.

Hill House Farm
In 2013 Brian and Megan Goulding became owners of the farm, following on from Brian's parents, Stan and Joan. Brian's brother, Derek, farms in Upleadon and between them they have 500 acres. At Hill House 70 acres are used for wheat, barley and maize and they rear beef cattle and sheep. There are three large stock sheds for cattle and a grain store. Buildings in the second yard are used as lambing sheds.

The building that adjoined the house with a second kitchen and a room over became dilapidated and was demolished by 1980. The pond at the back of the buildings was filled in. In 2012 the farmhouse was extended and the kitchen modernised. Megan worked as a teaching assistant for a number of years when farming was going through a difficult time. They have two daughters, Hannah and Joanne. Megan now cares for her grandson several days a week.

Two historic farmhouses, Crookes and Kews, which were not in the Onslow Estate sale but are in Oxenhall in 20013 are also important in the parish.

Crookes
The house, accessed from the Ross road, occupies a prominent position overlooking Oxenhall. The Hooke family has owned it and some of the land since 1415, when it was given to Thomas Hooke for saving Henry V's life at Agincourt. There has been virtually no break in ownership in 600 years. The pond in front of the house was the claypit from which the bricks were made for the house, and the sand on the other side was used for mortar. The Hooke family have rented out 100 acres of their land since the 1800s. Richard Hooke and Jane Neale came to Crookes in 1990 and have brought up their daughters there. The girls attended Gorsley Goff's School, Haberdasher's Monmouth School and university. They continue to enjoy riding their horses.

Three houses on Kews Lane which runs from the Kilcot Inn to Kilcot Cross are in the parish. One of these, **The Nest**, was a wooden bungalow with a tin roof when Daniel Goulding bought it in 1900 for £80. It was for sale again when Jane Goulding died in 1939. Lionel and

Joan Buckland bought it and lived there from 1959, bringing up their daughters there and adding a first floor. In 2012 they exchanged properties with a Newent family who rewired the building and renovated it with a new kitchen and bathrooms, roof, windows and dormers. The children go to Newent School and their parents work as a head cook in the Forest of Dean and a tyre repairer for heavy vehicles.

Kews

Kews was in the hands of the Goulding family for 120 years. Daniel Goulding rented the farm and lived there until he died in 1931. His son George purchased the farm in 1916 and started a sawmill and wood turning business for his son Reg, who was lame. When his mother died in 1961, Reg bought Kews, which then had 104 acres. He and his wife sold off land to his relatives and moved into their bungalow along Kews Lane. They rented out the house, buildings and remaining 40 acres of land to their nephew Wilfred when he married Sheila. They brought up their four sons, Anthony, Robert, Timothy and Simon here and in 1989 they bought the property.

Rob and Chris Cam and their children Isabelle and Laurie moved to Kews in 2007. Rob is a company director and Chris a local authority officer. They purchased the farmhouse, buildings and 5½ acres of land. They pulled down the pigsty and built stables and a hay store. The 17th-century house was renovated and rewired and the barn turned into a lovely residence.

John and Jean Cam, retired doctors, and their son, Peter, a retired engineer, moved into Kews Barn in 2012. The Gouldings continue to farm 26 acres.

Some of Oxenhall's landholders with their produce
Top (left to right): Richard Elgie, Ian Cracknell, Sam Wilkes, Roy Heath, Nigel Evans, Paul Jones
Middle: Genevieve Wilkes, Liz Taylor, Doreen Davies, Jenni Elgie, Chris Wright, Paul Wright, Gwyn Davies
Front: Ron Chapman, Don Meredith, Geoff Goulding, Gerald Jones

9   Cottages and Houses in 2013

In 1913 the cottages on the estate were small, two rooms up and two rooms down, and sometimes housed more than one family. They must have been very cramped, very basic and some were tied to the farm where the men worked. In contrast, the cottages of today have been bought, modernised and extended so that in some cases they are large houses. Many owners have stories of battles with the planning department, so these improvements have been hard won, but planning restrictions have also stopped too much ribbon development of new houses along the wider roads. The homes are still surrounded by rolling countryside and woods, but Dutch Elm disease in the 1960s destroyed many trees and opened up long distance views. Many neighbours can now see one another's properties and residents can see the Cotswolds, May Hill and Linton Ridge.

    The people who live in these cottages and houses today are no longer agricultural workers, though some families have links to earlier tenants. Most are owner occupiers, often

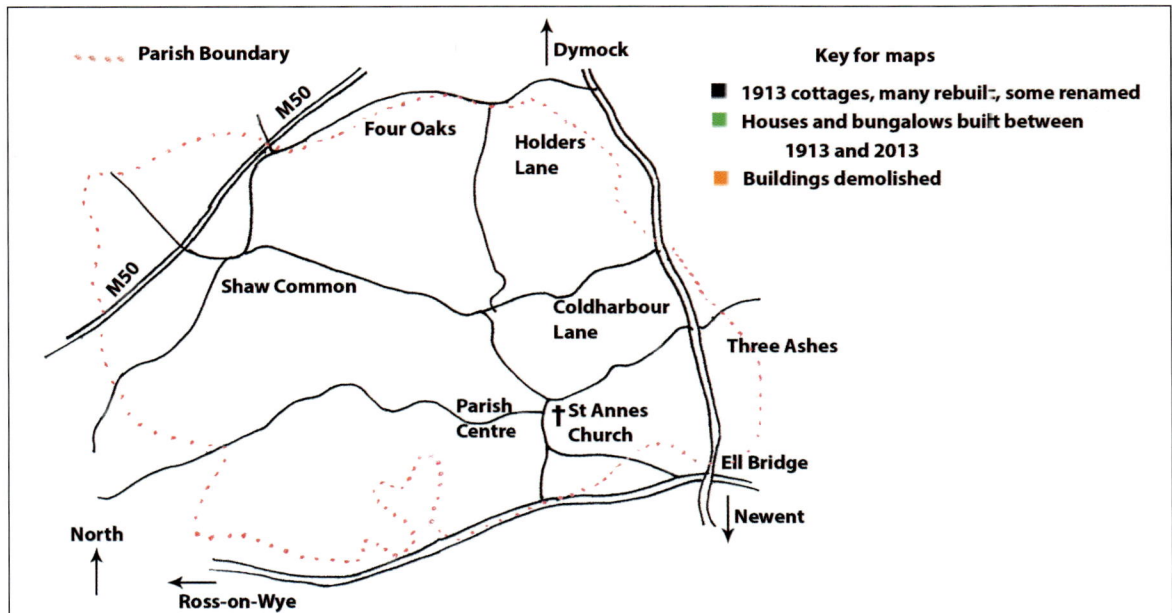

professionals and what might be termed 'middle class'. They work outside the parish and travel to work or further afield by car. Their children have mostly gone on to higher education and some have moved outside the area, even overseas. If one compiled a list of countries where Oxenhall residents have lived, worked or visited over recent decades, there might not be many parts of the world left off the list. Horizons have opened up for nearly everyone.

The best way to appreciate Oxenhall's different areas of cottages and houses, with their traces of the past, improvements and well-tended gardens is to walk or ride past them. The following route starts in Newent and ends at Oxenhall Church but each area can be accessed at different points along the way. The first two areas are on a busy road, so take care.

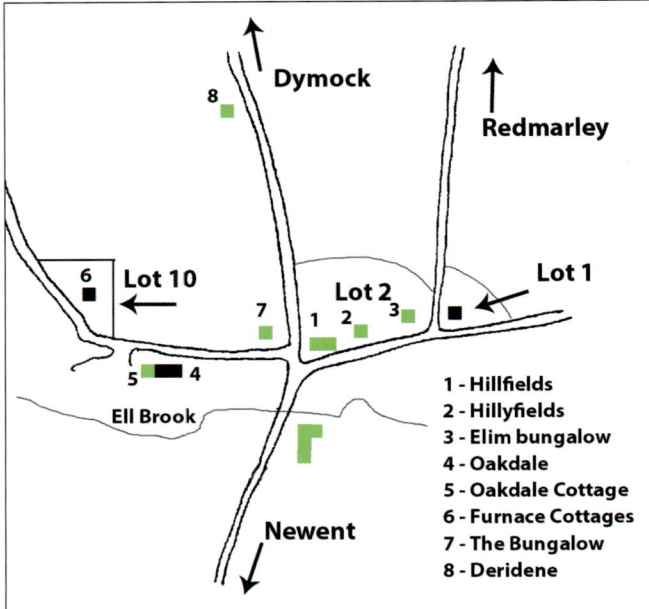

Ellbridge

Ellbridge – Tewkesbury Road

Starting from Newent, take the B4215 to Ledbury, passing between the buttresses of the old railway bridge. In the 1920s Cadburys built a milk depot close to Newent railway station from which milk could be easily transported by road and rail. The platform on which the churns were placed is still visible in the building to the right, now a depot for D.L. Dennis.

In the 1930s, a pair of semi-detached houses were built for workers at the Cadbury depot. These houses, since modernised and extended, can be seen along the Tewkesbury road to Upleadon.

No 1 Hillfields is occupied by John and Margaret Crisp and **No 2 Hillfields** by Colin and Carrie Hinton, who have lived here since 2008.

Two other dwellings built on this 'area of pasture land', sold as Lot 2 in 1913, are **Elim Bungalow,** occupied by Mr and Mrs Robin Fishpool; and **Hillyfields**, a smallholding, occupied by Alan Waters.

Retracing your steps and crossing the main road to head down Furnace Lane, you soon reach The Furnace, home of Andrew Richard Onslow until the early 1940s, when he sold it to R.H. Goulding who changed its name to **Oakdale**. This was a shrewd move, as very soon he was able to buy the old Cadbury depot from which he ran his haulage business, transporting milk, livestock and farm produce.

In 1996 Mr and Mrs Hall bought what then became **Oakdale House**, chosen as a suitable home in a convenient location in which to bring up their children. Robbie is a retired army officer and Helen a retired primary school teacher. Ben Hall was brought up at Oakdale House, and he and his wife Rachel live in **Oakdale Cottage** which adjoins the main house.

In the grounds of this large house is a building that housed the bellows for the furnace during the time of the iron industry. Planning permission has been granted and soon this interesting old building will be renovated and turned into a house.

Continuing along the lane with the large sandstone barn on the left you approach **Furnace Cottages**. In 1946 Leonard Smith bought the funeral services run by the Little family in Furnace Lane, moving from Ryton with his family in 1947. After completing his apprenticeship at a funeral directors in Hay-on-Wye Leonard had opened his own funeral services in Ryton at the age of 19. His daughter, Joyce, married Ken Tyler in 1963 and they took on the funeral service business. In recent years a new Chapel of Rest has been built, an office has been created and the workshop and garage have been rebuilt.

In order to get to Three Ashes, this tour returns to the main road where it turns left to pass **The Bungalow** built for Roy Heath's parents when they retired from farming at Furnace Farm. Roy and Rae's son Stuart lives here now with his wife Dawn and their three children. Stuart has his own business in agricultural engineering and construction and is also an on-call fireman.

As you climb the hill you pass **Deridene,** home of Steve and Jane Price. Steve has lived in this house all his life. He and Jane have extended the property. Steve is a principal mechanical engineer and Jane is a clinical administrator. Steve's great grand-father was superintendent at Newent Workhouse and his grandfather was registrar of births, marriages and deaths.

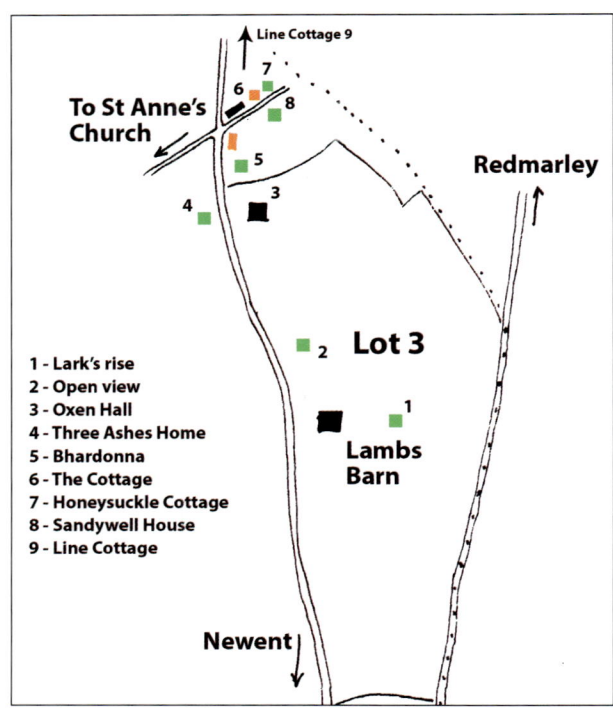

Three Ashes

1 - Lark's rise
2 - Open view
3 - Oxen Hall
4 - Three Ashes Home
5 - Bhardonna
6 - The Cottage
7 - Honeysuckle Cottage
8 - Sandywell House
9 - Line Cottage

The first properties in Three Ashes itself are on the right-hand side of the road. Lamb's Barn bungalow, now called **Lark's Rise**, was originally part of Lamb's Barn farm. It lies beyond the farmhouse and has an entrance from the Redmarley road. In the 1970s it was enlarged when an adjoining barn was renovated to create two-storey accommodation. In the 1980s it was bought by Mrs De'ath, and in 2001 David and Susan Ellis, both retired, chose to move here in order to be near relatives. They have added two extra bedrooms and a conservatory.

In the 1960s Robert W. Onslow built **Open View** on a field between Oxen Hall and Lamb's Barn. Following his death, his widow continued to live here until 2006. This bungalow, recently extended, is now occupied by their grandson Paul Davies and his family.

Oxen Hall

Oxen Hall, formerly the old Rectory, built in 1855 on glebe land, would have looked much the same then as it does in the photograph opposite, apart from the new chimneys. John and Mary Bowers, the present occupiers, bought it in 1974, having previously lived in Newent. They added a single-storey granny flat for Mary's mother at the rear of the property and a magnificent conservatory.

Directly opposite Oxen Hall is **Three Ashes Residential Care Home.** The original house, the only property in this area to be built on Onslow land, was occupied for many years by Mr Turner, then the Hedworth family and subsequently Mrs Nash.

When Richard and Judith Cockcroft bought it in the early 2000s they enlarged it, initially to run a bed and breakfast business, and in 2010 obtained permission for change of use to a respite care home. After further enlargement by owners Cleeve Care, it has become the residential care home seen today.

Further along, on the right-hand side of the road, the beautiful garden of **Bhardonna** is reached. The bungalow was built by Don and Barbara Markey in 1947/8 on land previously owned by the Rectory. The materials used were bricks from a demolished barn on the site and a new army hut bought from the Canadian Army. The bungalow was first extended by Graham and Madge Webb, and has been further extended and modernised since 2003 by Andy and Liz Crispe, who live there with Andy's mother Mildred. Andy is a builder, and he and Liz have two children, who attend Redmarley School.

Signpost – Three Ashes

As you turn into Three Ashes Lane the house on the corner, **The Cottage**, which Stuart and Sylvia Wilson bought in 1987, was 'the right property at the right price'. Outside they have erected fencing and built stables as well as converting half of the garage into an office used by Sylvia for her work as a veterinary surgeon. Stuart is a nuclear engineer with an office in Highnam.

This cottage was owned for many years by Reuben Jones, father of Barbara Markey. Reuben had previously lived in **Honeysuckle Cottage**, a tiny cottage further down the lane, once the home of the Buckland family and their nine children! Following the death of Mrs Anstey in the early 2000s, the new owners demolished the cottage and built a new house in the centre of the plot, since occupied by various tenants.

Sandywell House, on the right, was previously called The White House and when Kenneth and Patricia Brooks bought it in 1974 it was derelict. It was totally rebuilt on its original site. Having been part of the Sandyway Estate and there being a well in the garden, it was renamed Sandywell House. Tricia is an office worker in Newent.

This tour now returns to the main road where you turn left towards Ledbury until you see Three Shires Garden Centre. **Line Cottage** is directly opposite. Angela Humphries and John Addey, a married couple from Neath in south Wales, bought this cottage from the Revd Terry Williams and his wife Laverne in 2003. Terry was rector at St Anne's Church. During the 1980s, a developer rebuilt the small cottage, doubling the footprint by adding a mirror image extension. There are four bedrooms, two bathrooms, sitting room, dining room, kitchen and study. Terry and Laverne added a conservatory in 1999. There is no evidence of the piggery mentioned on the sale details of 1913 and only four plum and two pear trees remain from the orchard that originally surrounded the property.

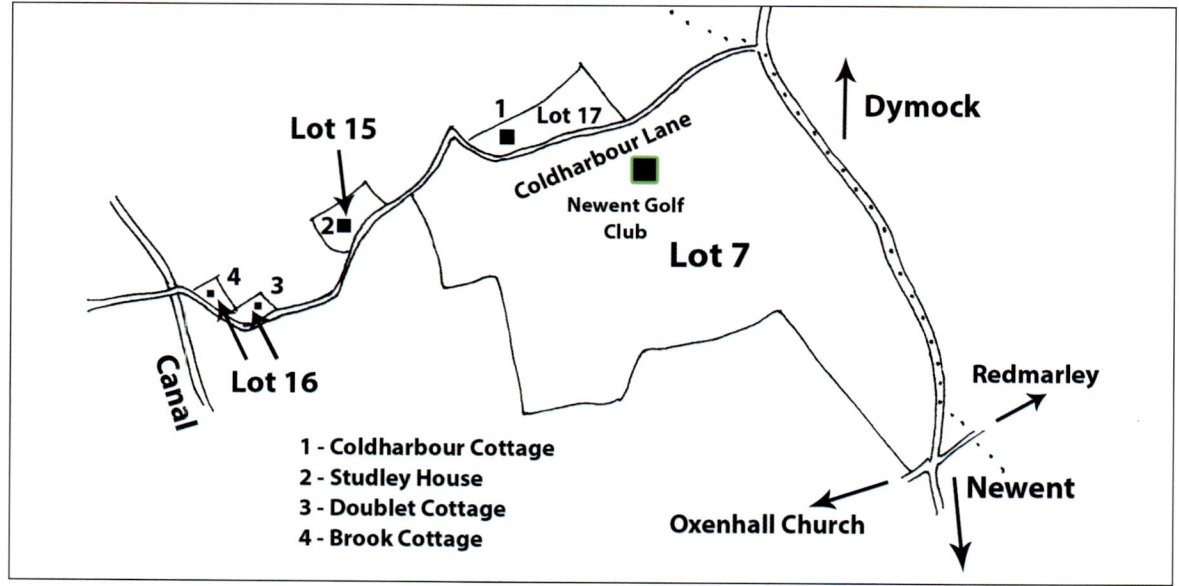

Coldharbour Lane

Coldharbour Lane is reached on the right-hand side of the road as you return towards Newent. The junction of Coldharbour Lane with the Dymock road was formerly sharper and steeper. Until the 1920s, a right-hand turn towards Newent was impossible. The improvement at that time included a little grass triangle at the junction, but it remained a hazardous approach until the main road was widened and the bend eased in the 1970s.

This narrow sunken lane, with just enough room for single vehicles, was tarred in the 1930s but it is often in a poor state, its high banks somewhat overgrown and sliding muddily onto a surface that is also pierced by springs.

Heading up the lane, you pass stone steps at the back of Newent Golf Club. Around the bend, on the right, is **Coldharbour Cottage**. This cottage was substantially modernised and extended firstly by Alison and Brian Smith, the county archivist, in the 1960s and then in the 1990s by Kath and Eifion Rees, who bought half an acre of adjoining farmland. In 2009 Chris and Libby Drew found their dream cottage in an ideal setting and since then, as well as general internal refurbishment and new plantings in the garden, they have added a garden room and rear porch.

The next cottage on Coldharbour Lane is **Studley House**, formerly Sandpit Cottages. In the early 1970s, after Ernie and Gertie Hale moved to Newent, some of the garden to the cottages was incorporated into Holders Farm. In 1973 Celia, daughter of Ken and May Goulding, and her husband David John, moved in and refurbished and extended the building. The sandstone rock used at one end of the original building came from the small quarry across the lane, now owned by Mr and Mrs John. In 2012 a small piece of land in front of the property was joined to the garden. David works from home as a chartered quantity surveyor.

Further down the lane is **Doublet Cottage**, a beautiful black and white cottage facing the old canal. Originally named The Cottage, this building acquired its new name when it was effectively doubled in size by its owners, Mr and Mrs Rose, in the 1970s. Anne Thompson, who has been living here since 2002, has added a small kitchen extension and created a new patio area in the beautiful garden which had been landscaped and redesigned by the previous owner, Rosemary Rimmer.

The Baldwin family occupied **Brook Cottage** for most of the 20th century. In 1941 Arthur Baldwin married Eileen Matthews. They had two sons, Michael and Christopher. Michael, a stonemason, married Cheryl Batchelor of Kempley/Oxenhall. A kitchen and bedroom were added by Alan Latter in 2001.

In 2003 Alan and Tina Hopkins bought Brook Cottage. They have re-roofed the cottage, completely refurbished the interior and built a detached garage, several patios and a pond. Alan works as a heating and plumbing engineer and Tina works in Newent as a medical administrator/receptionist.

Brook Cottage faces the canal, and if you stand on the nearby bridge looking to the left, the canal bed and towpath can be clearly seen, while to the right, rather overgrown, lies the route of the canal leading to the tunnel entrance.

The age of Coldharbour Lane may be judged from the depth to which it has been worn and this is very evident as you climb the steep incline almost totally enclosed by the high sandstone rock.

Coldharbour Lane

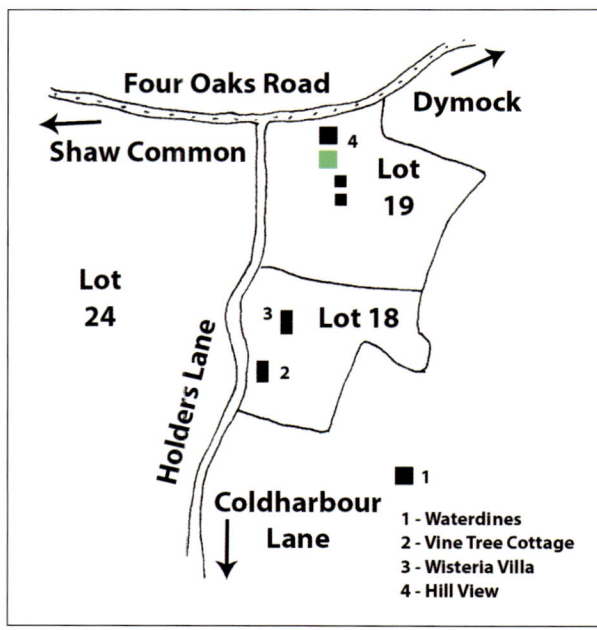

Holders Lane

At the end of the lane, this tour turns to the right along Holders Lane, passing Holders Farm on the right; here you can enjoy wonderful views of Oxenhall and the surrounding area. As the lane levels out, **Waterdines** can be seen in the fields to the right. In 1994 Dave Rogers retired from working at Holders Farm after 48 years of service. In 2004 he and Dot moved from Waterdines, where they had brought up their three daughters, Suzanne, Angela and Lesley, to Newent. Dave died in 2010. Dot is still a regular worshipper at Oxenhall Church and supports the parish by bringing her friends and neighbours to Oxenhall events.

Wilf and Sheila Goulding sold their home at Kews Farm, Kilcot and moved to

Waterdines in 2006 after carrying out renovation and modernisation. Wilf and Sheila are still actively involved in the owning and running of Holders Farm.

Almost at the end of the lane is **Vine Tree Cottage** where Gavin and Karen Refoy live. Karen is the great-granddaughter of Alfred Edward Jones, the local blacksmith who bought both Vine Tree Cottage and Wisteria Villa in 1913. Daniel and Rosa Howley were tenants here until Rosa's death in 1960 whereupon their daughter May Brown moved in. Karen has lived in Vine Tree since 1982 and Gavin moved there in 1999. The property has been extended by adding a side wing and a three-storey extension at the back. Gavin, an entrepreneur, works from home. Karen travels nine miles to her work as a hotel receptionist.

Vine Tree Cottage from Waterdines

Alfred Edward Jones lived at **Wisteria Villa** until his death in 1949. Earlier that year his mother-in-law, Sarah Parsons, who lived with the family, celebrated her 100th birthday. In the 1950s, a second borehole was sunk to reach the canal which runs under the property, a pump being used for water extraction. Alfred's daughter, Nellie, married William Huff in 1937 and they moved into Wisteria Villa in the early 1950s, on their retirement as farmers in Dymock.

A little further along you come to **Hill View**. This was built in 1967 by Colin Jones in an elevated position in front of the old cottage in which Colin's parents, George and Edith, lived following their marriage in 1930. George farmed 67 acres including the area around his house, three fields rented from his father at Pella and 26 acres at Tawneys Farm inherited in 1947 from Edwin J. Hanman – a grandson of John Jones born in 1798 at Shaw Common. George and Edith had two children, Colin and a daughter Mary who died of diphtheria at the age of six. When George died in 1973, the 24 acres, previously rented, reverted back to Pella. Paul and Ioanna Jones were married and moved here in 2008. Paul works with his father Gerald on Pella Farm and Ioanna is a care worker.

At the top of Holders Lane you join **Four Oaks** road, which forms the northern boundary of the parish with Dymock. If you turn left, there are four semi-detached houses on your right. These houses, named Orchard View, lie in Dymock Parish and were prefabricated in wood in the Swedish style in the 1950s. Several owners of the land adjacent to the road have connections with Oxenhall, and because of the distance to Dymock Church many of the residents of that parish in this area attended Oxenhall Church in the days before most people had cars.

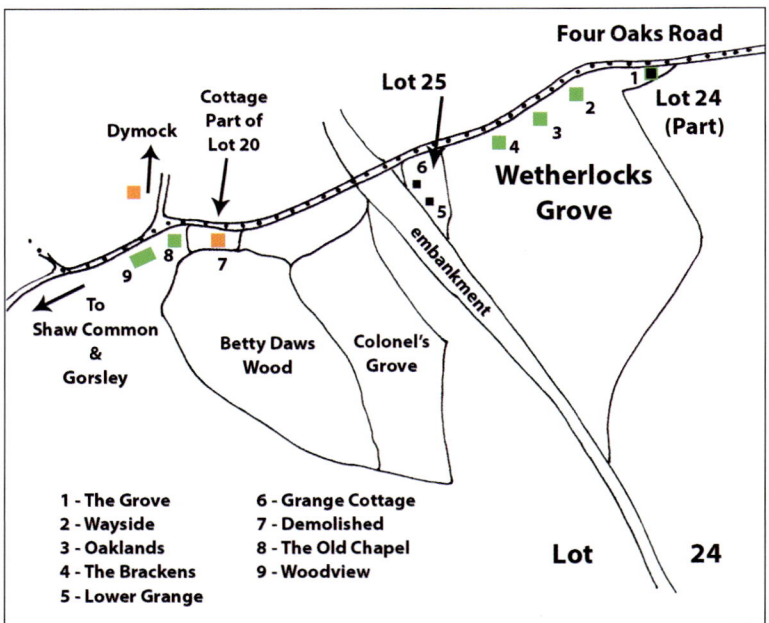

Four Oaks

All the dwellings on the left-hand side of the road are in Oxenhall.

In 2000 **The Grove** was bought by Alasdair Nicol and Patricia Alexander. They demolished the old cottage and completed the building of this large house in 2005. Alasdair is a

The Grove before restoration

The Grove in 2013

cross-country course builder and travels to venues in various parts of the country. In the 1930s, when the Hyett family lived here, cigarettes and sweets were sold through a hatch, and in the 1950s the Mann family used the property to run a small village store.

Near the roadside opposite Tawney's is the site where two bungalows have been built in succession. Reg Eversham and his wife lived here from 1945 until 1958. The owners of the second bungalow purchased additional land, once part of Wetherlock's Grove, and they replaced their bungalow with a house called **Wayside** that is further back from the road.

A large tractor tyre by the roadside, used by Reg Eversham to help customers locate his agricultural engineering business, stands in front of gates behind which can be seen some of the buildings in which Reg ran his business. Initially Reg was a contractor working on local farms. As farmers began buying their own equipment he concentrated on repairs and sales and enlarged his premises. During the 1950s he bought Wetherlock's Grove piece by piece from Pella. The family kept hens, grew Christmas trees and reared turkeys for Christmas, and grew soft fruit which was sent to market in Cardiff, before changing to 'pick your own'.

Reg built **Oaklands** and his family moved in during 1958. Mrs Eversham ran a small shop here for 30 years, selling groceries and sweets. Reg provided an essential service for the local farming community. He never retired but suffered a stroke in December 2009 and died the following October aged 97.

Reg's daughter, Sandra, lives in **The Brackens.** This wooden bungalow was built by Mr Chapel. Following the death of her husband, Mrs Chapel moved away and Reg bought it for Sandra and her husband, Richard Bishop, when they married in 1970. The kitchen and bathroom have been extended, storage heaters installed, the front porch enclosed and a garage built.

At this point traffic on the M50 can be heard. This road dramatically altered the landscape when it opened in the 1960s. However, it offered quicker and easier journeys for those who needed to travel to south Wales or the Midlands as well as faster transport of goods to and from the district.

In 1978 a lorry crashed into the bridge over the motorway linking Oxenhall and Kempley and the road between the two villages was closed for two years, badly affecting the Kempley residents. John Anderson opened an alternative route through the woods using an existing forest road which connected to the road going over Four Oaks bridge. This route was known locally as the '10mph' as motorists were going too fast!

Lower Grange, which can be glimpsed through the trees, was bought in 1967 by Ken and Joan Abbott. They had three children – Michael, Graham and Cathryn – who enjoyed a wonderful childhood playing in the adjoining woods and on the disused railway embankment. In 2007 Ken and Joan moved to Yorkshire and the present owners, Robert and Julie Willis, bought Lower Grange with their three sons Henry, Colin and Peter. Both Robert and Julie work away from Oxenhall and their children attend Newent Community School. Considerable internal refurbishment has been undertaken including the demolition of an old barn and single-storey kitchen, making way for more modern facilities.

Steve and Alison Bassi, eager to live in the countryside, bought **Grange Cottage** in 2010. They have two children – Louis and Rosa. Steve works in IT and Alison is a nurse. Internally they have altered the cottage considerably, have added a conservatory and built a double garage.

These two cottages overlooked the railway and the entrance to Lower Grange used to be alongside the line which ran below the old railway bridge which is crossed further along the road. The only indication that this was a bridge is the parapet on the right-hand side, for the deep cutting has been filled in by the Evershams and the Gouldings. There is no sign of the track but looking towards the motorway it is almost possible to visualise a train travelling through the meadow towards the bridge. Walkers on the Daffodil Way follow a path through this field, under the motorway, on their way to Dymock. Another sign of bygone days is the red telephone kiosk, once an essential means of communication for people living in Four Oaks.

A short stroll along the road takes you to Betty Daw's wood. There is no sign of a cottage, mentioned in the 1913 sale, which stood close to the entrance to the wood. The Howley family lived here for many years but in the 1980s it was demolished by the Forestry Commission. A perry pear tree marks the site of the old orchard.

Leaving the wood entrance, where there is space for parking, you pass a Victorian postbox and come to **The Old Chapel.** Four Oaks Baptist Chapel, built of Gorsley stone in 1924, was an integral part of the community until it was closed as a place of worship in 1990.

The site of the old railway bridge and telephone kiosk

In the 1960s, 60 children regularly attended Sunday School and 209 scholars received prizes for attendance between 1941 and 1973. Sunday School outings and parties were memorable occasions. JSU (Junior Scripture Union), held on Fridays, was popular from 1956. By the time the chapel closed most families had their own cars and chose to attend the parent church at Gorsley. The monthly Four Oaks Ladies meeting continues in Newent.

In 1995 **The Old Chapel** was converted into a house which was bought in 2006 by Henry and Laura Yates, who moved here with their two young children as they wanted to live close to family in the Newent area. Henry and Laura, who travel ten miles by car to their jobs in marketing and media, have made 'cosmetic' changes to the interior, with new flooring, a new kitchen and redecoration.

In 1953 a group of six council houses named **Woodview** were built next to the chapel on a plot purchased from Pound Farm. The original occupants included Mr and Mrs Tucker and three children, Les and Doreen Selwyn, and the Millards, Taylors and Merricks. The Boyce, Gardiner and Brown families have been amongst the residents. Four of the houses are now in private ownership.

When the motorway was built, the old road to Dymock was closed, leaving three Dymock houses in a cul-de-sac opposite the wood. The bridge to the west of Four Oaks carries traffic to Dymock and is an ideal spot from which to view one of the most beautiful stretches of the M50, especially in spring and autumn.

Continuing along Four Oaks road, **Greenaways** can be seen in the fields linked to this road by a long track. In the 1960s, the cottage was occupied by Fred Ellis, a steam engine enthusiast, together with his relatives Mr and Mrs Hooper. Kim and Sue Benniman bought this old cottage from relatives in 1990, living in a caravan while making it habitable. Kim is an engineer and Sue is an ex-teacher. They have three children, Hannah, Corinne and Robert; Robert attends John Kyrle High School.

Further along the road, the rear of **Woodbine Cottage** is visible. Les and Lily Millard, who lived here from 1948, worked for their landlord A.C. Jones of The Moors, the son of the blacksmith. Lily was a voluntary caretaker of Four Oaks Chapel for many years, following in her mother's footsteps.

Roger and Bronwen Carless bought Woodbine Cottage in 1993. They like the area and particularly this cottage, which they have extended by building a new kitchen, bathroom and bedroom plus altering the entrance. Roger is an engineer and Bronwen a speech and language therapist. They have three children – Edward, a plumber, Penelope, an RAF Medic, and Elizabeth, a nurse.

Shortly after passing Woodbine Cottage you reach the Newent/Kempley road with the old forestry depot on the right.

Turning right you find **Crown Lodge**, built in 1933 by the Forestry Commission for A.E. Walker and his family. Water was obtained from a well, but beneath the house there was also an underground tank into which water from the roof was collected and retrieved from the tank using a rotary pump.

Old Forestry Depot

In 1962 John Anderson, who worked for the Forestry Commission, moved into Crown Lodge with his wife Josie and son Mark. The family grew vegetables in the large garden. By the end of the 1960s John and Josie had three more sons, Simon, James and David. As James suffered from Muscular Dystrophy, the Forestry Commission built a one-room extension. Other alterations to the house have included a new entrance, sun lounge and utility room.

James died in 1980 and in the same year John was posted to the Forest of Dean as Head Forester. Later he had responsibility for the environment of the Forest of Dean district. This included recreation, picnic sites, landscape designs, conservation and information boards covering an area of 30,000 acres!

Road to Hay Wood

From Crown Lodge our journey continues to the nearby junction and takes the left fork signposted Linton/Gorsley. A very pleasant 10-minute walk through Hay Wood and down the steep Hay Wood Pitch will bring you to **Woodside**, on the right-hand side of the road. This house was renovated in 1946. Miss Head, a nurse, lived here in the 1990s and now the occupants are David Wells and Rebecca Collins.

The other properties in Shaw Common are reached by retracing your steps and passing Crown Lodge on the left, with a lovely view of Woodbine Cottage in front of you.

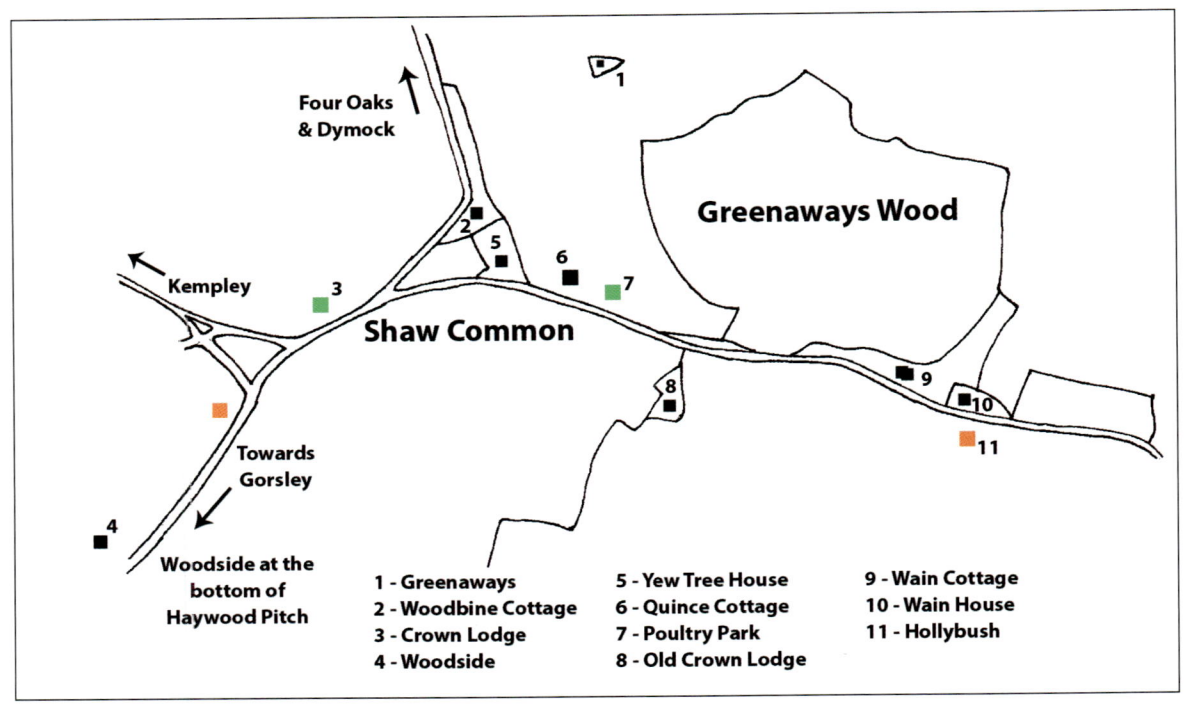

Shaw Common

Poultry Park

Chris Greenwood

In 1991 Chris Greenwood and Domenico Traversari bought both **Yew Tree** and **Quince Cottage.** They lived at Yew Tree during the time they were renovating and extending Quince Cottage. When they moved into Quince Cottage they sold Yew Tree Cottage to Alan and Pam Graham, who lived there with their young family until 2010. Mr and Mrs Peter Lea, the present occupants, enjoy the peace and quiet of Yew Tree House. In his retirement Peter is kept busy in the house and garden. Teresa works in retail, travelling nine miles to work.

In 2012 Anthony Watkins and Lindsay Perkins bought **Quince Cottage** having fallen in love with the cottage and its location. Andrew is a gardener and Lindsay an office worker.

The Poultry Park was opened by Chris Greenwood, who on his retirement seized the opportunity to realise a childhood dream. Chris remembers how at the age of 10 he had the thrill of collecting from the station a box of 12 Rhode Island Red day old chicks, which he reared in a cardboard box with an electric light underneath (for heat) and a mop head hanging in the box for comfort. In 2000 this hobby became a full time occupation when Chris began selling traditional breeds of poultry for farms and gardens.

Chris died in 2013 but Domenico, a rep for a pharmaceutical firm, is determined to carry on this wonderful enterprise and complete the good work Chris started.

Continuing along, **Old Crown Lodge** is reached. This was the Head Forester's cottage until the new Crown Lodge was built. The Webb family moved here in 1933 with their three sons, none of whom ever married. Albert worked in forestry for 40 years, George worked at Peters Farm, and from the war years Horace was employed at Oxenhall Court, working from 7am to 5pm each day. Both Bert and Horace were very enthusiastic gardeners, winning prizes at many flower shows. In the 1980s the brothers bought Old Crown Lodge, which they had rented up till then, and, at Horace's death in 1998, it was inherited by his relatives Fred and Peggy Baldwin. It is now owned by their son James Baldwin and occupied by John Cryer, a university lecturer. The kennels are still in use today.

Carrying on along this road the **Gwen and Vera Fields Nature Reserve** is reached on the left. The shape and size of these fields show they were probably once squatters' holdings, created from roadside common land. Following the demolition of the cottages and no cultivation, daffodils, wood anemones and other woodland flowers gradually encroached from Greenaways wood.

Another cottage that belonged to the Forestry Commission is next on the journey along this road. **Wain Cottage** looks very different from the description in the 1913 sale details, as the thatched roof has been replaced. Amos Griffin and his family lived here in the 1960s. After Amos' death, his daughter Rose was able to buy the cottage from the Forestry Commission in the 1980s.

Alan Smith has been living here since 1994 and, having retired from his job as a local government officer, he helps local people maintain their gardens.

A little further up the slope you arrive at **Wain House.** Brian and Ann Edwards moved here in October 1979, planted a vineyard containing a worldwide selection of vines, and extended the house to the present size. A shop, opened on the premises, sold a variety of locally produced wines. Brian and Ann left in 1994 and David and Paula Jenkins ran the business until 2012. During this period the property was known as St Anne's Vineyard.

In 2012 Oliver and Bethan Hunter bought Wain House, which is no longer a functioning winery. They are gradually renovating the cottage and altering the garden. Oliver travels six miles to his job at Weston's Cider and Bethan, a support worker for the local authority, travels 23 miles.

In 2013 Sally-Anne and Roly Bachelor left **Hollybush,** a wooden bungalow standing directly opposite Wain house, which they bought in 1994. It had been built in 1930 on land belonging to Peters Farm for Jane Niblett who lived at Peters. John Oram, a local postman and beekeeper, married Audrey Jones of Pella and in 1964 moved to Hollybush, where their children, Royston, Christine and Stephen were born. The bungalow has now been demolished and a local builder plans to build a new house on the site which will be called Fox's Hollow.

Continuing along the road towards Newent, another railway bridge is crossed. As you climb the slope beyond, you come to **Ashfield**, a house behind a hedge on the left. Ashfield, together with 13.9 acres of land, was bought in 2006 by Don and Linda Meredith. They are retired farmers from Welsh Newton and have six children between them. Some of the land is rented out and the large barn is used for storage.

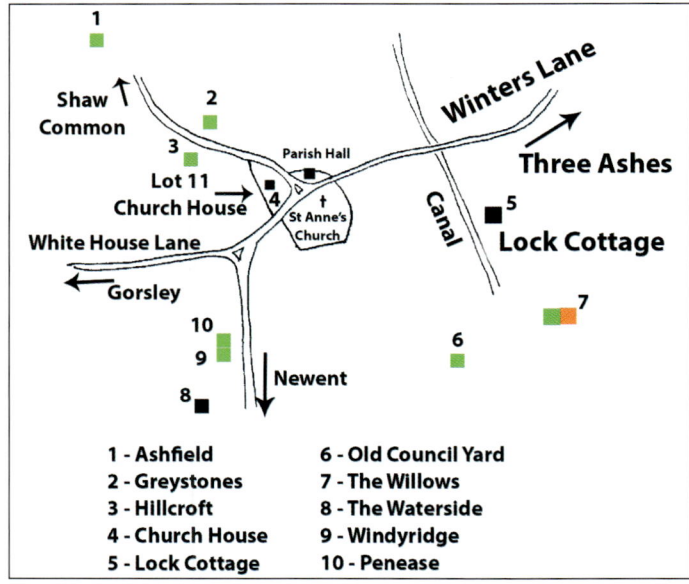

Centre of the parish

Veering to the right you pass Holders Lane, Coldharbour Lane and Hilters Fruit Farm before you see, on the left, a bungalow called **Greystones**. This was bought by Ian and Karen Crispe in 2000. Ian is a builder and the bungalow has been extended and modernised and a garage built. The garden has been cleared, fenced and planted.

In 1982 Lyndon and Barbara Cummins moved into **Hillcroft** further along the road on the right when they retired from farming, but retained one field from the Oxenhall Court Farm land. The bungalow was sold in 2002 when Barbara died and Lyndon went to live with his daughter near London. After refurbishment and extension, in 2008 the property was resold to Richard and Jane Muller, who chose a location that was convenient for work and lifestyle. Richard is managing director of a company based in Gloucester and Jane is a business consultant.

At the junction with Winters Lane and close to the Parish Hall and St Anne's Church is **Church House**. Formerly May Cottage, this was occupied from 1977 until 2006 by David and Nancy Jones, who moved in to care for Nancy's mother, Mrs Adamson. In 2006 Aidan and Sue Dowle bought Church House, moving just up the road from their home at Waterworks House. Aidan is a deputy head teacher and Sue a housewife. They have six children – Chris, a university student; Mike, a retail duty supervisor; Katie, an activities instructor; and Emily, Josh and Amy, who are still at school.

Aidan and Sue are gradually altering and re-decorating the inside of the house which has been insulated and rewired; a new heating system using 'biomasss' wood pellets has been installed. During the alterations they discovered the capped well, together with pump, under the coal bunker. While renovating the kitchen in 2010 they opened up the original bread oven, which is in excellent condition. Newspapers from 1934 were found packed into the chimney. Outside there are new buildings in the garden, and a pond.

From Church House the tour of the centre of the parish begins along the road between the church and the Parish Hall.

Turn right on to the towpath beside the canal. **Lock Cottage** has been occupied by various tenants over the last few years. The towpath leads to Horsefair Lane near the **Old Council Yard** occupied by a group of New Age travellers. The members of this community either work locally or look for seasonal work in other parts of the country.

Lock Cottage

Turning left towards Newent, **The Willows** was completely rebuilt on the site of the old garden nursery by Paul and Clare Gurney in 2004. They chose this site for its location in the countryside yet close enough to walk into Newent. Paul is a butcher and travels seven miles to work. Their two boys attend John Masefield School in Ledbury.

Returning past the Old Council Yard, the road, that runs parallel to the Ellbrook and past the old Council waste tip, is shaded by hazel trees. At the junction with Hydes Lane is a private road leading to Newent Pumping Station and **The Waterside**, formerly home to the superintendent of the pumping station. In 2011 Paul Jotcham and Nicola Roberts found this property while looking for a home in a quiet, peaceful location. Paul is a self-employed developer and Nicola a kitchen interior designer. Paul and the two boys, Arron aged 18 and Kieron aged 16, all work outside Oxenhall. Since living at Waterside the family have built a garage, cleared the garden and woodland area and built a bridge over the brook.

Returning to Horsefair Lane and thence the church, you cross an old railway bridge and pass two semi-detached cottages that were built in 1925 for the headmaster and bursar of Picklenash School in Newent. In 1996 Jan and Lindy Daines fell in love with and bought **Windyridge**, one of the cottages. Jan and Lindy are both teachers. They have extended the living accommodation by converting the attic.

Nigel and Judy Evans live at the adjoining cottage, **Penease**, with their children Thomas, Samuel and Lucy. As well as undertaking agricultural contract work, Nigel helps his mother run Peters Farm following the death of his father in 2013. Judy is a full-time mum helping out at the children's school.

Windyridge and Penease

10   OXENHALL IN 2013

So how has Oxenhall as a community changed in the last hundred years? What has happened to this small, rural place and what are the residents' hopes for the future?

One area of Oxenhall that draws visitors in 2013 is the woodland, especially in spring when the wild daffodils and then the wood anemones carpet the forest floor. In 1913 a fence surrounded the estate woodland and gamekeepers kept the public out. In contrast, nowadays public pressure has seen the 1960 programme of oak felling and conifer planting halted within ten years, trails and sites of Special Scientific Interest created, and attempts to sell off woods in 1994, and the Forest of Dean in 2011, overturned.

Daffodils grow in profusion in the cleared areas of Shaw Common wood

A Wildlife Trust walk in Betty Daw's wood

The Forestry Commission is still in public ownership, although the houses for forestry workers (Crown Lodge, Old Crown Lodge and Wain Cottage) were sold off, as well as the Forestry Office and sheds at Shaw Common. At one time 11 forestry workers reported to this office daily. The depot had its own mechanics' workshop and a road engineer's office. The sheds are now just used for storage. There is no longer a resident forester and the woodlands are managed from the Forest of Dean using contractors.

Since 1980 Betty Daw's Nature Reserve has been a Site of Special Scientific Interest managed jointly by the Forestry Commission and Gloucestershire Wildlife Trust. The nest box scheme was started in 1963 and ensures local volunteers help to protect the diversity and beauty of wildlife in the woods. The first trail through these woods was opened in 1970 and during Oxenhall's Daffodil Weekend, Betty Daw's wood is the venue for Gloucestershire Wildlife Trust Open Day, when members of the Trust lead walks. Shaw Common wood has been an acorn collection area since 1985. The oak trees are Sessile Oak (*Quercus petroa*), native to the English/Welsh border. Good crops of acorns occur every three to four years, called 'mast years'. To make it easier to collect the seeds the whole area is mown every autumn before the seeds drop, which also encourages the growth of the wild daffodils. Up until 1964/5 the Forestry Commission sold permits to the public allowing them to pick daffodils, and 'Daffodil patrols' checked whether those picking had a legitimate permit. Now visitors are encouraged to walk in the woods along the circular path, but picking flowers is forbidden.

The Forest Design Plan of 2000 envisaged a multi-purpose forest which will take decades to achieve. The aim is for timber production, landscape conservation and recreation to have equal importance. The forest will be oak dominated, with some mixed beech and other broadleaves, and a much diminished conifer area. The public, Oxenhall residents in particular, have strong feelings about public access and enjoyment of the woods, and forest management has had to take account of their views.

Oxenhall's water continues to be important in 2013. The Ell Brook, fed by many tributaries, runs through Oxenhall, Newent and Upleadon before joining the river Leadon near Highleadon. The brook provides a corridor and habitat for wildlife – kingfishers, wagtails, buzzards, otters, badgers and muntjac deer. Wild garlic, daffodils, snowdrops and lady's smock grow along the banks. Alder, formerly coppiced for furniture, floorboards and fuel, is the predominant tree. A sawmill at Kews Farm, Kilcot used the alder to make broom heads from the 1920s to the 1940s, but alder has not been coppiced for many years. An Environmental Agency survey in 1996 recorded good populations of wild brown trout, eel and a variety of other coarse fish on the upper Ell Brook. There is no comparable data for 2013, but there appears to have been a significant reduction in all populations. This may be because fallen trees have caused over-shading and barriers to upstream migration for spawning fish, and the silting up of gravels needed for successful spawning.

In 1992 the Herefordshire and Gloucestershire Canal Trust decided to aim for the full restoration of the 34 miles of canal and locks so that Hereford would once again be linked with Ledbury, Dymock, Newent and the rest of the inland waterway system at Gloucester. Work started at the south portal of the Oxenhall tunnel and then the Trust dredged the channel between Coldharbour Lane and Top Lock, close to Winter's Lane Bridge. Now there is a length of canal fully in water, providing an attractive walk along the canal and the adjacent lake. The next phase of the work was to excavate and repair the lock, to sell the grade two listed Lock Cottage to enable restoration by the owner, and restore the bridge, walls and Ell Brook aqueduct below the lock, with help from the Waterways Recovery Group. A bailey bridge with components donated by the army was erected across the top of the aqueduct to enable vehicles to cross the stream without overloading the weakened structure. Having created a wonderful asset for the Oxenhall community, the Trust is continuing to excavate the route of the old canal between Newent and Gloucester.

In 2013, Severn Trent PLC continues to use Oxenhall Pumping Station to pump water from the aquifers within the red sandstone underneath Oxenhall. Increasing demands from local housing, agriculture and horticulture mean they are close to the abstraction limits. The Environmental Agency's expectation is that no new abstraction will be available after 2019.

Oxenhall's lake, canal, brook and below ground aquifers have always been important features of our landscape and a resource for farmers. Periods of drought or heavy rainfall have become more common in recent years so methods of coping with too little or too much water will be vital in the future for our farmers, residents, visitors and wildlife.

The Gloucester/Ledbury railway, so important to residents and farmers in Oxenhall in 1913 with the station at Newent and a halt at Four Oaks, was in decline by the 1950s as the bus, lorry and car took over and electricity superseded coal. The last passenger trains ran on 11 July

1959, with freight trains continuing until May 1964. In 2013 the old railway bridges remain, narrowing the roads for motor traffic, and there are traces of the lines and embankments in the fields. The buildings at Newent station have been demolished and the platforms are overgrown. The Herefordshire and Gloucestershire Canal Trust has drawn up ambitious plans to restore the canal between the two platforms to create a unique site for tourists.

At the centre of the Oxenhall community are the church and Parish Hall. The non-conformist tenants who became owners in 1913 had active roles in churches outside of the parish. Today their descendants and some new residents attend the Baptist Chapel in Gorsley and Glebe Chapel in Newent, and they also support activities at St Anne's. St Anne's, now part of a group of nine local churches in the care of Revd Anthony Lomas, serves households in the scattered parish. It is the duty of the rector and the Parochial Church Council (PCC) to promote the whole mission of the Church – pastoral, evangelistic, social and ecumenical – and to maintain the building. However, this could not be achieved without the help of the many volunteers who care for the building and grounds and help with services and general church organisation, as well as visiting parishioners when they need support.

As an example of this care for St Anne's, dedicated local support raised funds in the 1980s to make the church spire safe. More recently, following two reports highlighting that urgent work was needed to the church roof, a parish meeting was held in October 2008 which harnessed

Daffodil Teas at the Parish Hall attract many visitors

support for the church from all the community, not just churchgoers. OCRA (the Oxenhall Church Roof Appeal) was formed. Grants were applied for and the community began vigorous and imaginative fundraising over several years. Grants were received from English Heritage, All Churches Trust, Langtree Trust, Gloucestershire Historic Trust and Gloucestershire Environmental Trust. In February 2012, at the final meeting of OCRA, the chairman John Bowers pointed out that in three years the church of St Anne's had been saved from possible closure and carefully made sound for the next 150 years. John emphasised what a wonderful community Oxenhall is and what the power of teamwork can achieve. Furthermore, the new roof had been completed without leaving any debt.

The annual Daffodil Teas, organised over a weekend by the PCC of St Anne's, have for many years attracted hundreds of visitors, some friends and families from outside the parish travelling long distances to meet up at Oxenhall for lunch or tea and to enjoy the beauty of walks in the local woods. There is a service at the church every Sunday with a small but dedicated congregation who enjoy chatting and refreshments either before or after the service. Realising the importance of children as the future of the church, family services are held every other month and the children are encouraged to take part. The same children meet regularly in the Parish Hall for activities related to church festivals throughout the year, again run by volunteers. The church is valued by many outside the regular congregation for its history and genealogy as well as for the christenings, weddings and funerals it is able to provide. St Anne's is a beautiful building, a landmark, a place of peace and contemplation and has been the spiritual heart of Oxenhall for centuries.

Gavin and Karen Refoy's wedding in July 2007. Gavin is a churchwarden. He married Karen, the great-great-granddaughter of Charles Jones, the blacksmith in Holders Lane

In 1997 the Parish Hall Trust was set up as a charity with local people as trustees and a committee of volunteers. The hall is the only public meeting place in the parish. In 1999 grants from several organisations were obtained to refurbish it and Nigel Freeman gave land to make a car park. In 2000, to commemorate the Millennium, the History Group organised the making of three fabric hangings by residents, depicting most of the properties in Oxenhall; these now hang in the hall. Two albums with photographs of each Oxenhall household and their property and an anthology of writing by Oxenhall people were also created.

Anne Thompson's birthday party in the Parish Hall where the Millennium banners hang

Strawberries grown at Hilter Fruit Farm are enjoyed by visitors

On Apple Day people are encouraged to buy fruit and to plant fruit trees

A display of apple varieties

Thanks to the Trust, the hall now has an extended kitchen with new equipment (which meets the standards required in the new regulations for hygiene in village halls), improved loft space and a capacious outside storage shed. These improved facilities were made possible by community fundraising and grants from Barnwood House, the Forest of Dean District council, Gloucestershire Environmental Trust, Grass Roots, Biffaward and Awards for All – Big Lottery. The improved facilities have contributed to popular community events like Strawberry Teas and Apple Day celebrating local produce, and enhanced the reputation of Oxenhall's ladies as master bakers and fine cooks! Before Christmas there is a parish get-together and meal in the hall, and a parish walk after Christmas.

A more recent innovation has been the music and theatre events organised by the committee in the hall, three or four times a year, made possible by the funding from the 'Air in G' Arts initiative, and attracting an audience which is sometimes mostly from outside Oxenhall and a more mixed age crowd. The revenue from these evenings has been a great help with the cost of maintaining the Victorian building, but is of course dependent on the Rural Arts Council subsidy continuing in the future. The hall is also hired out for private functions and local groups. Once a year it is the venue for the parish meeting because Oxenhall is one of the few parishes in Gloucestershire to opt for this simple and inexpensive alternative to a Parish Council. It means it is not charged a parish precept as part of the council tax! It is dependent on two volunteers prepared to run it and e-mail out to the parish all the information that flows in.

All these things are run by volunteers who are from Oxenhall or have been connected to it in the past, plus friends and family from further afield roped in to help! The hope is that the sense of community which exists, reflected in the Parish Plan of 2007 when 70% of residents said they felt community events and activities were very important, will help to keep Oxenhall's separate identity, while attracting more young families and drawing in younger residents to help.

One organisation in Oxenhall which is attracting youngsters is Newent Cricket Club, which plays on land at Three Ashes bought by the council in 1930 for the Grammar School playing fields. In 1935, 100 lime trees were planted to commemorate the Silver Jubilee of George V and these still surround the field today. Previously the club played on fields in Watery Lane in Newent, sharing a wooden pavilion with the Tennis Club, but had to move when Newent Community School was built on the fields. The club has also benefited from Lottery grants. In 1997, under Oxenhall resident Eifion Rees' chairmanship, they were awarded a grant to build a

Three Ashes cricket ground home of Newent Cricket Club

Celebrating the Queen's Diamond Jubilee
Middle left and right: A competition for best hats;
Bottom left: A marquee provided shelter from the rain; Bottom right: In February 2012
106 saplings were planted between the lake and the canal to commemorate the Diamond Jubilee

new clubhouse. Improvements have continued to be made thanks to local support and fundraising. In 2013 the club has two pitches and puts out five adult teams and six junior teams, including a girls team. The facilities are of a standard to host Gloucestershire County U17 matches. The Oxenhall community used the ground for its celebration of the Queen's Diamond Jubilee in 2012.

So in 2013 Oxenhall plays host to a variety of leisure activities sited along the Newent/Dymock main road – an equestrian business, a cricket club and a golf club. Along the lanes, horse riders, cyclists and walkers enjoy the countryside and woods at their own pace.

Left: The golf course's quick-draining, sandy soil allows golf to be played all year round
Right: A local horserider

The roads are busier than ever and while considerably improved, the Parish Plan showed that the state of the roads was still a priority for residents. Heavy machinery, large lorries and white delivery vans (the result of increasing internet shopping?) take their toll on road surfaces, sometimes damage the old railway bridges, and are a hazard for unwary pedestrians, particularly those with dogs or pushchairs. The proximity of the M50 with arguably the worst slip road off a motorway, onto the B4215 to Newent on the boundary of the parish, brings quicker journey times but also more traffic. A car is now essential to life in the country, as is delivery by road, but there is a downside.

Other concerns highlighted in the Parish Plan were the linked problems of Oxenhall's expensive houses with no plans to build affordable houses for younger people, and the ageing profile of the residents which sometimes causes concern about the future of the community. People living in Oxenhall don't want to become a suburb of Newent, or the fine views to become a sea of polythene tunnels and glasshouses. The community has shown that it cares immensely about its separate identity and values its heritage. Residents do want to support local farmers, protect wildlife and plan for climate change. Oxenhall's agricultural history and beautiful surroundings are what makes it special to residents and brings newcomers to live here – the oak woods, wild daffodils and wood anemones, the canal, lake, Ell Brook, rolling fields and orchards full of blossom. Residents in 2013 want to both share it and preserve it. The hope is that this book will help do that, both now and in the future.

Ewes on summer grazing at Oxenhall Court farm

The OPHG hope that this project has helped the understanding of Oxenhall's history and how the lives of its residents have changed in the last 100 years. We have tried our best to check our information and obtain permission to use it but inevitably we may have misunderstood or missed out something. Our archives, held at Oxenhall Parish Hall, contain more detailed information and anyone who has a particular area of interest can request our help to access them.

Bibliography

Printed sources
Beale, Catherine, *Champagne and Shambles – The Arkwrights & the Country House in Crisis*, 2006
Bick, David E., *The Hereford and Gloucester Canal and Gloucester-Ledbury Railway*, 1979
    The Mines of Newent and Ross, 1987
British Record Society, *Abstracts of Inquisitions Post Mortem for Gloucestershire 1236-1413*
Bruton, Knowles & Co., Particulars, Plan and Conditions of Sale of the Onslow Estate, 1913
Eldridge, Christopher, *Celebrating 150 years of Bruton Knowles Heritage*, 2012
Gethyn-Jones, The Revd J.E., *Dymock Down the Ages*, 1951
Goodland, Patrick, *The Greening of Wild Places – Story of Gorsley Baptist Church 1800-2002*, 2002
    The founding of Gorsley Goff's School, (a school leaflet), 2011
Goulding F.E. and R.A., *Four Oaks Chapel 1924-1974*, 1974
Hines, Lee (ed), *Millennium Memories – The History of Gorsley and Kilcot*, 2001
Juřica A.J.R. & N.M. Herbert, *Victoria Count History, Volume XII – Newent and May Hill*, 2010
Johnstone, B.L.C., *Foley Partnership – The iron industry at the end of the charcoal era*, 1951
Kirby, Darrel, *The Story of Gloucester*, 2007
Newent Local History Group, *Chapters in Newent's History Vol. 2*
Newent Grammar School, *Silver Jubilee School Magazine*, 1954
Newent Local History Society, *Chapters in Newent's History*, 2003
Pates, Stella, *The Rock and the Plough – John Grandisson, William Langland and Piers Plowman: A theory of Authorship*, 2000
Postle, David, *From Ledbury to Gloucester by Rail*, 1985
Pearce D. and Penney F., *Oxenhall Church Burial records*, 1998
Rudder, Samuel, *A New History of Gloucestershire*, 1779
Shambrook, John C., *Life of John Hall*, 1876
Skeet, Richard, *Rescued from Obscurity – Hereford and Gloucester Canal*, 2014
Torode Brian E., *John Middleton, Victorian Provincial Architect*, 2008

Private Publications
Bowers, John, *World War I 1914-1918 – Remembering those on Oxenhall's War Memorial*, 2013-14
Farnham, Cyril, *Life and Times of White House Farm 1800-1976*, 1976
Goulding, E.M., 'The Effect of the Iron Industry on Oxenhall (1639-1775)', M.A. Dissertation, 1999
Hinds, David, *A Farmer's Tale*, (private publication), 1992
Smith, Brian, *The History of Cold Harbour*

Archive material
Gloucestershire Archives
Bruton Knowles Collection, G.A. D2299
Gloucester Journal
Kelly's Directories
Land Belonging to Henry Finch, 1615, G.A. PC1194
Onslow records, G.A. D1882
Oxenhall School records, 1842-1935, G.A. S241
Stardens Estate Sale Book, 1910, G.A. SL80
Tithe Map and apportionment, 1841, G.A. D603
Who was Betty Daw? Research by Belinda Legge, G.A. D1/47/2

Hereford Record Office
Hereford Times

National Archives
Calendar of Close Rolls
Census returns for Oxenhall 1841-1911
Survey of Farms by Ministry of Agriculture and Fisheries 1941

Oxenhall Parish History Group
Oral research - War Memories, 1995
School Memories Project, 1997
The Oxenhall Anthology (ed Gwen Tutt), 1999
'Arts for All' Millennium Album, 2000
Exhibition – Oxenhall Then and Now, 2013

Oxenhall Parish Meeting
Oxenhall Parish Plan, 2007

Newent Community School Archives
Miss Morris and pupils, *Newent Grammar School's History*, 1946

Private
Onslow Estate Trustees, Abstract of Deeds of the Onslow Estate, 1910

Websites
www.ancestry.co.uk, Databases for baptisms, marriages and burials
www.ewyaslacy.org.uk, Ewyas Study Group, The History of Ewyas Lacy
www.forest-of-dean.net, Forest of Dean Family History
www.gloucestershirewildlifetrust.co.uk, Gloucestershire Wild Life Trust
https://en.wikipedia.org, for information of national and international events in Chapter 7

Index of Places

Apple Mill, Oxenhall Court farm 141, 164
Ashfield 134, 144, 192

Baldwin's Oak / Baldwyn's Farm, Newent 34, 70
Betty Daw's wood (see under woodland)
Bhardonna 179
Black House 31
Botloe Green 108
Brassfield's / Brassfields Farm 31, 36, 83-6, 125, 131, 132, 142, 144, 170
Bridge Cottage 118
Bridges Farm, Kempley 83
Brockmore Head 31, 36, 144
Brook Cottage 95, 118, 125, 134, 144, 181
Bull Hill Farm, Gorsley 31, 74
Bungalow, The 177

Castle (Fruit) Farm 148, 151
Church House 126, 128, 129, 134, 144, 193
Cleeve Mill 39, 30, 33, 42
Coldharbour 108
    Cottage 94, 128, 131, 137, 138, 141, 143, 144, 181
    Lane 94, 181-2
Conigree 108
Cottage, The (see also Doublet Cottage) 95, 118, 125, 134
Cottage by Betty Daw's wood 98-9, 132, 186
Crookes farm 33, 170, 172-3
Crown Lodge 115, 121, 131, 188-9

Dales 31
Deridene 118, 121, 177
Doublet Cottage (see also Cottage, The) 134, 137, 144, 181

Elim Bungalow 177
Ellbridge 90-92, 176
Elmbridge 31
    ironworks 15-17, 90

Four Oaks 97, 108, 109, 184
    Chapel 109, 116, 118, 128, 131, 134, 142, 186-7
    Halt 111, 122
Fox's Hollow 192

Furnace Cottages 126, 177
Furnace Farm 30, 34, 36, 64-6, 122, 125, 131, 132, 134, 141, 143, 145, 146, 159-60
Furnace House 18, 22, 30, 32, 91, 125, 177

Gamages, Much Marcle 43
Gorsley Court Farm, Gorsley 31, 34, 36, 81
Gorsley Goff's School 22
Grange Cottage 118, 186
Great Pound 36
Greenaways 165
Greenaways cottage 101, 122, 132, 141, 187-8
Greystones 118, 144, 192
Grove, The 97, 121, 129, 184-5
Gwen & Vera Fields Nature Reserve 191

Haines Oak 108
Halls Barn Farm 74
Hawthorne Hill Farm 144, 146, 168-9
Herb House 167
Herefordshire and Gloucestershire Canal 19-20, 110, 141, 142, 145, 197
    Oxenhall Tunnel 19, 20
Hill Brook farm, Kempley 165
Hill House Colliery 19
Hill House Farm 31, 36, 86-8, 125, 126, 131, 137, 144, 145, 171
Hill View 97, 121, 132, 183
Hillcrest 129
Hillcroft 137, 144, 164, 192-3
Hillend Green 108
Hillfields 177
Hillyfields 177
Hillyland 91
Hilter Fruit Farm 137, 140, 141, 146, 157-8, 159
Hilter's / Hilters 30, 34, 36, 67-70, 121, 123, 125, 126, 131, 134, 135, 138, 156, 159, 161
Hilters Farmhouse 137, 140, 156
Holder's / Holders Farm 23, 24, 30, 36, 72-5, 108, 118, 121, 125, 131, 132, 133, 144, 160-1, 182, 183
Holders Lane 96, 182
Holly Bush Cottage 121, 192
Hydes 31

Keeper's Cottage 51, 101, 115
Kews (Farm) 33, 73, 116, 121, 144, 160, 161, 164, 170, 173-4, 197
Knapp Farm, Aston Ingham 70
Knapp farm, Kempley 125
Knappers Farm 83

Lamb's Barn 29, 30, 36, 53-5, 108, 126, 134, 152, 178
Lamb's Bungalow / Lark's Rise 134, 137, 144, 178
Lancaster Saw Mills 32
Lands End Farm 141, 146, 169
Lea
    Crown Inn 65
    Rock, The 70
Lime House 108
Lime Tree 108
Little Furnace 23
Little Pound 30, 34, 36, 43, 44-5, 48, 49-50, 161-2
Lock Cottage 128, 138, 144, 193
Lock House 66
Lower Cottage, The 91
Lower Grange 98, 131, 132, 186
Lower House 31, 34, 36, 70, 86-88, 131, 134, 144, 164, 170-1
Lower House Cottage 108
Lyne House / Line House 30, 34, 36, 52, 55-8, 108, 125, 126, 144, 151
Lyne Cottage 128, 138, 144

Malswick 41, 64
Marshall's / Marshalls 30, 32, 34, 36, 59-60, 70, 118, 125, 141, 152-3
May Cottage 69, 103-4, 121, 125, 128
Moors The, Dymock 118, 188
Murrell's 30, 43, 44-5, 50-51

Nelfields 31, 42
New Barn 108
Newent 2, 27, 28, 65, 112
    Baldwins 108
    Bury Bar 64
    Colliery 19, 23, 27, 80, 168
    Court 23
    Cricket Club 142, 201-2
    George Hotel 1, 33, 64
    Golf Club 141, 152-3, 203
    Manor 16

    Market 24, 119
    Market House 24
    pumping station 112
    schools 25, 119, 128, 131
        Picklenash School 107, 128
    Station 21

Nest, The 172
Newport House, Almeley 17-8
Newtown 31

Oak Cottage 177
Oakdale 125, 177
Oaklands 185
Old Chapel, The 186-7
Old Council Yard 193
Old Crown lodge 121, 137, 142, 164, 191
Onslow Estate 29-36
Open View 132, 178
Orchard House 145
Orchard View, Dymock 184
Overton Farm 141, 158
Oxen Hall 26
Oxenhall Court Farm 12, 30, 36, 69, 70-1, 80, 121, 137, 161, 164, 170, 193
    Apple Mill 141, 164
Oxenhall Parish
    blacksmiths 92, 96
    brickmaking 17
    cider & perry 17, 52, 148
    coalmining 19-20, 29
    foot & mouth 1967 132, 133, 134, 161
    ironworks 15-17, 19, 29, 90
    isolation hospital 26
    mills 27, 42
    Parish Hall 3-6, 142, 198-201
    railway 20-22, 110-2, 122, 130, 131, 197-8
        Daffodil line 110-2, 130, 131
    school 24-25, 107-9, 122
    tenancy terms 17
    tithes 18
    turnpike roads 28, 92
    water supply/waterworks 27, 64, 65, 68, 69, 75, 104, 113, 128, 129, 142, 197
    wheelwrights 92

Parks, The 24, 30, 34, 38-41, 121, 125, 130, 142, 144, 149-50

Parks Farm 30, 34, 36, 41, 65, 117, 121, 134, 150-1
Parks Farm Nurseries 134, 150-1
Pella Farm 30, 36, 76-78, 108, 121, 127, 129, 141, 144, 145, 165, 183, 185
Penease 118, 194
Peters Farm 19, 30, 34, 36, 79-81, 121, 136, 145, 166, 192
Picklenash School 25
Poplars 31
Poultry Park, the 141, 190, 191
Pound Farm 29, 30, 34, 43-49, 118, 123, 125, 128, 134, 141, 162
Poyke's Farm, Newent 64

Quince Cottage 191

Rectory (see also Oxen Hall) 93
Rose Cottage, Hillend Green 108

St Anne's Church 8, 12, 24, 25-26, 69, 105-6, 135, 145, 198-9
    lead font 11, 12
St Anne's Vineyard 15, 138, 142, 145, 157, 192
Sandpit Cottages 94, 121, 161, 181
Shaw Common 45, 99, 108, 131, 189, 190
Stardens 24, 29, 31, 32, 33
Stoke Edith 16
Studley House 121, 134, 181
Sunnydale (see also, Villa, The) 145
Sysum's Pitch 108

Tawneys Farm 183
Three Ashes 92-93, 108, 178-9
Three Ashes Care Home 144, 179

Villa, The (now Sunnydale) 88, 131
Vine Tree Cottage 183

Wain Cottage 99-100, 132, 137, 142, 191-2
Wain House 100, 135, 142, 145, 192
Waterlocks / Waterdi(y)nes 23, 73, 99, 121, 123, 128, 135, 144, 161, 182

Waterside, The (see also Waterworks Cottage) 194
Waterworks Cottage / House (see also Waterside, The) 104, 193
Way House 15, 23
Wayside 185
Wenryl 131
Whitehall Cottage 48, 129
Whitehouse / White House 30, 34, 36, 80, 81-5, 118, 120, 121, 123, 125, 128, 129, 130, 134, 136, 137, 141, 142, 166-8
    Colliery 23
Willows, The 104, 194
Windyridge 118, 194
Winter's / Winters 30, 34, 36, 52, 61-4, 66, 68, 108, 121, 132, 134, 137, 138-9, 142, 154-5, 157, 161
Winters Farm Lodge 142, 155-6
Wisteria Cottage / Villa 126, 128, 137, 183
Woodbine Cottage 48, 103, 126, 141
Woodside 100, 141, 189
woodlands 36, 43, 101, 113-4, 117, 131, 195-7
    Betty Daw's wood 133, 196
    Dymock Wood 51
    Ellis' Cross 51
    Forestry Commission 101, 188, 191-2, 196
    Great Haywood 114
    Greenaways wood 15, 48, 51
    Haines Oak Coppice 114
    Hill House Grove 51, 85, 86
    Mount Pleasant Plantation 51
    Park Wood 48
    Shaw Common wood 195, 196
    Upper Wayhouse Wood 15
    Wetherlocks Grove 51, 78, 99, 128, 165, 185
    Woodground 51
Woodview 128, 187
Wyatts, Gorsley 108

Yew Tree Cottage 126, 131, 141, 144, 191
Yew Tree Farm, Huntley 71
Yewtree House 48

Index of Names

Abbott, Cathryn 98, 133, 186
    Graham 186
    Ken & Joan & family 132, 133, 186
    Michael 186
Adamson, Thomas & Catherine 129
    Marjorie 129
    Mrs 193
Addey, John 144
Addis, Alice 82
Alexander, Patricia 184-5
Allen, C.E. 128
    E.I. 128
    M. & C. 128
    Mr 30
Anderson, David 140
    John & Josie 8, 10, 117, 131, 133, 137, 140, 186, 189
Arthur, Bert 126
Aston, Mr 29

Bachelor, Sally-Anne & Roly 192
Baldwin family 181
    Arthur & Eileen 94, 125, 126, 134, 181
    Christopher 181
    Edith 94, 108
    Fred & Peggy 105, 125, 126, 142, 191
    Gertrude 94
    James 191
    Margaret 94, 108
    Michael & Cheryl 134, 181
    Richard (woodward d.1866) 22
    Richard (woodward) 33, 36, 114
    Richard Snr & Louisa 94
    Richard Jnr & Martha 94, 108, 118, 125
    William (Bill) 94, 161
Barter, Mr 167, 169
Barton, Revd J. 131
Bassi, Louis 186
    Rosa 186
    Steve & Alison 186
Bates, Lt Commander James 125, 126, 129
Barnwood, Josias 26
Batchelor, Cheryl 131
    Roy & Margaret 131
    Wendy 131

Bayliss, Frederick H. 116
Beale family 18
    Ernest 108
    Florence 108
    Henry 108
    William Henry 108
Beaman, Michael & Geraldine 126, 151
    Rowley 130
Beard, Charles 108
    Ernest 108
    Florence 108
    Gladys 108
    Herbert 108
    W. 31, 34
    William Henry 108
Beckett, W. Fowler 30, 55
Bendle, Caroline 126
    Celia 126
    Francis 126
Bennett, Andrew 134, 138, 141, 157
Benniman, Corinne 188
    Hannah 188
    Kim & Susan 141, 188
    Robert 188
Benson-Bunch, Rick & Rosie 144, 149
Bentley, Michael & Christiana 148
Berkley, Mrs 107, 117
Bigland, Maud 104
Bird, Reginald 70
Birks, Doug & Diana 135, 157
Bisco, Mary Ann 111
    Robert 111
Bishop, Richard & Sandra 186
Blewitt, Alice 64
    Florence 64, 65
    Frank 64
    Hubert 64
    Walter & Sarah 64-5
    William Snr 64
    William Jnr 65
Boswell, Robin 167
Boto, Mrs 95
Boulter, Thomas 30
    William 77, 97
Bowers, John & Mary 2, 179, 199
Bowkitt, Joseph 82
Boyce family 128
Bridgetts, Ralph 93
    Rose 93

Brook, George 30
Brooks, William & Hannah 99
Brown family 128
    Ian 153
    Margaret 153
    May 183
    Tom & Susan 141, 153
Bruton, Henry W. 33, 34, 35
    William 33
Buckland, Lionel & Joan 172-3
Burford, Jo 14
Burroughes, Charles 32-3
    Revd Robert 29
Byron, Capt. 30, 91

Cadle, S.A. 30
Calvert, Herbert & Jessie 121, 126
Cam, Isabelle 173
    Laurie 173
    John & Jean 174
    Peter 174
    Rob & Chris 173
Campbell, A.W. Montgomery 30, 38, 39, 41, 98
Carless, Edward 188
    Elizabeth 188
    Penelope 188
    Roger & Bronwen 141, 188
Chamberlain, Lillian 110
Chapel, Mr & Mrs 186
Chapman family 45
    Frederick 43
    George & Alice 30, 34, 43, 44, 47, 49, 109, 116
    George Jnr 128
    Howard 43, 47, 109, 115, 116, 123, 125, 128
    John 128
    May 43
    Ron 122, 127, 128, 134, 162, 174
Cockcroft, Richard & Judith 144, 179
Collins, Rebecca 189
Cornall, Henry & Mildred 121
Cother family 23
Cracknell family 144
    Alfred 75
    Ian & Julia 168, 169, 174
    Josh 169
    Naomi 169
    Ruth 169

Theo 169
Crook, Roger 134
    William 31
Cummins, J. 30
    John 31
    Joseph 31
    Lyndon & Barbara 121, 129, 137, 144, 164, 192-3
    William & Beatrice 121, 129, 164
Cox, Ethel 108
    Revd Stanley 115, 118
    William 108
    William Henry 116
Crisp, John & Margaret 177
Crispe, Andy & Liz 179
    Ian & Karen 144, 192
Cryer, John 191

Daines, Jan & Lindy 194
Davies family 144
    Craig 155, 156
    Gwyn & Doreen 137, 155-6, 174
    James 30
    Laura 142, 155, 156
    Paul & family 178
Davis, Albert 108
    Byron 108
    Caroline 108
    Charles 67
    Ernest 108
    Eva 108
    John 108
    William 108
Daw, Betty & Edward 99
    Robert & Mary 99
Dawkins, Anne 149
    Edwin & Elsa 125, 149
    Peter 149
Day, Dorothy 108
    Gladys 108
    Thomas 108
    William 86, 108
De'Ath, Mrs 127, 178
De Grandisson family 12-13
De Lacy family 11
Deykes, William 18, 22
Dobbins, R. 31
Dowdeswell, Daniel & Emma 31, 34, 83, 84, 86, 88
    Daniel Jnr 86
    Joseph 86
    Samuel 86
    Thomas Snr & Emma 30, 31, 86
    Thomas Jnr 86

Dowle, Aidan & Sue 144, 193
    Amy 193
    Chris 193
    Emily 193
    Josh 193
    Katie 193
    Mike 193
Drew, Chris & Libby 144, 181
Drinkwater, Alfred 31
Dyer, Eva 128

Edwards, Brian & Ann 135, 192
Elgie, George 157
    Richard & Jenni 137, 138, 140, 141, 157-8, 174
    Thomas 157
    William 157
Elliott family 122
    Matthew & Ruth 95
Ellis, David & Susan 144, 178
    Fred 132, 187-8
Evans family 121
    George Snr & Emily 54
    Dora 54
    Elizabeth 91
    Eric & Dilys 121, 166
    George Jnr 54
    Kathleen 54
    Lucy 194
    Revd Mervyn 131, 134
    Nigel & Judy 145, 166, 174, 194
    Samuel 194
    William & Hilda 121
Evesham, Reg & Mrs 128, 165, 185
    Sandra 186

Farnham, Cyril & Flossie 128, 130, 166-7
    Robert 167
Farrants, Dave 2
Faulks, C.J. 30
    William 30
Fender, William & Kathleen 121
Finch family 13
    Francis 15
    Henry 13-15
Finch Dawson, Margaret 32
Fishpool, Mr & Mrs Robin 177
Foley family 15-18
    Andrew 17-18
    Elizabeth 23, 24, 25
    Harriet 23
    Paul 16
    Richard 15

    Thomas Snr 15-16
    Thomas Jnr 18
    William 18
Fowler family 88
    Bruce 2
    Philip & Beryl 118
Freeman, Nigel 199
Fumpson, Mr and Mrs 26

Gardner family 128
    Mr 30
Gayther, Sue 135
Gethyn-Jones, Canon D. 128
Gladwin, Joseph 98
    Joe 126
    Mr 118
Gladwyn, Wilf 127
Glegg, Mrs 38, 39
Goff, Edward 22
Goldring, Joy & Will 125, 131, 170
Goodland, Revd Patrick 134, 142
Gorin, Kate 93
    William 93
Gough, George 158
    Gilly 158
    James 158
    Philip & Carrol 141
    Victoria 158
Goulding, Anthony 161, 173
    Arthur & Sophie 86, 88, 170
    Brian & Megan 137, 144, 145, 171
    Celia 161, 181
    Christopher & Karen 145, 170, 171
    Daniel & Jane 30, 31, 34, 55, 56, 72, 73, 76, 88, 117, 172, 173
    David 126
    Derek 171
    Dorothy 75, 108
    Edith 116
    Emily 116
    Ethel 86, 88
    Evangeline 161
    Florence (Flossie) 75
    Geoff & Shirley 131, 134, 164, 170, 171, 174
    George & Annie 30, 39, 41, 50, 55, 56, 72, 73, 75, 94, 95, 108, 116, 121, 160, 173
    George (son of Tim) 161
    Gertrude 75, 108, 118
    Gilbert & Gladys 55, 56, 151
    Hannah 171

Harold 75, 108, 160
Harriet 76
Horace 55, 56, 58, 108
Jacob 161
Jane 76
Joanne 171
John & Charlotte 30, 39, 41, 55, 56, 58, 151
Kenneth & May 73, 131, 132, 134, 154, 161
Leslie 75, 160
Lillie 75, 118
Lily 86, 88
Mabel 75
Marjorie 55, 56, 58, 118
Mark 170
Millicent 75
Olive 55, 56, 58, 108
Phyllis 55, 56, 58
Reginald C. (son of George & Annie) 75, 108, 173
Reginald H. (son of Samuel & Ada) 86, 88, 91, 122, 124, 125, 126, 142, 177
Richard 170
Robert 173
Rosemary 161
Rosie 161
Sam (son of Mark) 145, 171
Samuel & Ada 70, 86, 88
Simon 173
Stan & Joan 125, 126, 132, 144, 170
Tim & Beth 144, 161, 173
Van 2
Violet 86, 88
Wilf & Sheila 144, 161, 164, 173, 182-3
Graham, Alan & Pam 141, 191
Gregorie, Mrs 30
Green, Charles 108
 Gilbert 108
 Joseph 93
Greenwood, Chris 141, 191
Grey, Lord, of Wilton 13
Griffin family 102
 Alec 73
 Amos 100, 108, 132, 192
 Bill & Harriet 73
 Eliza 95
 John & Mehetable 45, 50, 100, 108
 Lillian Louise 102, 108

May 108
Phyllis May 102
Revd 105
Richard Frederick 102
Rose (dau. of Amos) 137
Rose (dau. of John) 100
Sidney Albert 100, 108
William 71
Griffiths, Arthur & Ruby 121, 156
 Brian 121, 156
 Jean 121, 156
 John 121, 123, 156
Grimes, Mr 92
Grimmett, Thomas 93
Gurney, George 30, 34, 45, 49, 50, 70, 71, 121, 164
 Elijah 30
 Paul & Clare 194
Guppy, John 60

Hale, Ernest & Gertrude 121, 161, 181
 Thomas 30
Hall, Ben & Rachel 177
 Mrs C.M. 31
 John 22
 Robbie & Helen 177
Hanman, Edwin J. 183
Harcombe, Joan 141
Hartley, John 31
Head, Miss 141, 189
Heane, James 60
Heath family 145
 Albert & Dorothy 122, 125, 136, 159, 177
 Georgina 160
 Julia (Judy) 159
 Roy & Rae 132, 159-60, 174
 Stuart & Dawn 177
Heaysman, Andy & Penny 137
Hedworth family 179
 Thomas 126
Herbert, William 155
Herrick, Fred & Iris (1st wife) 157
 Fred & Doris (2nd wife) 126, 134
 Jennifer 157
Higginbottom, Edith Ethel 104
Higgins, Edmund 31
Hill, Jame 14
 Revd J.B. 134
 John 26
 Raymond & Patricia 142, 149
 Thom 14
 Major William 29, 32

Hinds family 141, 153
 David & Margaret 118, 153
Hinton, Colin & Carrie 177
Hodson, Revd H.E. 30
Holman, Oliver J. 93
Honeyfield, James
 R.J.C. (Jack) & Agnes 31, 34, 83, 84, 86
Hooke family 33, 172
 Commander 126
 Richard 172
Hooper, Mr & Mrs 188
 R.E. 125
Hope, Elizabeth 94
Hopkins, Alan & Tina 144, 181
How, Major 31, 32
Howley family 102, 186
 Beatrice May 108
 Cyril 97, 108
 Daniel & Rosa 30, 77, 97, 108, 127, 183
 May 97
 Michael 129
 Richard 45, 51
 Winifred Violet 97, 108
Huff, William 121, 183
Hulme family 149
 Charles Snr & Hannah Mary 34, 38, 41, 121, 150
 Charles Jnr & Evelyn Elizabeth 41
 William 41, 150
Humphries, Angela 144
Hunt brothers 89
 Caleb & Annie 104
 Joseph 104
 Sarah 104
Hunter, Oliver & Bethan 145, 192
Hutt, Will 14
Hyett family 185
 Ann 64
 George 108
 Grace 108
 Mary 121
 Raymond 108

Innes, Henry 128
Irving, Revd William Swain & Dora 93, 105, 106, 107, 116

Jeffrey, Revd W.G. 134
Jenkins, Clara 108
 David & Paula 142, 192
 Frank 108

John, David & Celia 134, 181
Johnson, Gertrude 70
Jones, A.C. (son of Alfred Edward) 188
   Ada 92
   Alfred Edward & Ellen Sarah 34, 96, 98, 103, 118, 126, 183
   Albert Stanley 108, 115, 117, 118, 122
   Alfred Snr 96
   Alfred Charles 96, 108
   Annie 50
   Arthur 86
   Audrey 165, 192
   Betty 123
   Carey 76
   Charles (blacksmith) 42, 96
   Charles H. 42
   Colin 132, 183
   David & Nancy 134, 193
   Edith May 76
   Edwin & Anne 30, 82
   Elsie (dau. of Henry & Harriet) 76
   Elsie Lilian (dau. of Wm Charles) 61, 63, 64, 108
   Mrs F. 30
   Florence (Flossie) 82, 166-7, 128
   Frederick 91
   Geoffrey 165
   George 76
   George & Edith Annie 121, 183
   Gerald 141, 165, 174
   Henry 30, 50, 108, 165
   Henry Charles & Harriet 76, 77, 97, 116
   Hubert 92, 111-2
   Humphrey & Florence 42
   Ivy 76, 108
   Jane 76
   James 30, 34, 50
   John the elder 103
   John 30, 31, 50
   Kate Dorothy 61, 64, 121
   Keith 165
   Lydia 82
   Margaret 42
   Mary 123, 128, 183
   Nellie (Ellen Mary) 121, 183
   Paul & Ionna 165, 174, 183
   Raymond & Kathleen 76, 165
   Reginald Edwin (son of Samuel & Alice) & Madge 82, 121
   Reginald (son of Henry Charles & Harriet) 76
   Samuel & Alice (1st wife) 30, 34, 45, 50
   Samuel & Mary (2nd wife) 81, 82, 121, 166
   Revd T. Madoc 131
   Wilfred 82, 121, 166
   William Charles & Julia 30, 34, 50, 61, 63, 64, 82, 94, 108, 121, 154
Jotcham, Arron 194
   Kieron 194
   Paul 194

Kerfoot, Robert 26
Keyse, Charles Snr 108
   Charles Jnr 108
   Edith 108
   Ellen 108
   Fanny 101
   Mrs 45, 51, 101
   Richard 108
   Thomas 101
   William 108
Kidney, Joseph 42
King, Joseph 67, 70
Kingham, Cornelius 92
Kingscott, Julia Mary 64
Kirby, Albert James 108
   Oliver 108
Knowles, Andrew 32
   Andrew Brooks 116
   William 34
Kyrle, John 15

Lancaster, Herbert 22
Lane, Charles 30, 45, 50
Latter, Alan 181
Lawrence, J.H. 42
Lea, Mr & Mrs Peter 144, 191
   Teresa 191
Leeke, Mr & Mrs W.J.D. 134, 167, 168
Lewis, Jim 157
Little family 177
   Arthur, John 116
   Clara 89, 92, 107
   Edward 26
   Harry & Lucy 34, 91, 92
   William 91
Load(e), Henry & Naomi 45, 51, 100
   Jane 100
   John 100
   Nora 100
   Percy 100

Lodge, James & Mary 34, 64, 65
Lomas, Revd Tony 144, 198

Markey, Don & Barbara 179
Mann family 129, 185
Manns, Mike & Janet 134
Martin, Richard & Lyn 5, 137, 140, 157
   Revd R.W. 137
Matthews, Charles 31, 45
   Eileen 181
   Rene 150
Meredith, Don & Lyn 144, 174, 192
Merrick, Charles & Maria 103, 108
   Arthur 103
   Ethel 103, 108
   George 103
Middleton, John 24, 26
Millard, Les & Lily 126, 188
Monkley, Harold 121, 166
Morris, William 81
Muller, Richard & Jane 144, 193

Nash, Mrs 179
Neale, Jane 172
Niblett, Albert 34, 79, 81
   Florence 81
   Frederick 79, 80, 81, 164
   John & Jane 30, 79, 81, 121, 192
   Mary 79, 81, 82
   Miss 104
Nicol, Alasdair 184-5
Nicholson, John 150
Notley, Ruth 26
Nutte, Jo 14

Oates, Stephen 162
Onslow family 22
   Capt. Andrew George & Mary 29, 31, 32, 91
   Andrew Richard 29, 32, 86, 91, 177
   Catherine 22, 24, 26
   Emma 91
   Capt. George 31
   Margaret 32
   Mary Charlotte 32
   Richard Foley 18, 22, 23, 24, 25, 26, 29, 35, 60
   Richard Francis & Harriet 23
   Robert William & Martha 126, 132, 134, 178
   Revd William Arthur 29, 30

Oram, Christine 192
   John & Audrey 192
   Royston 192
   Stephen 192
Overton, Thomas 31
Owen, Mary Frances 91

Palmer, Arthur 108
   Beatrice 108
   Ernest 108
Parlour, Ruby 60
Parry, Carey 63, 64, 116
   Edith 116
   Ethel 82
Parsons, Sarah 126, 183
Peachey, Phil 5
Pearman family 126
Perkins, Lindsay 191
Peters, Richard 92
Phelps, Lionel 131
   Matthew 93
   Phillips, Revd Pat 144
   Thomas 26
   William & Julia 91
Piggott family 13
Pippete, Jo 14
Pope, W.W. 30, 31
Powell, Jo 14
Powis, Sydonia 91
Preece, Ambrose & Margaret 49, 50, 162-3
   Adolphus 50, 162
   David 50, 106, 117, 162
   Francis 50, 162
   John 104
   Mabel 50, 162
Preedy, Mr & Mrs Charles 91
Price, O.T. 91
   Steve & Jane 177
   William & Ivy 121
Pritchard, Anne 23
   John & Herbert 125, 156

Reece, Muriel Lucy 104
   Stanley Murrell & Adah Lavinia 104
Rees, Eifion & Kath 137, 138, 141, 181, 201
Refoy, Gavin & Karen 183, 199
Riley, Edna 133
Rimmer, Rosemary 137, 181
Roberts, Nicola 194
Robinson, Dennis 70

   Harold 70, 108
   John & Edith (1st wife) 70
   John & Alice (2nd wife) 34, 70, 108, 126, 156
   L.B. & J. 30
   Muriel 70
   Noel 70
   Oswald 70
   Sheila 70, 116
Roderick, Revd Havelock 122
Rogers, Angela 182
   Dot & Dave 135, 161, 182
   Lesley 182
   Suzanne 182
   William (Bill) 121, 161
Rose, D.P. 134
   Mr & Mrs 181

Savidge, Albert 70
   Alice 67, 70
   Charles Frank & Kate 64, 67, 70, 121, 154
   Elsie 64, 120
   George Snr & Ruby 30, 34, 59, 60, 67, 70
   George Jnr 59, 60
   John 134, 154
   Kenneth & Edna 64, 129, 131, 154
   Lilian 67, 70
   Mary Snr 64
   Mary Jnr 134, 154
   May 67, 70
   Norman 64
   Peter 134, 154
   Richard 134, 154
   Robert (Frank) & Charlotte Ann 30, 34, 59, 67, 68, 70
   Robert Henry (Harry) 67, 70
   Stuart 129
Schofield, Revd 118
   Craig & Georgina 160
Scott, Amos & Eliza 30, 34, 70, 71
   Annie 70
   Cecil 70
Selwyn, Amos 108
   Les & Doreen 128, 187
   Mr 118
   William 108
Shotton, Albert 127
Smart, William 126
Smith, Alan & family 142, 192
   Brian & Alison 131, 181
   Leonard 126, 177

   Joshua 31
   Joyce 131, 177
   Michael 167, 168
Spiers, Agnes 91
Spragg, Albert 93
   Arthur 93
   Walter & Eliza 93
Stapleton, Revd L.G. 128
Stephens, Chris & Mrs 123
Strutt, Mabel 126
Symonds family 18
   Mary Ann 18
Sysum, Alice Maud 100
   Anna Maria 104
   Edmund 45, 51, 100
   Georgina 100
   Matilda 82
   Wallace Henry 100, 115

Tarberth, Mr 104
Taylor family 132
   Albert 170
   Bob & Liz 7, 134, 150, 174
   Catherine 150
   Clare 150
   Joseph & Helen 142, 170
   Michael & Sandra 169, 170
   Thomas & Ann 64
Teire, Anna 142, 154
   Lucy 142, 154
   John & Sue 137, 138, 154
Tennant, Lt-Col 33, 116
Thackwell, Revd J. 131
Thompson, Anne 144, 181, 200
Thorkell 11
Thursby, Hugh 33
Thurston, Mrs 24
Toomey, Charlotte 56
Tranter, George 30
   Neah 93
Traversari, Domenico 141, 191
Treasure, Frank 64
Trigg family 86
   Mary 104
   Peter & Emma 96
Trilloe, Rhoda 91
Tucker, Mr & Mrs 187
Turner, Mr 179
Tutt, Roger & Gwen 2, 8, 137, 142, 167-8
Tyler, Ken & Joyce 131, 177

Vickery, Hugh & Martine 134, 157

Wakefield family 134, 163
   Gary & Debbie 163
Walker, A.E. 101, 121
Warne, Richard 23
Waters, Alan 177
Watkins, Anthony 191
   Elizabeth 73
Webb family 121, 137
   Albert 191
   George 191
   Graham & Madge 126, 179
   Horace 164, 191
Weller, Archibald 34, 49, 50, 100, 101
Wells, Albert & Sarah 93
   David 189
West, Henry & Ann 91
Wetherlock, Henry 99
Whilows, Jo 14
White, Josiah 81

Whittes, Jo 14
Wilkes, Sam & Genevieve 144, 151, 174
Williams, Alick 116
   Arthur 51, 101
   Edith 73
   Percy & Minnie 56
   Revd Dr Terry & Laverne 138, 141
Willis, Colin 186
   Henry 186
   Peter 186
   Robert & Julie 186
Winters, Albert 108
   Elsie 108
   George 108
   Lyndon Samuel 108
   Percy 108
Wintour, John 15

Wood, Bert & Alice 121, 128
   Samuel & Mrs 31
   Thomas 98
Woodbridge, F.W. 128
Wright, Martin & Helen 164
   Paul & Christine 137, 164, 174

Yates, Arthur (Joe) & Lavinia 118, 152-3
   Henry & Laura 187
   Margaret 118, 125, 152-3
Yeates family 141, 168
   Nick & Nicole 144, 168-9
   Roger 168

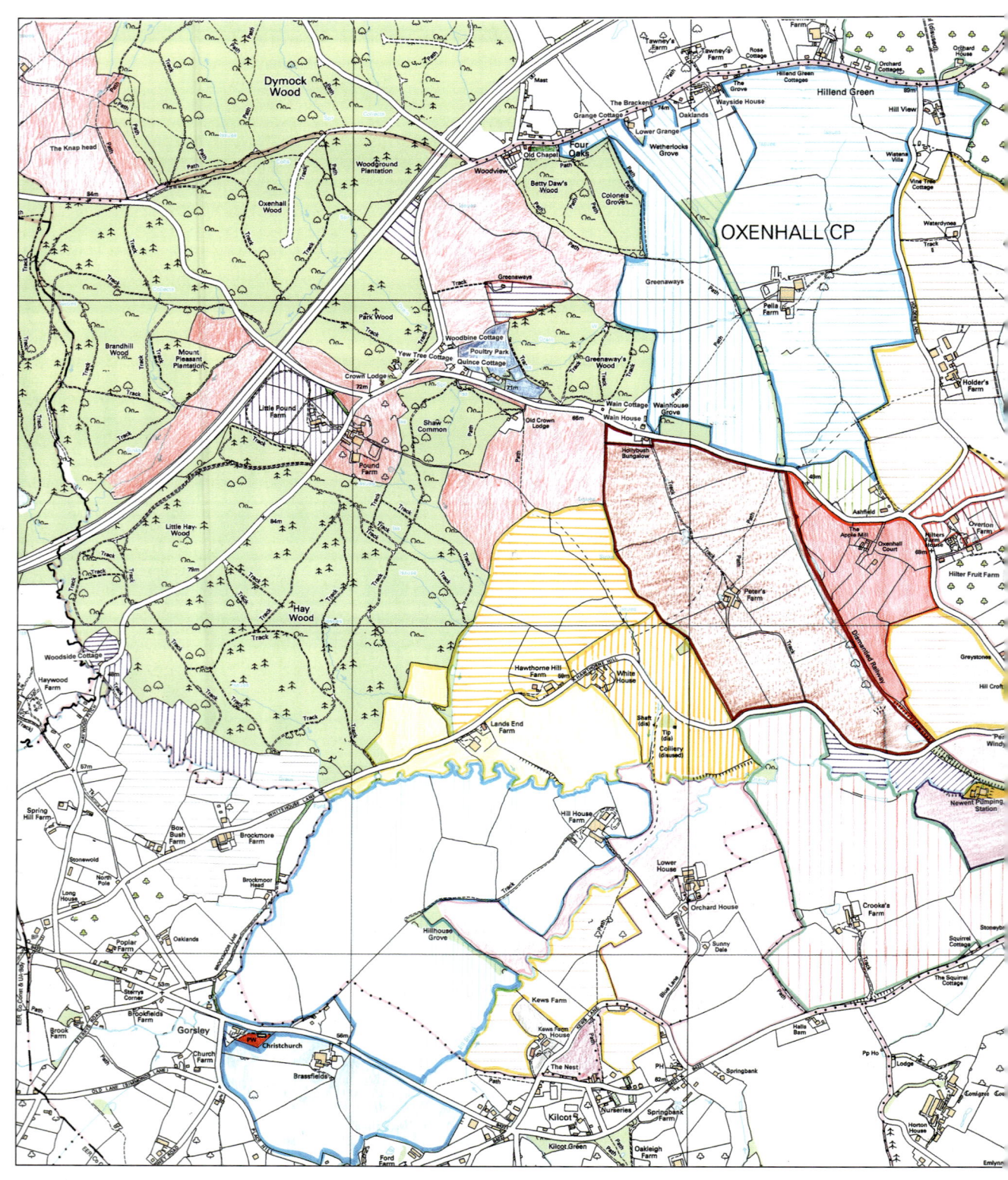